RODALE'S
SUCCESSFUL ORGANIC GARDENING®
HOUSEPLANTS AND CONTAINER GARDENS

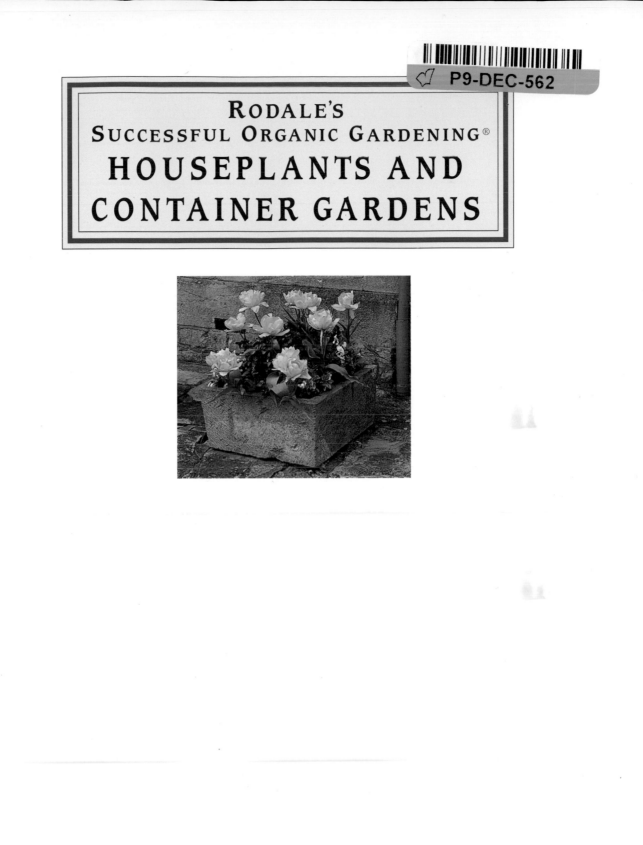

RODALE'S
SUCCESSFUL ORGANIC GARDENING®
HOUSEPLANTS AND
CONTAINER GARDENS

TEXT BY CHERYL LONG
PLANT-BY-PLANT GUIDES BY JUDYWHITE

Rodale Press, Emmaus, Pennsylvania

Our Mission

We publish books that empower people's lives.

RODALE BOOKS

If you have any questions or comments concerning this book, please write to:

Rodale Press
Book Readers' Service
33 East Minor Street
Emmaus, PA 18098

Library of Congress Cataloging-in-Publication Data

Long, Cheryl.
    Houseplants and container gardens / text by Cheryl Long : plant-by-plant guides by judywhite
        p.   cm. — (Rodale's successful organic gardening)
    Includes index.
    ISBN 0–87596–673–X (hardcover : alk. paper). —
    ISBN 0–87596–674–8 (paperback : alk. paper)
    1. House plants. 2. Indoor gardening. 3. Container gardening.
    4. Plants, ornamental. 5. Organic gardening.   I. judywhite.
    II. Title. III. Series.
    SB419.L64   1995
    635.9'86—dc20   95–31983
                                                  CIP

Produced by Mandarin Offset, Hong Kong
Printed in China on acid-free ∞ paper

Rodale Press Staff:
    Editorial Director, Home and Garden Books: Margaret Lydic Balitas
    Managing Editor, Garden Books: Ellen Phillips
    Editor: Nancy J. Ondra
    Copy Editor: Carolyn R. Mandarano
    Editor-in-Chief: William Gottlieb

Produced for Rodale Press by Weldon Russell Pty Ltd
107 Union Street, North Sydney NSW 2060, Australia
a member of the Weldon International Group of Companies

    Chief Executive: Elaine Russell
    Managing Editor: Ariana Klepac
    Editor: Libby Frederico
    Horticultural Consultant: Cheryl Maddocks
    Copy Editor: Yani Silvana
    Designer: Honor Morton
    Picture Researcher: Elizabeth Connolly
    Illustrators: Tony Britt-Lewis, Barbara Rodanska, Jan Smith,
        Kathie Smith
    Indexer: Michael Wyatt
    Production Manager: Dianne Leddy

A KEVIN WELDON PRODUCTION

Distributed in the book trade by St. Martin's Press

2 4 6 8 10 9 7 5 3 1 hardcover
2 4 6 8 10 9 7 5 3 1 paperback

Opposite: Mixed spring containers
Half title: Tulips and pansies
Opposite title page: *Agave* sp.
Title page: *Mammillaria* sp.
Opposite contents: *Aphelandra squarrosa*
Back cover: Spring bulbs (top), *Euphorbia pulcherrima* (bottom)

CONTENTS

INTRODUCTION

Growing plants in pots offers all the enjoyment of in-the-ground gardening—and so much more! Indoors and out, containers give you the freedom to move plants around, creating a constantly changing display of foliage and flowers. Plus, containers allow you to grow many kinds of plants—including flowers, shrubs, trees, herbs, vegetables, and fruit—even if you don't have any land to have a regular garden. You can enjoy flower-filled planters on your porch, deck, or patio or perhaps a little window box salad garden outside of your kitchen window. If your living space has no bright windows for growing plants, you can still grow a variety of plants with the help of artificial lights.

Houseplants seem to have universal appeal—perhaps because they bring nature's beauty to the indoor spaces where we must spend so much of our time. Growing plants indoors means that you get to live in a garden all year long. The plants will produce fresh oxygen to renew the air you breathe. The growing leaves and colorful blooms will add constantly changing accents to any room. And sweet flower fragrances will linger in the air, scenting your home the way no artificial perfumes can.

Each and every day, you will be able to enjoy the beauty and wonders of the plant world right in your own home.

Outdoor container gardening also helps you bring plants closer to your daily life. Pots, planters, and hanging baskets provide movable accents of color and fragrance to brighten up porches, patios, decks, balconies, and other outdoor living spaces. As you work with container plants outdoors, you may find that a few carefully placed flower pots can enhance your yard more effectively and easily than planting an entire new flower bed or border.

Indoors and outside, container gardening lets you control the weather and the seasons. You can create your own hardiness zones, growing orchids in Anchorage or oranges in Iowa. If you enjoy a challenge, you can grow just about any plant you want in a container, at least until it gets too big for your space. But there are some plants that adapt better to container growing than others and some that are better suited to growing inside than outside. *Rodale's Successful Organic Gardening: Houseplants and Container Gardens* is your guide to selecting and growing a wide range of beautiful and dependable plants in either indoor or outdoor containers.

Well-planned containers can give you a garden's worth of beauty in just a tiny space. Plus, growing plants in pots gives you the freedom to change your displays to match the season or your mood.

HOW TO USE THIS BOOK

Whether you're an experienced gardener looking for new challenges or a beginner getting ready to buy your first houseplant, this book is designed to answer all of your questions about growing plants in containers. Because indoor and outdoor gardening involve unique conditions, we've divided the book into two parts: one on indoor container plants (houseplants) and one on outdoor container plants. Since some plants grow equally well indoors and out, you'll also find information on how to move plants back and forth, growing them outdoors in the summer and then bringing them inside to enjoy during the colder months.

To grow great houseplants, begin by reading "The Basics of Healthy Houseplants," starting on page 12. This chapter explains key aspects of houseplant care—providing the proper light levels and the correct amounts of water and fertilizer. It also includes tips on keeping your plants healthy and looking good with proper grooming, training, and pest control, as well as pointers on propagating your favorites.

The next chapter, "Living with Houseplants," starting on page 34, presents a variety of options for displaying houseplants throughout your home. You may enjoy using flowering plants for seasonal color or training foliage plants into attractive topiary shapes for year-round interest. Other topics covered here include growing indoor bulbs, caring for terrariums and dish gardens, and gardening under lights. This is also where you'll find the details on moving plants outdoors for the summer and back inside for winter.

The second half of this book covers growing plants *outdoors* in containers. In "Gardening in Containers," starting on page 92, you'll learn about basic design principles for success with all kinds of containers, from pots and planters to window boxes and hanging baskets. There are also sections on growing less common container plants, including trees, shrubs, and edible crops.

"Caring for Container Gardens," starting on page 104, is your source for container planting and maintenance guidelines. You'll learn how to choose the best type and size of containers for outdoor growing, how to buy or blend container growing mixes, and how to water and fertilize for healthy growth all season long.

Throughout this book, you'll find out how to use nature's nontoxic, organic methods to grow beautiful indoor and outdoor containers, as well as safe, simple techniques to protect your plants if pests appear. As we all know too well these days, reliance on toxic pesticides and synthetic chemical fertilizers is polluting our drinking water and harming wildlife and humans. And considering the problems those materials can cause when used outdoors, we certainly don't want to think about using them within our home, where we'll come in contact with them daily. In these chapters, you'll learn about the organic gardening principles that will help you create a rich organic soil to grow strong, healthy container plants without using harsh chemical fertilizers and pesticides.

Plant-by-Plant Guides

In addition to all the information on growing and displaying potted plants, *Rodale's Successful Organic Gardening: Houseplants and Container Gardens* includes two encyclopedia sections: the "Guide to Houseplants," starting on page 50, and the "Guide to Container Plants," starting on page 116. Here's where you'll turn to find color photographs and complete descriptions of over 75 flowering and foliage houseplants and over 65 top choices for ornamental *and* edible container gardening.

If you're looking for ideas of new plants to try, skim through these sections to look at the photographs and read the entries of the plants you are interested in. If you already have a particular plant, look up its entry to find out which growing conditions it prefers, what kind of care it needs, and what common problems it has. These entries are arranged alphabetically by each plant's botanical name. Only know the common name? Look it up in the index, and you'll find a cross-reference to the plant in question. Below is a diagram of a sample page from one of the plant-by-plant guides, showing what to look for on these informative pages.

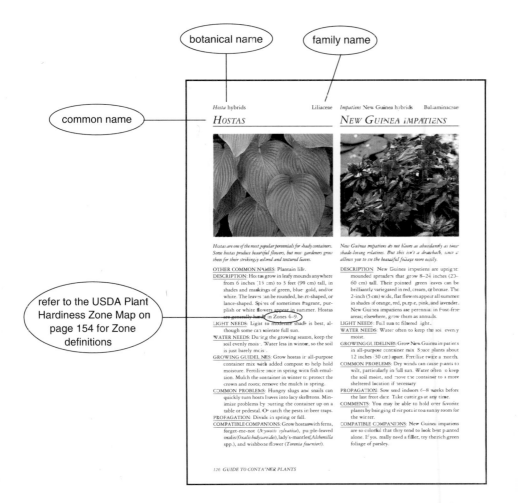

Sample page from a "plant-by-plant guide."

THE BASICS OF HEALTHY HOUSEPLANTS

Most common houseplants are truly easy to grow if you understand their basic needs for light, water, and fertilizer. Even the blackest thumb can grow a drought-tolerant jade plant or ponytail palm. But why settle for just the most common, easiest plants when there's a wonderful world of colorful flowers, sparkling variegated leaves, dramatic cacti, and exotic orchids waiting for you to explore? Whatever time and skills you have and whatever the conditions in your home, there are dozens of beautiful houseplants you can grow! This chapter will show you the way.

You'll start off by learning how to choose the right plants to suit the conditions in your home, as explained in "Buying the Best Plants" on page 14. Once you bring your plants home, giving them the right amount of light is probably the single biggest key to keeping them healthy and happy. "Providing the Right Light" on page 16 will help you to understand how to estimate how much light each location receives, so you can pick the ideal location for each plant.

Some people have trouble knowing how much to water their plants, and too much or too little water can spell trouble. But with the tips and techniques covered in "Watering Wisely" on page 19, you'll be able to know exactly when to water and when to wait.

Many houseplants can grow just fine in the temperatures and humidity levels found in the average home, but some need special treatment to really thrive. If you choose a fern that needs high humidity, for example, there are special techniques you can use to give it a more humid environment. "Humidity and

Temperature" on page 22 will tell you what you need to know about these important factors.

The foundation of all organic gardening is nutrient-rich, disease-preventing compost. You'll want to combine compost with slow-release organic fertilizers to feed your houseplants. In "Fertilizing for Healthy Growth" on page 24, you'll find out how to mix your own fertilizers using household wastes such as coffee grounds and wood ashes, along with organic products such as bonemeal and bloodmeal.

As your houseplants thrive, they will eventually outgrow their containers. "Potting and Repotting" on page 26 will tell you how to know when repotting is in order and exactly how to do it.

Another aspect of keeping your houseplants in peak condition is covered in "Grooming and Pruning" on page 28. This section covers basic plant pruning techniques that you can use to keep plants vigorous but still compact and well shaped.

The best defense against pests and diseases is strong, healthy plants. And that's what you'll get using the organic techniques explained throughout this book. If pest or disease problems do show up on your plants, you'll find safe, nontoxic solutions in "Handling Pests and Diseases" on page 29.

When you find out how much fun and rewarding it is to grow gorgeous, vigorous houseplants, you'll probably want to expand your collection. In "Making More Plants" on page 32, you'll learn all the basics of propagating your existing stock to fill every part of your home with lush and lovely houseplants.

One secret of growing houseplants successfully is grouping plants that have similar light and watering needs. The plants will look good together, and you won't have to bother remembering which ones require special care.

Buying the Best Plants

Let's face it. If you're out shopping, you see a houseplant you like, and the price is right, you're probably going to bring it home. It may not be the best way to get the perfect plant to match the conditions in your home, but most of the time it works out just fine. Check the plant tag, or look up the plant in the "Guide to Houseplants," starting on page 50; then find a site in your home that can provide the right growing conditions.

If, on the other hand, you want a plant that will thrive in a particular location, you need to be more careful to choose just the right one. A little advance planning is especially helpful if you intend to buy a large (and therefore more expensive) plant.

Plant-shopping Guidelines

When you're looking for just the right plant for a particular spot, remember to keep these key points in mind:

- Decide where you want the new plant to grow and estimate the light level available in that location.
- Browse through the entries in the "Guide to Houseplants," starting on page 50, and make a list of plants you like that have light requirements that match the conditions you can provide. (Or you can check the tags on the plants as you shop to see if the ones you like can take the conditions you can offer.)
- Shop around for the best color and size selection and prices.
- Choose a well-shaped plant. When buying a flowering houseplant, also look for one that has plenty of buds, with just a few flowers beginning to open.
- Be sure there are no signs of insect or disease problems before you buy. You don't want to take home any problems that could spread to your other plants!

Flowering houseplants generally need high light levels, so make sure you have a bright spot for them.

Estimate the Light

Your first step in buying the right plant is to consider how much light is available in the location you've chosen. Unless you're planning to place the plant directly in front of a large south, east, or west window, you should avoid buying houseplants that need bright light or direct sun. Instead, stick with those that only need medium light. Flowering plants require more light than plants grown only for their attractive foliage, so if you're expecting flowers, it's especially important to be sure the plant gets enough light. If you have to place a plant well away from the windows, try to select a plant that can tolerate low light levels. (For details on estimating light levels, see "Providing the Right Light" on page 16.)

Do a Little Research

Once you've estimated the light levels available in the location you've chosen, turn to "The Right Plant for the Right Place" on page 36, and make a list of plants suitable for your chosen location. Look up each of the plants listed in the "Guide to Houseplants," starting on page 50, and use the color photographs and descriptions to help you decide which plants you like best. Jot down the names of your favorites.

Now that you know what you're looking for, you can shop around a little. Prices can

Specialty greenhouses and catalogs are the places to look for unusual species, such as *Spathiphyllum wallisii.*

Look for flowering plants that have plenty of buds but few open blooms; that way, you'll get the longest show

vary a lot, especially for large plants, so it's worth investigating several sources; check out the garden centers, florists, and grocery stores in your area. Talk to the employees and find someone who can help you make a good plant selection.

When you've decided exactly which kind of plant you're going to buy and where you're going to buy it, look over all the plants of that type that the seller offers. Some plants will have a nicer overall shape than others; look for those that you find most appealing. Once you decide which plant you want, inspect it closely for any signs of insect or disease problems before you take it home. (For specific tips on identifying common problems, see "Handling Pests and Diseases" on page 29.)

Consider Flowering Habits

If you're buying a flowering plant for your home, there are some extra factors to consider. First of all, be aware that many flowering houseplants are grown under special controlled conditions in commercial greenhouses and are not likely to rebloom for you next year unless you have a greenhouse or can give them special care. Some, such as Persian violet (*Exacum affine*), are actually annuals that won't live more than a year or so, even with the best care.

Even though they can be relatively short-lived, flowering plants are still a good choice for brightening up indoor spaces. Live flowering plants will last at least two to three times longer than cut flowers, and some—including florist's cyclamen (*Cyclamen persicum*), orchids, and African violets (*Saintpaulia* hybrids)—will bloom nonstop for many months. So go ahead and bring flowering plants home to enjoy; just don't feel like it's your fault if they don't bloom again next year.

When choosing a flowering houseplant, always try to pick one that has lots of buds, with just a few already open. That way you'll get the maximum bloom time as the unopened flower buds bloom over the next several weeks.

Clivias may take a few years to start flowering, but to many gardeners, they are worth the wait!

Providing the Right Light

When you're growing plants indoors, light is the factor you need to consider most carefully. Indoor light, whether it's from sunlight coming in through the windows or from electric lights, is not nearly as bright as the sunlight plants receive when they're growing outdoors. The light intensity in a room may seem almost as bright as sunlight, but in reality it's usually only about one-tenth as bright. (The brightness seems similar to us because the pupils in our eyes open wider to make dim light appear brighter.)

Most common houseplants have become popular precisely because they can tolerate the lower light conditions found inside our homes. As long as you know whether a plant prefers low, medium, or high light, you'll do fine in providing the right conditions.

Find the Right Spot

South-facing windows let in the most light, and most houseplants will flourish there. Although east and

Most bromeliads thrive in sunny windows, but they can also adapt to bright north windows or fluorescent lights.

west exposures don't provide as many hours of bright light as south windows, many bright-light lovers (and all plants that need medium light) will grow well in most east- or west-facing windows. Save north-facing windows for low-light plants. To identify plants suitable for the varying light intensities in your home, see "The Right Plant for the Right Place" on page 36.

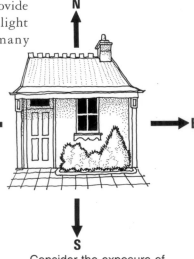

Consider the exposure of each window, as well as features that may block light.

There are several things besides direction that affect the amount of light coming in a window. A very large east-facing window might actually be brighter than a small, south-facing one. Shade from trees may make a west-facing window more like a northern one. Fortunately, most houseplants are adaptable. Your plants should do fine, as long as you do your best to match the right plant to the right window.

If you're the type of person who feels more comfortable with a little more precision, you can buy an inexpensive light meter,

A light meter can give you an accurate idea of light levels.

Defining Light Levels

What exactly do "high light," "medium light," and "low light" mean? Check the descriptions below to see which apply best to your available conditions.

- **High Light:** Areas directly in front of most south-facing windows and large, unobstructed east or west windows. These locations usually provide 4 to 6 hours of direct sun per day.
- **Medium Light:** Areas directly in front of unobstructed small or medium-sized east or west windows. Plant will also get medium light from partly shaded, large south, east, or west windows.
- **Low Light:** North windows and other windows shaded by large trees, porches, buildings, or awnings. Low light also applies to all locations more than a few feet away from windows.

Stephanotis floribunda needs sun in winter but some shade in summer.

A sunny south window is a perfect spot for a collection of cacti and succulents. A sunny east or west window could also be suitable.

which will measure the actual amount of light at any given spot. These meters usually measure light in units known as "foot-candles" and come with a chart that tells you how many foot-candles various plants require.

Place Plants Properly

Matching your plants to the best available windows is important, but placing each plant so it's right up near the glass is probably even more important than having the right window. The intensity of light drops off very rapidly as it enters the room, so a plant even a few feet from the window will get only half as much light as it would if you keep it right next to the window.

If your windowsills are too narrow to hold plants, consider adding a shelf to make the sill wider, or place a table in front of the window so you can set plants on it. Keep the windows clean and remove any sheer curtains that might cut down the light intensity.

Move Plants to Manage Light Levels

There may be times when you want to put a plant in a spot that you know doesn't provide enough light for it. For example, say you buy a spectacular flowering azalea and you really want to keep it on the dining room table where everyone can enjoy it. You can usually get away with this for a week or so; then

Aglaonema 'Silver Queen' is a great choice for a low-light area.

If you plan to grow herbs indoors during the winter, give them a sunny kitchen windowsill so they'll be within easy reach for cooking.

To give all of your plants ample light, you may want to rotate them so each has a chance to be near the window.

move the plant back into brighter light in a window. Most plants won't suffer much from such a procedure. Obviously, the lower the plant's light needs, the longer it can tolerate a dim location.

Another way to keep plants thriving in low light locations is to rotate two plants between the dark location and a bright window every few weeks or so. That way you get to enjoy a plant right where you want it all the time, and the two plants will get enough light to thrive. This is how shopping malls and offices keep their plants looking so good: The plants are moved back to a greenhouse periodically to recuperate, then they go back to the mall.

By the way, placing a plant close to an incandescent light bulb doesn't help much, but there are other types of lights that work very well for growing houseplants if your window space is limited. For more information on selecting and using the appropriate kinds of lights, see "Gardening under Lights" on page 40.

Is Your Plant Getting the Right Light?

If your plant isn't getting the right light, it may show symptoms that tell you it needs a new location. Sometimes, you may notice that plants growing in bright windows develop a yellowy tinge or white or brown patches on the leaves that get the most sun. This may be a signal that the plant is getting too much light. This doesn't happen often with houseplants, but it could be a problem if you put a low-light plant like a Chinese evergreen (*Aglaeonema* spp.) directly in a south-facing window. If these symptoms occur, move the plant away from the window a bit or move it to a less-bright window.

The opposite problem—plants not getting enough light—is far more common. A plant trying to grow where there's not enough light will gradually become leggy and spindly, and its lower leaves may turn yellow and drop. Or the plant may just sit, not putting out any new growth at all. If you notice a plant is not growing, or if there's new growth but it looks weak and spindly, try moving the plant to a brighter location.

Some plants, such as weeping fig (*Ficus benjamina*), may drop a lot of their leaves when you first bring them home. This is because they were probably grown outside in very bright light. When you move them to the much dimmer interior of your home, they simply don't need as many leaves because there isn't as much light, so they drop them. Don't be alarmed at this. Keep the plant in the brightest location you have, water it moderately, and wait for it to adjust. It should stop dropping leaves after a few weeks.

If a plant continues to drop leaves or to grow very poorly, consider moving it to a brighter location. Too often when houseplants grow poorly, people give them more water or fertilizer thinking that will solve the problem. Some plants do drop leaves when their soil gets too dry, but if the real cause is low light levels, extra water or fertilizer is the last thing that will help.

Watering Wisely

Next to getting the light levels right, watering is probably the most important aspect of houseplant care. You can't just water this plant once a week and that one twice a week; there are too many different factors that will affect how much water a plant needs. If you understand what those factors are and how they increase or decrease your plants' water requirements, then you'll know what to expect and be better able to give each plant the right amount of water for healthy growth.

The major factors that will affect how much water a certain plant needs include:

- **The plant's particular moisture preference.** The entries in the "Guide to Houseplants," starting on page 50, will tell you if a plant needs dry conditions (as succulents and cacti do) or if it needs constantly moist soil (as many ferns prefer). Most houseplants fall in the middle and need a steady supply of moisture with the soil surface drying out between waterings.

- **The container the plant is growing in.** Plants in clay pots will dry out faster than those in plastic pots. Large plants growing in small pots will also need water more frequently. (That's one of the reasons plants either need to be divided or repotted into larger pots as they grow.)

Cacti adjust well to life as houseplants since they are naturally adapted to low humidity.

- **The soil the plant is growing in.** Soil mixes containing ample compost or peat moss will absorb and hold more moisture than mixes containing lots of sand.

- **The amount of light the plant gets.** Plants growing in bright light will need more water than those placed in dimmer areas.

- **The weather conditions.** Plants will use much more water during bright, warm, summer periods when they are actively growing than in the winter, when temperatures are cooler and the daylight hours are much shorter. They also need very little water during sustained periods of cloudy weather.

Considering all these varying factors that affect how fast the soil dries, it's easy to see why it's so important to check each plant's soil before you water.

If you're having to water often to keep a plant moist enough, try moving it to a larger pot.

Don't wait until your plants are wilting to water! Repeated wilting leads to dropped leaves and poor growth.

When to Water

Your first clue about when to water should be the soil surface, which usually turns a lighter color when it's dry. If it's dark colored and damp, do not water. If the surface is dry, you can use your finger to check the soil an inch or two below the surface. If you still feel moisture, wait a day or two and test again. When that top layer feels dry, it's generally the right time to water.

Another way to check soil moisture is to lift the pot. You can tell immediately if the plant feels really light and thus needs water or if it feels relatively heavy, in which case you should wait a few more days before you water. This technique works especially well for small to medium-sized plants in lightweight plastic pots.

Some pots are just too big to lift, and the soil near the surface may dry out while there's still plenty of moisture deeper in the soil. Always check for moisture several inches deep in large pots; if you go only by whether the soil surface is dry, you could easily overwater. When in doubt, always underwater rather than risk giving too much water and thereby destroying the roots.

Clay pots tend to dry out quickly, so pay special attention to watering plants that need even moisture.

How to Water

Once you're sure a plant needs watering, you should water it thoroughly so that a little water runs out into the saucer under it. When you apply more water than the soil can absorb, the excess flows out the bottom into the saucer. This flow of water through the soil, similar to what happens in the garden when it rains, serves an important function in container plants. As

Water-quality Considerations

Not all water is equally suitable for irrigating your houseplants. Tap water can contain various additives, depending on where you live. Its pH can also vary.

The chlorine in our drinking water doesn't seem to harm plants, although some gardeners like to let tap water sit overnight so the chlorine can evaporate. Fluorine, on the other hand, has been shown to cause slight damage to some plants. If you use city water that has fluorine added (because of its ability to protect our teeth against decay), then you might want to capture rainwater and use it on your plants when you can. Home water softeners add salts to the water, so avoid using soft water for container plants; otherwise, the salts can build up to toxic levels in the soil.

If you have water that is naturally hard or alkaline, it may eventually cause the pH of the potting soil to become too high. (pH is a measure of how acid or alkaline the soil is. A pH below 7.0 is acid; a pH above 7.0 is alkaline. Most plants grow best when the soil pH stays around neutral, between pH 6.0 to 7.5.) You can offset the effects of hard water by using compost in your potting mix and adding vinegar to your watering solution once a month. (Use 1 tablespoon of vinegar per gallon [4.5 l] of water, and water as usual.) The pH level is more important for some plants than others; check the entries in the "Guide to Houseplants," starting on page 50, to find out if the plant you're growing has specific pH preferences for healthy growth.

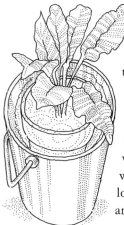

If the soil dries out, you may be able to revive a plant by soaking it in water.

the water runs down through the soil, it pushes out used air and allows fresh air to move into the spaces between soil particles. (Plant roots need both water and air to thrive. That's why it's so important to have a loose, well-drained potting soil and to always water thoroughly.)

By the way, always use pots with drainage holes, and always put saucers under them. Without drainage holes, it's too easy to over-water and make the soil soggy. (The excess water trapped in a pot without drainage holes could cause the roots to rot and the plant to die.) And if you don't have a saucer under the plant, you'll be tempted to underwater to avoid having water run out the bottom and make a mess.

Occasionally when you water, you may notice that the water seems to be running rapidly through the soil and out the bottom without being absorbed by the soil. When this happens, you've let the soil get too dry. When potting soil dries out, it shrinks away from the sides of the pot, leaving space where water can just run right through. To water a dried-out pot, you need to set the entire pot in a bowl or sink full of water up to the pot's rim and let the soil slowly absorb the water. After the soil is thoroughly rewetted, let the pot drain, then return it to its saucer.

To avoid overwatering, touch the soil with your finger or lift the pot to check the moisture level.

Signs of Overwatering and Underwatering

Overwatering is just as bad for your plants as underwatering—maybe even worse. When plants are too dry, their leaves will droop, so at least you have a clue that they need to be watered (although it's best to water just before leaves start to droop).

When plants are kept too wet, you may see the same symptom—drooping leaves—but it will be because the roots are rotted and the plant can no longer get the food and water it needs from the soil. If this happens, your plant may or may not recover; your only hope is to reduce watering and cross your fingers.

Watering for Vacations

If you'll be away for more than a few days, there are several techniques you can use to get extra water to your plants. If you're only going to miss one of your usual watering days, you can water the plants thoroughly and add some extra water to the saucers. (While you shouldn't make a habit of leaving water standing in the saucers, it's okay to do it occasionally as a way to give them some extra water while you're gone.)

If you're going to be gone for more than just a few days, you can set your plants up to be wick-watered. To do this, use a strip of nylon pantyhose, a rolled-up paper towel, or some other absorbent material for the wick. Insert one end of the wick into the bottom of the pot, making sure it makes good contact with the potting mix, then run the other end into a container of water. Recycled margarine tubs with lids work well for small plants; just cut a hole in the lid, fill the tub with water, run the wick down through the hole, and set the plant on top of the reservoir. Capillary action will draw water up along the wick and into the pot. (This method also works well year-round for plants that need constant soil moisture, such as gardenias and ferns.)

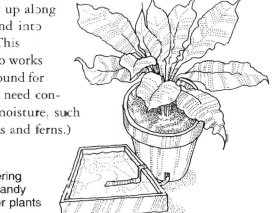

A wick-watering setup is a handy way to water plants while you're away.

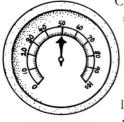

Humidity and Temperature

Although humidity levels and temperature levels are not as critical for good growth as light intensity or proper watering, they can have an effect on the health and vigor of your plants.

Handling Humidity

Almost all houseplants will grow better if you can give them higher humidity levels than those found in the average home. Indoor air is usually much drier than outdoor air, especially during the winter when heating systems drive away moisture. Summer air-conditioning also creates dry indoor air.

In general, plants with thin, delicate leaves tend to be more sensitive to low humidity, while plants like Chinese evergreen, with their thick, waxy leaves, can tolerate typical home humidity levels. There are some plants on the market, such as bird's nest fern (*Platycerium bifurcatum*), that look great at the store (because they just came from a greenhouse) but usually grow poorly in most homes unless you provide extra humidity. Always check the label and avoid buying a plant that needs extra humidity, unless you just like it so

humidity gauge

Gloxinias, sinningias, and African violets need high humidity to produce healthy leaves and flowers.

much that you are willing to give it that extra care.

You can buy an inexpensive humidity gauge (at hardware stores) to monitor the water vapor in the air. Most plants thrive in humidity levels very similar to what humans like—around 40 to 60 percent humidity. It's more likely, however, that the humidity in your house is below this. In winter, in fact, the humidity level may be as low as only 10 or 20 percent (which is as dry as a desert!).

Symptoms of low humidity include brown leaf tips and edges and leaf curling. If you notice these signs on your plants, consider the following techniques for increasing humidity levels.

A bit of moisture is good, but don't let water cling to flowers or leaves.

The blooms of potted spring bulbs and primroses will last longest if you keep them in a cool spot. Grouping the pots will help to keep the humidity level adequate.

Clustering several plants together will help to raise the humidity level around the leaves.

If you choose to mist your plants, do it lightly and during the day to prevent disease problems.

Grouping Plants One way to increase humidity is to cluster your houseplants. This happens naturally when you place plants in groups near windows. As the leaves release water vapor, the extra moisture creates a more humid microclimate for the plants. Using clay pots instead of plastic also helps a little because water vapor evaporates from the sides of the clay pots.

Misting Some people like to mist their plants directly to increase humidity, and this does help a little. However, as soon as the mist evaporates, the humidity level will drop. Misting plants so heavily that water stands on the leaves is not good, either, since that can lead to disease problems. If you decide to mist, do it during daytime hours and do it lightly.

Pebble Trays A better choice than misting is to grow your houseplants on trays containing pebbles and water. You can use any kind of saucers or shallow trays to hold the water—plastic cafeteria-type trays work well; even baking sheets are fine. Set the plants on a 1- to 2-inch (2.5 to 5 cm) layer of pebbles or gravel. Add enough water to bring the water level just below the top of the pebbles. (You don't want the bottom of the pots to be sitting in water.)

A shallow tray filled with pebbles and some water is a great way to provide extra humidity.

Moisture will evaporate steadily from the trays and rise to increase humidity around the plants' leaves. This is a very effective way to raise the humidity levels in a certain area, and humidity-loving plants like ferns will definitely benefit if you grow them over these water-filled trays.

Humidifiers If you happen to have a room humidifier or an automatic humidifier installed in your heating or air-conditioning system, you'll be able to raise the humidity in the whole growing area. Both you and your plants will be very comfortable year-round.

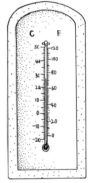

thermometer

Providing the Right Temperature

Most common houseplants prefer typical home temperatures of around 65°F (18°C) during the day and 55° to 60°F (12° to 15°C) at night. However, some do need cooler temperatures during part of the year. Certain flowering plants, such as azaleas and camellias (*Camellia japonica*), won't bloom well unless you can give them a period of cooler temperatures. Be sure to check the "Guide to Houseplants," starting on page 50, to find the temperature preferences of each kind of plant.

Spreading coffee grounds on the soil can provide the acid soil conditions that gardenias need to thrive.

If you notice a white crust or buildup on pots, run water through the soil to leach out harmful salts.

Fertilizing for Healthy Growth

If you want your houseplants to thrive, you have to give them food as well as water. The best organic fertilizers for houseplants are the same ones that work well outside—things like bloodmeal, bonemeal, and fish and seaweed products. You can also use household "wastes" such as wood ashes and coffee grounds. But the first item on your fertilizer list should always be compost, the organic gardener's secret for success.

Compost is especially good for container plants because it releases nutrients slowly over a long period of time, just the way plants growing in the wild receive their nutrients. Compost will never burn roots or cause major salt buildup like synthetic chemical fertilizers. Plus, compost doesn't just feed your plants—it prevents disease and improves the structure of the soil, so air and water reach the roots better. Ample compost also helps the soil retain moisture, so you won't have to water as often. If that's not enough, compost contains the major plant nutrients nitrogen,

Mix compost into the soil and add a bit to the soil surface each year.

phosphorus, and potassium, plus minor nutrients and trace elements not provided by chemical fertilizers.

If you aren't already making your own compost, consider starting. It's easy, and there's just nothing any better for making plants grow well. And if you can't make your own compost, check with your local government—many communities are now composting yard wastes and offering the compost free to anyone who wants it.

A Simple Program for Feeding Houseplants

Use compost whenever you pot up a new plant or repot old ones, adding up to 1 part compost for every 3 or 4 parts potting soil.

Each spring thereafter, take your plants to a sink or bathtub and water them heavily with warm water until water runs steadily out the bottom for a few minutes. This leaches out any harmful salts, which can build up over time. It's a good idea to do this once a year, but you should also do it any time you notice a crusty deposit in the saucers or around the pot rims. Rinse the leaves thoroughly, too, to remove dust.

After you've completed the spring leaching treatment, add a ½- to 1-inch (12 to 25 mm) layer of fresh compost to all of the pots. (If there's not room in the pot, just wash away some of the soil with a hose.) Mix a small amount of a balanced organic fertilizer into the compost before you apply it to the pots.

That should feed most plants well into midsummer. (Check the fertilizer packages for guidelines on how much to apply.)

Most houseplants will be getting much more light during the summer than in the winter, so a couple of months after the spring compost/fertilizer treatment, begin feeding them about once a month with a half-strength liquid fish fertilizer. The fish fertilizer contains plenty of nitrogen, the nutrient most likely to be in short supply. It also contains the other major plant nutrients—phosphorus and potassium—and important trace elements. Keep feeding the plants until growth slows in fall. Always remember that too much fertilizer can be just as bad as too little. Go easy when you fertilize plants in dim locations, and don't fertilize at all during the short days of winter unless you have a plant that continues to grow actively then.

Orchids demand excellent drainage, so use foliar fertilizer sprays rather than adding compost to the mix.

Understanding Organic Fertilizers

The three major nutrients plants need the most of are nitrogen (N), phosphorus (P), and potassium (abbreviated as K by scientists). All fertilizer labels carry these "N-P-K" numbers, which tell you the percent of each nutrient. Bonemeal, for example, typically has a ratio of 1-11-0, meaning it contains 1 percent nitrogen, 11 percent phosphorus, and no potassium.

To keep your houseplants happy, you want a rough balance of all three of these nutrients. It doesn't have to be exactly 5-5-5 or 2-2-2, but try to get the numbers as similar as possible. If you're growing flowering plants, switch to a formula with more of the middle number (phosphorus) when it's time for the plant to set flower buds. (The extra phosphorus will stimulate flowering.) Nonblooming foliage houseplants generally prefer a high-nitrogen formula, such as 5-3-3.

You can buy balanced organic fertilizers blended especially for houseplants, or you can mix your own. Listed here are some of the most common organic fertilizer materials. Choose a container (such as a margarine tub or paper cup) to measure out your fertilizer ingredients. Exactly how much you'll use of each ingredient depends on the specific materials you have available.

To determine the N-P-K ratio of any combination of ingredients given here, just add up the percent of each nutrient in all of the ingredients you plan to use, and divide by the total number of parts to get the N-P-K ratio of the mixture.

Here's an example. Say you have combined 2 parts bloodmeal (2 x 11-1-1 = 22-2-2) with 1 part bonemeal (1-11-0) and 2 parts wood ashes (2 x 0-2-8 = 0-4-16). Add up each part of the ratios, and you get 23-17-18. Divide each part of the ratio by 5 (since you're using 5 equal parts of fertilizer), and you'll see that the resulting mix has an N-P-K ratio of 4.6-3.4-3.6, a good balance for most houseplants.

Nutrient Contents of Organic Fertilizers

Bloodmeal:	11-1-1
Bonemeal:	1-11-0
Coffee grounds:	2-0.3-0.2
Compost:	0.5-0.5-0.5 to 2-2-2
Cottonseed meal:	6-2-1
Fish emulsion:	4-1-1
Granite dust:	0-0-4
Greensand:	0-2-7
Kelp meal:	1-0.5-2
Manures:	1-1-1 (typically)
Phosphate rock:	0-3-0
Tea leaves:	4-0.5-0.5
Wood ashes:	0-2-8

When potting up amaryllis (*Hippeastrum* hybrids), choose a pot that's just a bit larger than the bulb, and leave the top third of the bulb above the soil.

Succulents needs good drainage, so add extra sand to the potting mix.

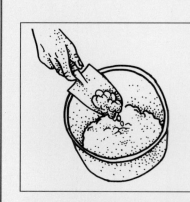

Potting and Repotting

Your houseplants will eventually need to be repotted, either because they grow too big for their pots or because they need to be moved into fresh potting mix.

Generally, you should repot your plants about once every year or two in the spring or summer, when plants are actively growing. If they get too big for their pot, they can become "root-bound," which means they have grown so many roots that there's not enough soil left to support further growth.

Most (but not all) plants shouldn't be allowed to become root-bound. You can check to see how crowded the roots are becoming by lifting the plant and tapping the pot until it slips loose. Lift out the plant to examine the root ball. If you see lots of soil with some roots, all is well. But if you see mostly roots and little soil, it's time to repot.

How to Repot a Houseplant

You have a choice when you repot—you can move the plant to a larger pot size, or you can keep the plant in the same pot. If you want the plant to grow bigger and don't mind going to a larger container, choose a new pot that's only 1 to 2 inches (2.5 to 5 cm) in diameter larger for small to medium-sized plants or

Repotting a Houseplant

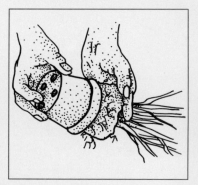

Choose a new container that is slightly larger than the old one. Add a layer of potting mix.

Carefully turn the plant over onto one hand, and use the other hand to pull off the old pot.

Settle the plant at the same level in the new pot, and fill in around the sides with mix.

4 to 6 inches (10 to 15 cm) larger for bigger plants. (If you move a small plant into a very big pot, you run a risk that the excess soil around the plant's roots will stay too wet and cause the roots to rot.)

When you're moving a plant to a larger pot, add some potting mix to the bottom—enough so that the soil level will be an inch or so below the pot rim when you set in the plant to allow room for watering. Then remove the plant from the pot it's growing in. Holding the base of the pot in one hand, lift the plant slightly and tap around the rim with your other hand to loosen the pot. Carefully lift the plant out and set it on the soil in the new pot. Then add potting mix around the edges, using a trowel or stick to gently settle the soil around the root ball. That's it—easy as one, two, three.

If you'd prefer to keep the same pot, remove the plant and shake away as much of the old soil from the roots as you can. If the plant's root ball is so dense and tangled that the soil won't shake loose, use a large knife to slice away an inch or two of the root ball on all sides and the bottom. Add fresh soil to the bottom of the pot, then set the root-trimmed plant back in

Early spring is a good time to check your houseplants and see which ones need repotting, since most will be entering a growth period then.

and add fresh soil in the space you created around the sides. This root pruning allows you to keep the plant to a manageable size. If the plant itself can be pruned, trim it back a bit to bring the top into better balance with the reduced roots. (See "Grooming and Pruning" on page 28 for details on pruning.)

If you're repotting a very large plant, you may want to ask someone to help you. Removing the plant will be easier if you lay the container on its side, then carefully pull out the plant.

Potting Soils

You can use any commercial potting soil for most houseplants, but your plants will grow much better if you add some compost and slow-release organic fertilizers before you plant. If you want to blend your own growing mix, see "Making Your Own Potting Mix" on page 108 for some recipes. There are a few plants that prefer special soil mixes. Cacti and succulents, for instance, appreciate extra sand for drainage, while African violets (*Saintpaulia* spp.) thrive with extra peat moss for acidity and moisture retention. Orchids generally prefer a very loose, bark-based mix. The entries in the "Guide to Houseplants," starting on page 50, will indicate if a plant has a particular soil preference.

If you see roots circling the outside of the root ball when you remove the pot, it's time to do some repotting.

If you want to use the same pot but the root ball is dense and tangled, trim the root ball before repotting.

Miniature roses bloom on new wood, so they need regular trimming to promote fresh flowering growth.

Passionflower vines can get unruly unless you trim out tangled growth and wayward shoots as needed.

Grooming and Pruning

It's natural for houseplants to lose some of their older leaves as they grow. Shrubby plants such as weeping fig (*Ficus benjamina*) may also shed leaves when they're moved to a new location, sometimes leaving a tangle of bare twigs in the center of the plant. If you spend a few minutes now and then trimming off these yellowing leaves or dead twigs, your plants will look much better.

Many houseplants don't require pruning beyond this regular grooming. If all of the leaves grow out from a single center or crown of the plant and there are no stems or branches (as on African violets [*Saintpaulia* hybrids] and florist's cyclamen [*Cyclamen persicum*]), then you can't (and don't need to) prune the plant.

Trailing or vining plants (such as wandering Jew [*Zebrina pendula*] and passionflowers [*Passiflora* spp.]), on the other hand, benefit from pruning. Pinch or snip off unwanted leaves and stems with your fingers or scissors; use pruning shears or loppers to remove woodier stems cleanly.

There are three basic reasons to prune your houseplants, as follows.

• **Pruning for shape:** Regular trimming improves a plant's appearance by eliminating any long, awkward stems or branches that grow out of proportion to the rest of the plant. Don't hesitate about this—cutting back gangly branches will help, not harm, the plant.

• **Pruning to promote new growth:** Pruning is also very helpful to trailing plants, such as Swedish ivy (*Plectranthus australis*). Cutting back the growing tips causes the plant to put out more shoots and become bushier. Always make your pruning cuts right above a side branch or leaf node (the spot where a leaf joins the stem). In many cases, the plant will produce two new stems from the cut point, leading to bushier, more attractive growth.

If trailing plants look a little stringy, trim the stems back to promote bushier growth.

• **Pruning for size control:** The third way in which pruning is helpful is in keeping plants a manageable size. If a bushy plant, such as a hibiscus or a citrus tree, has become larger than you want it to be, you can prune it back really hard, cutting off as much as a third of the leaves and stems. In this way, you keep the top in balance with the roots without having to move the plant to a larger pot.

To find out if your particular plant has any special pruning needs, refer to the individual entries in the "Guide to Houseplants," starting on page 50.

Handling Pests and Diseases

Outdoors, organic gardeners keep plants healthy by protecting and encouraging the natural balance between bad bugs and good bugs (the ones that prey on the bad guys). But plants growing indoors don't have any good bugs around to keep the pests in check, so sometimes the pests may multiply and cause problems. Indoor plants also face a few disease problems.

The most important thing you can do to prevent insect or disease outbreaks is to keep your plants healthy and vigorous: Give them sufficient light and fertilizer and the correct amount of water and humidity. For reasons scientists don't yet fully understand, pest insects are actually attracted to plants that are weak or stressed. Strong, organically grown plants are far less likely to have pest problems than plants that are weak and unhealthy.

The second important pest-prevention technique is to learn the symptoms of common houseplant problems and inspect your plants regularly for any hints of trouble. Most houseplant pests don't cause serious damage until they've been around awhile; if you spot an outbreak early, you can nip it in the bud (so to speak!). For

Aphids are one of the most common pest problems. Rub them off with your fingers, or spray with water or soap.

descriptions of the pests that are most likely to appear, see "Common Houseplant Pests" on page 31.

Controlling Houseplant Pests

You can treat houseplant pests with just a few simple nontoxic materials.

Sticky Traps Sticky traps are basically just pieces of cardboard or plastic (usually yellow and about the size of an index card) that are covered with an adhesive material. When flying pests, such as aphids and whiteflies, land on the trap, they get stuck. Hang a few traps around your houseplants, or attach them to the ends of stakes and insert the stakes into the plant pots.

Water Sprays A spray of plain old water is often enough to knock pests off your plants. You need a spray that's forceful enough to remove the pests but not strong enough to damage the plant. Wash the plant off in the shower, or take it outside and spray it thoroughly with your garden hose.

Insecticidal Soap Insecticidal soap is specifically formulated to kill pests such as aphids and mites without harming you or your plants. It's widely available in garden centers in both ready-to-use spray bottles or in a liquid concentrate that you mix with water. (The concentrate is a much better value than the ready-mixed sprays.) If you have "hard" tap water, mix the soap with distilled water, or it won't work well. (You'll know you have hard water if soap makes a scummy ring in your bathtub.)

Horticultural Oil Horticultural oil works by smothering insects and eggs. It is also effective in helping prevent certain leaf diseases, especially when

It's easy to overlook scales until plants are infested. Check leaves and stems frequently for these tiny bumps.

combined with baking soda. The oil now comes in several grades, so be sure you buy the superior grade oil that is labeled for use directly on plant leaves. (Until recently, horticultural oil was less refined and could only be used on outdoor plants that were dormant and leafless during the winter, such as fruit trees.) Mix and apply oil sprays according to package directions.

Dealing with Diseases

Most popular houseplants aren't likely to have leaf diseases—that's one of the reasons they're so widely grown. Keeping plants healthy by providing good air circulation and adequate light, water, and fertilizer is your best defense against disease.

sprayer

One common disease that may show up is powdery mildew. It causes distinctive white powdery spots on the leaves of begonias and other susceptible plants. If you notice mildew or other suspicious spots on leaves, remove the infected leaves and spray the plant with either a sulfur solution or a homemade spray of baking soda and oil (follow the recipe in "Homemade Sprays for Pests and Diseases").

Keep in mind that these sprays only work to prevent the spread of disease, not to cure infected leaves. Always try to spray at the first sign of disease, and remove all infected leaves first. If a plant becomes severely damaged by disease, it may be best to discard it.

Diseases can also attack plant roots, where they are difficult to detect or treat. Sudden wilting or poor growth for no apparent reason are the main symptoms. Be sure you aren't over-watering, as this can promote root disease. Try letting the plant dry out some between waterings; it may recover. If it doesn't, throw it out and be more careful not to overwater in the future.

Homemade Sprays for Pests and Diseases

Commercial organic pest and disease sprays are convenient, but it's also easy to mix your own. You'll find two easy recipes here.

Whenever you spray, always cover the top and bottom surfaces of every leaf. If the plant can be pruned, do it before you spray. Repeat the spraying a week or so after the first spray to catch any bugs you missed or to prevent any remaining disease spores from attacking. To avoid marking walls, floors, and furniture, you should always move plants to some place where you can clean up easily—perhaps your shower, kitchen sink, or laundry tub, or outdoors if the weather's warm—before you spray.

Soap-and-oil pest spray: For a homemade insecticidal soap spray, mix 1 cup of vegetable oil and 1 tablespoon of dish soap. When you need to spray, mix 1 to 2 teaspoons of this oil/soap stock with 1 cup of water. Homemade soap-and-oil sprays may have a slightly greater risk of burning leaves than a commercial spray; test them on a few leaves, then wait a few days to make sure no damage appears before spraying a whole plant.

Homemade fungicide: Mix 1 tablespoon of baking soda, 1 tablespoon of horticultural oil or vegetable oil, and a few drops of dish soap with 1 gallon (4.5 l) of water. Try to use this spray solution before disease symptoms develop or as soon as you notice a problem.

Powdery orange spots on leaf undersides are a sign of rust.

Wilt diseases cause browned and drooping leaves; there is no cure.

Botrytis blight usually attacks flowers; pinch off affected blooms.

Common Houseplant Pests

The trick to handling houseplant pests is identifying them correctly, so you can choose the most effective control measure. Below you'll find descriptions of the pests you're most likely to encounter, along with suggested control techniques.

Aphids

Appearance: Aphids are small insects about $1/16$ inch (2 mm) long. They may be white, green, black, brown, or even orange. They may or may not have wings. They are often found in clusters on tip growth and flower buds; look closely—they are hard to see.

Controls: Rub off the aphids by hand or prune out infested leaf tips. To control serious infestations, take the plants to the shower or outside and blast them weekly with a strong spray of water, or use a soap spray.

Fungus Gnats

Appearance: Fungus gnats are small, slow-moving, dark-colored insects that you may notice when they run across the soil or fly up when you water. They lay their eggs in the soil, and the larvae that hatch feed mostly on dead organic matter. The larvae do only minor damage, sometimes feeding on plant roots, but the adult gnats can be something of a nuisance as they fly about the room.

Controls: Control measures usually aren't necessary. If you have many flies, you can drench the soil with Gnatrol, a microbial pesticide containing a bacteria that kills the larvae of fungus gnats.

Mealybugs

Appearance: Mealybugs look like tiny tufts of white cotton. They are usually found clustered in sheltered areas of stems or on the undersides of leaves.

Controls: Apply rubbing alcohol to individual mealybugs using a cotton swab. Be persistent in inspecting plants and repeating treatment as needed.

Mites

Appearance: Mites are tiny—about the size of a grain of salt. You are likely to notice the symptoms before you actually see the pests themselves. Leaves attacked by mites are stippled or mottled; flowers may be deformed.

If you look closely, you can usually see fine webbing over the damaged areas. Webs alone don't necessarily mean the plant has mites; they may just be webs from small spiders. Leave those spiders alone, and they'll help you control the pest insects.

Controls: Wash mites off the plant with a strong spray of water. (Be sure to spray both the top and bottom of all leaves.) Insecticidal soap or oil sprays will also control these pests.

Scales

Appearance: Scales are odd little insects. They spend most of their life underneath a shell-like house (about $1/8$ inch [3 mm] in diameter) You will probably never see the actual insects—they only move around outside their scale when they are very young and very tiny.

Scales can be difficult to notice because they blend in well against the leaves and twigs. The first clue of a scale outbreak is often sticky specks on plant leaves or the tabletop. Check the leaves and stems directly above the sticky area for little bumps that can be rubbed off. Young scales are flat and semitransparent; they turn darker and get larger and easier to see as they get older.

Controls: Scales can be difficult to eradicate. Inspect plants regularly, and rub off scales by hand or spray with horticultural oil. Move plants outside in warm weather to allow natural enemies to control the scales.

Whiteflies

Appearance: Whiteflies are easy to identify because they will fly up into the air whenever you disturb the plant. They are tiny white bugs about $1/16$ inch (2 mm) in length. If you notice white specks flying up when you brush against a plant, you'll need to spray promptly, or the whiteflies will multiply quickly.

Controls: Use yellow sticky traps to capture adult flies. Spray with insecticidal soap or oil to control immature wingless nymphs (which are usually found on the undersides of leaves).

Cottony white clusters on leaves and stems tell you that mealybugs are present; spot-treat them with alcohol.

Making More Plants

With just a few simple materials, you can propagate a wide variety of wonderful houseplants. Once you learn how to take cuttings, prepare air layers, or divide plants, you'll have dozens of new plants to expand your collection or share with friends.

Some plants can be reproduced several different ways; others propagate best with one particular technique. To find out what's recommended for your plant, check the entries in the "Guide to Houseplants," starting on page 50.

Taking Cuttings

Cuttings are pieces of stem (or sometimes just a single leaf) that can produce roots and grow into new plants. This is a fairly easy way to reproduce bushy or vining plants, such as ivies (*Hedera* spp.) and passionflowers (*Passiflora* spp.). Here's how:

1. Cut short pieces from the shoot tips of the plant, so there are about two nodes (those joints where the leaves come off the stem) below the three or four leaves on the tip.

2. Remove the leaves from the two bottom nodes.

3. Insert the base of the cutting in water or moist sand or vermiculite, so the two exposed nodes are covered. (You might want to try a few cuttings in each of these materials; different plants root better in some conditions over others.)

Use your finger or a pencil to make a hole for planting the cutting, so you'll avoid damaging the stem.

Some succulents, such as burro's tail (*Sedum morganianum*), can reproduce from just a single leaf.

4. Slide a clear plastic bag over the pot of cuttings to keep the humidity high until the stems root.

5. Place the cuttings in a warm, bright spot out of direct sun.

Some cuttings root very quickly; others will take weeks. You can tell when roots have formed because the plant will begin to send out new growth. When this happens, replant the rooted cuttings into regular potting mix and fertilize them.

Air Layering

Dracaenas (*Dracaena* spp.), diffenbachia (*Dieffenbachia amoena*), rubber tree (*Ficus elastica*), and some other plants make great houseplants, but they tend to gradually grow taller and taller until they reach the ceiling. You can't prune these plants because they grow from a single center point. But there

Cut off the top of the layered plant just below the new roots.

is a way to return this type of plant to a manageable height. It's called air layering, and it works on many plants that have single trunks. Here's how you do it:

1. First, get some fibrous sphagnum moss. The stuff you want is coarse, stringy, and light-colored. Moisten the moss well.

2. Make a shallow cut across the plant's trunk where you want new roots to form—about a third of the way through, at an angle.

3. Press a little moss into the cut, then take a large handful of the damp moss and wad it around the trunk at the cut point.

Many plants can be propagated several ways. Chrysanthemums, for instance, can be propagated by cuttings or division.

4. Wrap the moss tightly with plastic wrap so it's held firmly in a ball all around the trunk. Secure the plastic-wrapped ball of moss with tape or rubber bands.

5. Check the moss every few weeks to be sure it's still moist (open the wrapping and add a little water if it isn't), and watch for roots. Eventually they'll become visible through the plastic. When they seem well formed, cut off the plant just below the new roots, and pot up your new shorter plant.

So what do you do with the now-topless trunk and roots? Well, in some cases you can cut pieces off of the trunk, lay them sideways in a fresh container of potting soil, and just barely cover them with more potting soil. The pieces will sprout new shoots and turn into additional new plants for you. Keep the remaining trunk base in the pot, and water it lightly; it too may sprout new leaves.

Dividing

Some houseplants grow from a center point but produce additional offshoots as they grow, expanding into larger and larger clumps. The popular aloe plant (*A. barbadensis*) grows this way; so do asparagus fern (*Asparagus densiflorus*) and moses-in-a-boat (*Rhoeo spathacea*). You can produce new plants from these clump-formers simply by lifting the clump out of the pot and breaking it apart into several smaller clumps. Repot the pieces right away.

Break divisions apart with your hands, or use a knife to carefully separate touch clumps.

Leaf Cuttings for Even More Plants

It's hard to believe that a single leaf—or even just a small piece of a leaf—can turn into a new plant, but it's true. Succulents such as jade plant (*Crassula argentea*) and burro's tail (*Sedum morganicnum*) will readily sprout new plants from single leaves that fall from the main plant. Just stick the fat fleshy leaves halfway into a sandy potting mix and water them as usual. Soon you'll have a handsome crop of new succulents.

Other plants are not quite as simple to grow from leaf cuttings, but rex begonias (*Begonia rex*) and cape primrose (*Streptocarpus* hybrids) leaves can be pinned onto moist potting soil after you make small cuts through the larger veins on the leaf. Keep the leaf moist by covering the pot loosely with plastic wrap, and tiny plants will eventually form at the cuts. You can produce new African violet (*Saintpaulia* hybrids) plants by standing a leaf in moist potting mix, with its stem inserted into the mix. New plants will gradually form on the leaf stem.

If your plants produce offsets at the base, division is an easy way to increase your collection.

MAKING MORE PLANTS 33

LIVING WITH HOUSEPLANTS

ouseplants can be so much more than just a spot of greenery on a windowsill. Use them to fill your home with sweet scents, such as those of orange blossoms and jasmine. Brighten up the dull days of winter with the brilliant flowers of amaryllis and long-lasting orchids. Grow lush tropical plants to decorate the living room, and raise tasty herbs for the kitchen. Create a gift for a friend or a special feature for your own houseplant collection by planting a terrarium or training a fragrant rosemary plant on a circular topiary frame. With a little imagination, you'll find many wonderful ways to brighten your life with houseplants.

To grow a wide range of houseplants, you'll need to know each kind's specific preferences for light, temperature, water, and humidity. "The Right Plant for the Right Place" on page 36 will show you at a glance what each plant needs, so you can be sure you'll get the right ones for the conditions your home has to offer.

Even if you don't have big, sunny windows, you can still enjoy growing houseplants by using electric lights to create a garden even in the darkest corner of your home. In "Gardening under Lights" on page 40, you'll learn how to select the right lights and the right plants for your available space.

Whatever ways you choose to bring plants into your home, they will bring you much pleasure. They are a source of living and changing beauty, providing color, form, and fragrance throughout the year. If flowers are your favorite, check out the tips in "Flowering Houseplants" on page 42. "Growing Indoor Bulbs" on page 44 also has ideas on adding beautiful blooms to your home with amaryllis, paperwhite narcissus, and other easy-to-grow bulbs.

To have even more fun with your houseplants, you can learn new ways to grow and train them. "Terrariums and Dish Gardens" on page 46 tells how to combine a variety of different plants to create compatible and attractive groupings. You can also prune and shape some houseplants into fascinating tree, wreath, or spiral forms; see "Training Houseplant Topiaries" on page 47 for details.

To keep your houseplants happy and healthy, consider giving them a summer vacation outdoors. When you bring them inside again in fall, you can also pot up garden plants such as rosemary, geraniums, and other tender herbs and flowers to enjoy indoors over winter and then move out again next spring. You'll find all the details on shifting plants around safely in "Inside Out and Outside In" on page 48.

To get the most enjoyment out of your houseplant collection, spend a little time arranging the plants in pleasing groupings. A mixture of flowers and foliage, for instance, adds a welcoming touch to a sunny entryway.

The Right Plant for the Right Place

The key to growing houseplants successfully is matching your plants to the growing conditions they prefer. To help you make the best choices for the conditions you have, the following chart summarizes the specific needs of over 75 flowering and foliage houseplants. You can see at a glance exactly which plants grow fine in low light, which need bright south windows, and which prefer cooler temperatures or need extra humidity to thrive. (If you're not clear on the definitions of low, medium, and high light conditions, see "Defining Light Levels" on page 16 for an explanation.) Pick the plants that will thrive in the growing conditions your home has to offer.

Flowering Houseplants	Light Needs	Water Needs	Comments
Chinese lantern (*Abutilon* hybirds)	High	Moist; drier in winter	Keep at 50° to 60°F (10° to 16 °C) at night. Pinch shoot tips and fertilize for bushy growth and best flowering.
Chenille plant (*Acalypha hispida*)	Medium to high	Evenly moist	Needs warmth and high humidity.
Lipstick vine (*Aeschynanthus* hybrids)	Medium	Moist; drier in winter	Good for hanging baskets.
Flamingo flowers (*Anthurium* spp.)	Medium	Constantly moist	Must have warmth and high humidity.
Begonias, flowering (*Begonia* spp.)	Medium	Allow to dry slightly between waterings	Discard Reiger types after flowering, as they will not usually rebloom next season.
Bougainvilleas (*Bougainvillea* spp.)	High	Allow to dry between waterings; water less after flowering	Needs warmth indoors; grow outdoors in summer.
Ornamental pepper (*Capsicum annuum*)	High	Evenly moist	Grow plants in the garden in summer and move them inside to a warm spot for the winter.
Chrysanthemums (*Chrysanthemum* spp.)	Medium	Moist	Prefer cool temperatures. Discard or plant outside after bloom.
Citrus (*Citrus* spp.)	High	Allow to dry slightly between waterings	Outstanding winter fragrance and fruit if you keep the plants outside for the summer.
Clivia (*Clivia miniata*) (E-Z)	Medium to high	Moist in summer, drier in winter	Keep cool (40°F [4°C]) in fall. Long-lived, reliable bloomer.
Coffee plant (*Coffea arabica*)	High	Constantly wet and high humidity	Needs a warm spot. Seldom produces flowers or beans when grown indoors.
Cigar plant (*Cuphea ignea*)	High	Allow to dry between waterings	Blooms readily.
Florist's cyclamen (*Cyclamen persicum*)	Medium to high	Evenly moist	Prefers cool nights. Blooms over a long period, but may not rebloom.
Crown of thorns (*Euphorbia milii*)	High	Allow to dry between waterings	Easy to grow.
Poinsettia (*Euphorbia pulcherrima*)	High	Allow to dry slightly between waterings	Prefers cool nights. May not rebloom.
Gardenia (*Gardenia jasminoides*)	High	Evenly mosit with high humidity	Keep plants warm. 'Prostata' blooms more readily than standard types.
Hibiscus (*Hibiscus rosa-sinensis*)	High	Evenly moist	Keep plants warm. Hibiscus may grow to 6 feet (1.8 m) tall.

None of the plants in this chart is difficult to grow once you have provided the conditions it needs. If you're just getting started, though, you might want to try some of the plants that are marked with "E-Z" after their name. These are some of the very easiest, almost-impossible-to-kill houseplants you can grow. They can tolerate some neglect, they're not fussy about how they're watered, and they're not particularly susceptible to pest or disease problems. These "E-Z" plants are also easy to find: They're popular precisely because they're so undemanding. You'll find them at almost any garden center or grocery store. Once you've gained confidence with these easy plants, you can start looking for more challenging kinds in specialty catalogs and greenhouses.

Flowering Houseplants	Light Needs	Water Needs	Comments
Amaryllis (*Hippeastrum* hybrids) (E-Z)	Medium; high when flowering	Moist while in active growth	Keep bulbs warm to start new growth after the rest period. Amaryllis will rebloom every year with minimal care.
Wax vine (*Hoya carnosa*) (E-Z)	Medium to high	Allow to dry between waterings	Very durable vining plant.
Jasmines (*Jasminum* spp.)	High	Evenly moist	Jasmines generally prefer warmth, but some need a cool period in fall to flower. Superb fragrance.
Kalanchoe (*Kalanchoe blossfeldiana*)	High	Allow to dry between waterings	Thrives in average to cool temperatures. May not rebloom.
Orange jessamine (*Murraya paniculata*) (E-Z)	Medium to high	Evenly moist	Easy to grow, with superb fragrance.
Orchids	Ranges from low to high	High humidity; allow to dry between waterings	Moth orchids have very long-lasting flowers.
Sweet olive (*Osmanthus fragrans*)	High	Allow to dry slightly between waterings	Plants prefer cool conditions. The small flowers have superb fragrance.
Oxalis (*Oxalis* spp.)	High	Evenly moist	Some types require a dormant (rest) period after flowering.
Passionflowers (*Passiflora* spp.)	Very high	Keep moist while growing	Plants need warmth. Many types are fragrant; robust vines will require a trellis.
Geraniums (*Pelargonium* spp.)	High	Allow to dry between waterings	Geraniums can take average to cool temperatures. Grow them outside in summer.
African violets (*Saintpaulia* hybrids)	Medium	Allow to dry slightly between waterings	Keep African violets warm. They make excellent long-blooming houseplants.
Christmas cactus (*Schlumbergera bridgesii*) (E-Z)	Medium to high	Moist while blooming; then drier	Requires long, dark nights and cool temperatures in fall to set flower buds.
Gloxinias (*Sinningia* hybrids)	Medium to high	Keep moist and provide high humidity	Gloxinias prefer warmth, but they appreciate a cool rest period after flowering.
Jerusalem cherry (*Solanum pseudocapsicum*)	High	Keep moist	Keep plants cool. May grow to 4 feet (1.2 m) tall.
Stephanotis (*Stephanotis floribunda*)	High	Keep moist	Vining plants produce clusters of fragrant star-like flowers.
Cape primrose (*Streptocarpus* hybrids)	Medium	Keep moist	Cape primrose offers a long period of colorful bloom.

Foliage Houseplants	Light Needs	Water Needs	Comments
Century plant (*Agave* spp.) (E-Z)	High	Allow to dry well between waterings	Dependable, slow-growing plant.
Chinese evergreen (*Aglaeonema* spp.) (E-Z)	Low	Evenly moist	Prefers warm temperatures; otherwise, very easy.
Aloes (*Aloe* spp.) (E-Z)	Medium to high	Allow to dry between waterings	Juice from the leaves will relieve pain from burns.
Zebra plant (*Aphelandra squarossa*)	High	Keep moist and provide high humidity	Keep plants warm. Cut the stems back hard after flowering to promote new growth.
Norfolk Island pine (*Araucaria heterophylla*)	Medium to high	Evenly moist	Excellent houseplant; can grow to 10 feet (3 m) tall in containers.
Asparagus fern (*Asparagus densiflorus*)	Medium to high	Just moist	Plants prefer average to cool temperatures. Divide and repot when roots fill the container.
Cast-iron plant (*Aspidistra elatior*) (E-Z)	Low	Evenly moist	Very sturdy houseplant.
Ponytail palm (*Beaucarnea recurvata*) (E-Z)	Medium to high	Allow to dry between waterings	Sturdy and slow-growing.
Begonias, foliage (*Begonia* spp.)	Medium to high	Allow to dry between waterings; give extra humidity and warmth	Some types need a dormant (rest) period for part of the year.
Schefflera (*Brassaia actinophylla*)	High	Allow to dry between waterings	Prefers warm temperatures. Very tough plant. May grow to 8 feet (2.4 m) tall.
Bromeliads	High	Water in leaf cup	Prefer extra humidity and warmth.
Cacti	Medium to high	Allow to dry well between waterings; no water in winter	Many different types and sizes are available.
Spider plant (*Chlorophytum comosum*) (E-Z)	Medium	Allow to dry between waterings	Easy to grow; excellent in hanging baskets.
Grape ivy (*Cissus* spp.)	Medium or high	Evenly moist	These trailing plants look good in hanging baskets.
Croton (*Codiaeum variegatum*)	High	Keep moist and give extra humidity	Fast-growing. Must have warmth and high light for best colors.
Jade plant (*Crassula argentea*) (E-Z)	Medium or high	Allow to dry well between waterings	Excellent, sturdy houseplant.
Dumbcane (*Dieffenbachia amoena*) (E-Z)	Low to high	Allow to dry between waterings	Very easy to grow. May reach 6 feet (1.8 m) tall.
False aralia (*Dizygotheca elegantissima*)	Low to medium	Allow to dry between waterings	May be short-lived.
Dracaenas (*Dracaena* spp.) (E-Z)	Low to high	Moist	Prefer warm temperatures; otherwise very sturdy and adaptable.
Aralia (*Fatsia japonica*)	High	Just moist	Prefers cool temperatures. Fast-growing; prune in spring.
Ferns	Medium to high	Moist	Very graceful; many different types and sizes.
Figs (*Ficus* spp.)	Medium to high	Allow to dry between waterings	Many types are excellent houseplants.
Fittonia (*Fittonia verschaffeltii*)	Low	Must have high humidity; keep moist	Beautiful leaves but may be difficult to grow; needs warmth.

Inexpensive "cool white" or "warm white" bulbs work just fine for most flowering and foliage houseplants.

high-intensity discharge (HID) light. HID lights use special sodium or metal halide bulbs, and they are very bright—wattage ranges from 175 to 1,000.

The 1,000-watt units are probably too intense for use anywhere except in a greenhouse or basement—you just wouldn't want to have such a bright light on in your living areas. But the 400-watt type is perfect for a spare corner in your living room or bedroom. It will provide an ample amount of light for a growing area about 6 feet (1.8 m) square. HID lights are bright enough to grow virtually any plants you want—even large, sun-loving vegetables such as peppers and

tomatoes. The lights aren't as bright as outdoor sunlight, but you can make up for some of the difference by leaving the lights on for up to 16 hours per day.

HID lights are generally available from specialty suppliers (such as those that sell equipment for greenhouse or hydroponic gardening). To find a source, look for ads in gardening magazines, or check your local phone book for greenhouse suppliers.

Special Growing Guidelines

If you grow plants under electric lights (especially the brighter HID types), you'll need to fertilize regularly to keep up with the plants' growth. (Unlike outdoor or window plants, which slow down during cloudy weather, plants under lights keep growing steadily.)

Regular light bulbs can release too much heat, damaging plant leaves.

To provide the right amount of light every day, you may want to buy a timer to automatically turn the lights on and off. Timers are available at hardware stores, home-improvement centers, and department stores for about $10. Most experts suggest that you set the timer to leave the lights on for 14 to 16 hours per day, unless you're growing day-length-sensitive flowering plants—such as Christmas cactus (*Schlumbergera bridgesii*) and poinsettia (*Euphorbia pulcherrima*)—which need short (12 hour) days to trigger flowering.

A light setup can expand your houseplant options if your windows aren't bright enough for good growth.

A timer will turn lights on and off for you every day, so your plants will always get the light they need.

Flowering Houseplants

Foliage houseplants are attractive and dependable, but it's the brilliant colors and fantastic fragrances of flowering plants that grab and hold the interest of houseplant-lovers of all levels. Flowering plants tend to demand a little extra attention and care, but it's all worthwhile when you get to enjoy the beautiful blooms.

To get an idea of the wonderful plants you have to pick from, stroll around any local greenhouse, or flip through the "Guide to Houseplants," starting on page 50. When you find a plant you simply must have, use the guidelines here to help keep it happy and vigorous.

Choose the Right Site

To grow flowering plants successfully, you must consider the available light levels carefully. If you put a foliage plant in a location where it gets less light than it would really like, it may still grow reasonably well. But without the necessary amount of light, a flowering plant will bloom poorly or may refuse to flower at all. Most flowering plants, such as hibiscus (*Hibiscus rosa-sinensis*), require high light—at least 4 hours of direct sun in a south window, for example. A few, such as the popular African violet (*Saintpaulia* hybrids),

Flower production takes lots of energy, so blooming plants generally need all the light they can get.

will flower in medium light levels, but almost none will bloom well in low light.

Generally, you should always give flowering plants your brightest windows. And if you can, move them outdoors for the summer. In many cases, a few months of brighter outdoor light will be enough for the plant to grow strong and set flower buds, even if you can only give it medium light during the rest of the year indoors. (Be sure to read "Inside Out and Outside In" on page 48 for information on how to safely move houseplants outside.)

After they produce their gorgeous flower display, gloxinias need a cool, relatively dry rest period.

Try Moth Orchids for Months of Bloom

One of the best-kept secrets of indoor flower growing is the lovely moth orchid (*Phalaenopsis* hybrids). Orchids have a reputation of being difficult to grow, but these elegant hybrids will thrive easily in a bright windowsill.

The most amazing thing about colorful, winter-blooming moth orchids is that their graceful, arching flower sprays can last for many weeks. For the price of a bouquet of cut flowers (which only last a week or two), you can enjoy the beautiful blooms for up to months at a time. Just water and fertilize them regularly, and give them a few weeks of cooler nighttime temperatures in the fall to set new flower buds. For more details on succeeding with orchids as houseplants, see the Orchids entry on page 62.

African violets bloom dependably and come in a wide range of colors.

The stunning flowers of florist's cyclamen certainly brighten dull winter days, but it can be tricky to get plants to bloom again next year.

Fertilize for Flowers

Besides giving them plenty of light, you'll also need to fertilize flowering houseplants carefully for the best blooms. To flower well, plants must have plenty of phosphorus, which is the middle number in the N-P-K rating you'll see on any bag or bottle of fertilizer. (If you're not clear on how N-P-K ratings work, turn back to "Understanding Organic Fertilizers" on page 25 for a review.)

If you buy a plant that's already in flower, you don't need to worry about fertilizing it while it's blooming. But when it finishes flowering, and if it's a kind that's likely to flower again for you (check the individual entries in the "Guide to Houseplants," starting on page 50, for that information), then you should begin feeding it. Give the plant a regular "balanced" fertilizer (one with roughly equal amounts of N, P, and K) as long as it's actively growing. Shortly before it's time for the plant to flower again, change to a fertilizer with extra phosphorus (such as a 5-7-4 fertilizer) to stimulate flower bud formation.

Don't Expect Miracles

Despite your best care, there are some flowering houseplants that simply refuse to bloom again the following year after you bring them home. Some may need special greenhouse conditions; others demand carefully maintained periods of light and darkness each day to repeat their colorful show.

Poinsettia (*Euphorbia pulcherrima*), Reiger begonia, and florist's cyclamen (*Cyclamen persicum*) are a few examples of houseplants that are difficult or nearly impossible to get to rebloom without a lot of fussing. (If you're not sure whether your plant will reflower, check the entry in the "Guide to Houseplants.") If you really like looking at the leaves, you can keep these as foliage plants when they are done blooming; otherwise, discard them after flowering and buy replacement plants next year.

Clivias may take several years to reach blooming size, and they seem to flower best when crowded.

Growing Indoor Bulbs

Indoor bulbs are a terrific way to enjoy brilliant flowers and fragrance, especially during the winter months. Two no-fail choices include amaryllis (*Hippeastrum* hybrids) and paperwhite narcissus. Once you get the hang of handing these, increase your enjoyment by bringing garden bulbs, such as crocus and hyacinths, indoors for winter or spring bloom.

Easy Amaryllis

You've probably seen an amaryllis or even received one as a gift. The large bulbs produce huge red, white, or pink flowers and long, strap-like leaves. These bulbs are easy to grow, and they will bloom year after year. You can buy them at florists and garden centers in the fall and winter months.

If your amaryllis doesn't come preplanted, choose a pot just slightly larger than the width of the bulb itself. Put some growing mix in the bottom of the pot, set in the bulb, and fill around it with more mix. Leave the top quarter of the bulb exposed.

Set potted bulbs in a bright, warm window, and water them lightly until they start growing. You'll be amazed at how fast the plant will grow once the flower stalk appears—it takes just a few weeks until the flowers open. Turn the plant regularly so the stalk won't become lopsided. Use a bamboo stake (be careful not to stick it into the bulb!) and a rubber band to hold the stalk steady once the giant flowers begin to open.

Most cultivars of spring crocus respond well to forcing. You can pack many bulbs into a single pot.

While the amaryllis is flowering, you can move it to a table where everyone can enjoy it. When the flowers fade, cut off the stalk and return the plant to a bright window. During the summer, put the plant in its pot outside in light shade. Water and fertilize it, and let it grow to replenish the bulb. (You can continue growing it inside if you prefer, but it will probably grow better outside.)

Before frost in the fall, bring the plant back inside and gradually reduce watering. As the leaves begin to die back, place the plant in a cool (50° to 60°F [10° to

Name	Bulbs per 6-inch (15 cm) Pot	Weeks of Chilling	Recommended Cultivars
Crocus	10 to 12	15	Most cultivars force well
Daffodils	3 to 7	15 to 17	'Cheerfulness', 'Dutch Master', 'February Gold', 'Sir Winston Churchill', 'Tete-a-Tete', 'Yellow Cheerfulness'
Hyacinths	3	11 to 14	'Anne Marie', 'Ostara'
Tulips	6 to 7	14 to 20	'Apricot Beauty', 'Beauty Queen', 'Monte Carlo', and many others

Outdoor Bulbs for Indoor Bloom

16°C]), dark area. The leaves will die down, and the bulb will go dormant. Don't water the plant during this period.

After a month or two, top-dress the pot with 1 inch (2.5 cm) of fresh growing mix and a teaspoon of bonemeal. Bring the plant back into a warm spot, water it lightly until new growth begins, and then return it to a bright window and watch those wonderful flowers appear all over again!

Paperwhite Narcissus

Another great candidate for super-easy indoor bulb growing is paperwhite narcissus. These bulbs are sold in the fall, along with daffodils, tulips, and other outdoor bulbs. Paperwhites are not hardy outdoors in most regions, however; they are sold specifically for indoor growing.

Some forced bulbs will grow on in the garden if you plant them outdoors after their foliage dies back. But always start with fresh bulbs for indoor forcing.

Paperwhites are perhaps the easiest flower in the world to grow. Just pot them up in regular potting mix or coarse gravel, with the tips of the bulbs showing. You can even grow them with their roots in water, using a special vase designed for bulbs. Once the bulbs have some moisture and begin to grow, the flower stalk will quickly become visible among the leaves, and you'll have flowers in just a few weeks!

Paperwhite flowers have a spicy, musky fragrance, and they will last for several weeks, especially if you can keep the plant in a cool, bright location. Staking the plants with small bamboo stakes and string will help keep them looking nice as the leaves and flowers grow taller. To have flowers in bloom all winter long, buy a couple dozen bulbs in fall and store them in your refrigerator; then pot up a few every 3 to 4 weeks.

Unfortunately, you can't really expect the bulbs to bloom again another year (because they don't get enough light indoors to replenish the bulbs), so it's best just to discard the plants when the flowering is done.

Spring Bulbs

If you love the hardy spring-flowering bulbs that grow outdoors, why not grow them inside, too? All you have to do is pot them

in the fall with pointed ends up and just the tips showing. Store them in a cool (40° to 45°F [4° to 7°C]), dark place for the minimum number of weeks given in "Outdoor Bulbs for Indoor Bloom." Water occasionally to keep the soil from drying out and protect them from mice. Then bring them inside to a bright windowsill. In just a few weeks, you'll have daffodils, crocus, and tulips blooming indoors even if there's still snow on the ground outdoors.

Add extra punch to displays of spring bulbs by combining them with other early-blooming plants.

Terrariums provide ideal growing conditions for moisture-loving plants, such as Venus fly-traps.

Dish gardens are an excellent way to display a collection of low-growing succulents.

Terrariums and Dish Gardens

To get even more enjoyment out of your collection, you can create decorative groupings of colorful houseplants in terrariums or dish gardens. These simple projects are fun and easy, and they provide great movable accents for any part of your home.

Try a Terrarium

Terrariums are simply clear glass containers in which you grow a group of plants. They work especially well for plants that require high humidity, such as ferns and insect-eating bog plants (like Venus fly-traps).

You can purchase beautiful, leaded-glass terrariums made specifically for plants or use a container of virtually any shape. Old aquariums work very well, as do brandy snifters and recycled, clear glass wine jugs.

Next, decide what type of plants you want to grow. Tropical plants, which like warm temperatures and high humidity, are generally a good choice. If you have a cool room, you could select a group of temperate woodland plants that like shade, humidity, and cool temperatures. Just be sure

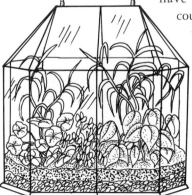

Keep terrariums away from direct sunlight; they can heat up quickly.

all the plants you choose like reasonably similar conditions. And unless you're using a really large container, choose plants that won't grow very big.

Once you've chosen your container and selected your plants, place 1 inch (2.5 cm) of coarse sand or gravel in the bottom. Then add several inches of soil mix and set in your plants. If you're planting in a bottle with a small opening, you may need to use special long-handled tools to slide plants into the container. Water the plants to settle them into the mix.

Give the finished terrarium whatever light level the plants you selected require. Be aware, however, that the clear glass sides of the container will trap considerable heat, so you must keep the terrarium out of direct sunlight. And don't overwater—there are no drainage holes, and the container will trap and recycle most of the moisture that evaporates from the soil and plant leaves. You may have to water only once a month, especially while the plants are small.

Dish Gardens

A dish garden is any open container in which you grow several different plants to create a miniature garden. This technique works especially well for smaller kinds of cacti and succulents, which grow well in a wide, shallow dish. As with the terrarium, you should choose relatively small plants that all have similar requirements.

If you plant a dish garden of cacti or succulents, use a special cactus soil mix, or make your own by mixing equal parts of standard potting soil and sand. For other plants, standard potting soil should work fine.

Fuchsias make particularly pretty standards, but they need lots of light to stay bushy and blooming.

Training Houseplant Topiaries

Topiary is the art of training plants to a particular shape. It's actually quite easy, and there are many houseplants that adapt well to topiary training. The shapes are limited only by your imagination, so you can continually experiment with new topiaries to add to your collection.

Setting Up Standards

The simplest topiaries are known as "standards." To create a standard, train a single-stemmed plant up a long stake, then trim the tip to form a round ball on top of the stem. One of the best houseplants to train as a standard is myrtle (*Myrtus communis*). It grows slowly in medium light, so you can enjoy the same plant for many years. Plus, the leaves have a sweet fragrance when cut or crushed.

Top Picks for Topiaries

Many plants can adapt to life as a topiary, but some tend to be better than others. You want a plant that will grow fast enough to give you results fairly quickly but not so fast that it will outgrow its shape without weekly trimming. Here's a sampling of some of the best choices for indoor topiary projects.

English ivy (*Hedera helix*)
Lantana (*Lantana camara* or *L. montevidensis*)
Lavender (*Lavandula* spp.)
Myrtle (*Myrtus communis*)
Rosemary (*Rosmarinus officinalis*)
Scented geraniums (*Pelargonium* spp.)

Training Plants to Topiary Forms

You can also make topiary by training an ivy or other vining plant onto a special wire form. Circles and heart shapes are common, but you can find them in a practically unlimited range of other shapes, too. To train a plant to a form, simply insert the form in the pot, then fasten the stems to whatever part of the form you want to cover. Use coated wire or soft string ties to secure the stems to the form as they grow.

Maintaining a Topiary

Care for topiaries the same way you would any other plant of the same kind. The only extra thing you need to do is trim the plant regularly to maintain the shape you want. Fast-growing plants may need trimming every few weeks to keep their shape; slower-growing species may only need clipping once or twice a year.

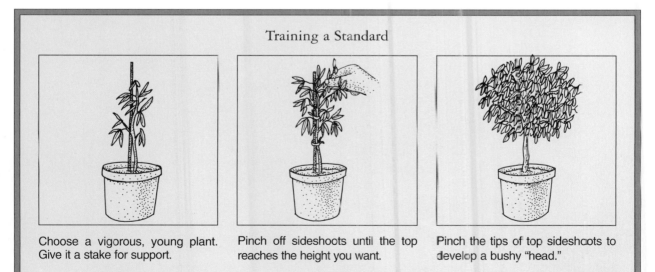

Training a Standard

Choose a vigorous, young plant. Give it a stake for support.

Pinch off sideshoots until the top reaches the height you want.

Pinch the tips of top sideshoots to develop a bushy "head."

Inside Out and Outside In

Just like people, many houseplants appreciate a vacation. Moving your plants outdoors for the summer is a great way to keep them healthy and happy. When you bring them back in for the winter, you can also dig and pot up rosemary, geraniums, and other flowers and herbs for indoor enjoyment. To help your plants through these transitions between house and garden, try the tips here.

Moving Indoor Plants Outside

Many indoor plants benefit from spending a summer outside. Flowering plants, which require bright light, will especially appreciate some time outdoors. If your plants have aphids, scales, or other pests, moving them outdoors can give beneficial insects a chance to attack the unwanted insects, solving your pest problems. If you have a large number of plants growing indoors, you may want to move the bright-light-lovers outside for the summer and shift some medium-light plants to the brighter spots vacated by the high-light-lovers.

Before you move plants outside, wait until the weather is warm and settled. Also, you must introduce indoor plants to outside sunlight gradually. If you don't, their leaves can show brown or white scorched spots—the plant equivalent of sunburn.

Before bringing outdoor plants inside, check them thoroughly for pests, and apply any needed controls.

To give your houseplants time to adjust, always place them in full shade when you first move them outside. After a few weeks in the shade, you can move the kinds that enjoy brighter light out from the shade to partial or full-sun locations.

Plants growing in the brighter, airier conditions of the great outdoors will grow much faster than they do indoors, so they'll need more water and fertilizer than normal. Pay special attention to make sure they don't dry out; they may need daily watering when temperatures peak in midsummer. Check the entries in the "Guide to Houseplants," starting on page 50, to see if your particular plants have any other special needs when living outdoors.

To avoid sunburned leaves, always put indoor plants in a shaded spot when you first move them outside.

Pots will dry out much more quickly outdoors, so make sure you check them frequently to prevent wilting.

Geraniums are dependable favorites for outdoor containers, but they also make great indoor plants.

In warm climates, you can keep tender plants outdoors through the winter, unless a cold snap is predicted.

Bringing Outdoor Plants In

Many plants typically grown outside can also be enjoyed inside. Plants classified as "tender perennials" will keep on growing if you protect them from freezing temperatures by moving them indoors for the winter.

Geraniums (*Pelargonium* spp.) are a perfect example. You can enjoy their colorful flowers or pleasant scents in the garden all summer, then bring them indoors in fall and keep them in a bright window. Other great plants for indoor growing include rosemary (*Rosmarinus officinalis*), wax begonias (*Begonia* Semperflorenscultorum hybrids), and coleus (*Coleus* x *hybridus*), just to name a few. You can even bring hot pepper plants inside to hold them over for the next year.

To move plants indoors, you can dig them up and set them in a pot. Usually you'll want to trim them back pretty hard to bring the top growth into balance with the now much smaller root ball. After they're potted up and trimmed, keep them well watered, and let them stay outside for a few weeks in part shade. This transition period will help them recover from the shock of being transplanted, so they can grow back nice and bushy. Be sure to bring any cold-tender plants inside as soon as frost is predicted.

If you'd rather have smaller plants (which fit better on windowsills), you can easily root cuttings from many garden plants in summer or early fall. Cut off 3- or 4-inch (7.5 to 10 cm) long shoot tips, and remove all but two or three of the top leaves. Insert the bottom 2 to 3 inches (5 to 7.5 cm) of each cutting into a small pot of moist sand, vermiculite, or potting soil, and cover the cuttings with a clear plastic bag to keep the humidity high. Place them in a warm, medium-bright location until they root and begin growing, then remove the plastic and move them to your brightest south windows for the winter. You can move the plants back out to the garden in spring, after all danger of frost has passed.

When you bring any outdoor plants inside, there's always a chance you may bring in some pest problems as well. Once those pests are inside, they can spread to your other plants quickly, since there are no natural enemies to keep them in balance. To minimize the chance of problems, inspect your plants carefully before you bring them in; refer back to "Common Houseplant Pests" on page 31 to remind yourself of what to look for and how to control any problems you find.

Certain garden plants are very susceptible to aphids when grown indoors. Hot peppers are a good example. If you find that aphids keep coming back even when you have sprayed the plant several times, it may be best just to enjoy that particular plant outdoors each summer and not try to keep it indoors. Or, if it's a plant you really love, you can order specific beneficial insects from mail-order suppliers and release them to munch on the aphids or other troublemakers.

GUIDE TO HOUSEPLANTS

With so many wonderful indoor plants to choose from, it can be hard to resist buying one of each kind you see. Start with a few dependable foliage plants, branch out into some of the more challenging flowering plants, and pretty soon you'll have every available space filled with a wide array of houseplants. While collecting indoor plants is a fun hobby, you'll get the most satisfaction if you choose your plants carefully, with an eye toward those that are best adapted to the growing conditions your home has to offer.

To help you quickly find the knowledge you need to make an informed buying decision, we've included this handy guide to over 60 popular indoor plants. "Flowering Houseplants" starts on page 52; "Foliage Houseplants" begins on page 68. In each section, the individual entries are arranged alphabetically by the plants' botanical names. If you don't know the botanical name, look up the common name in the index, and you'll be directed to the right place.

In each entry, you'll find a photograph and description of the plant to help with correct identification. You'll also discover the details on that plant's needs—its preferred light, humidity, water, and temperature conditions. "Growing Guidelines" tells what kind of care the plant will need to keep it healthy and vigorous: how often it needs to be repotted, what kind of soil mix it prefers, and related tips. And if you decide you like the plants so much that you want to make more of it, you'll also find propagation pointers.

With this kind of practical information at your fingertips, you'll be able to easily identify which plants should thrive in your home. And if you find a plant that you absolutely must have, even though it isn't naturally suited to your conditions, you'll know what special care you'll need to provide to keep it happy and healthy.

Once you find plants that grow well for you, start looking for their relatives to expand your collection. If you like snake plant (*Sansevieria trifasciata*), for instance, you could also try some of the variegated selections.

Abutilon hybrids   Malvaceae

FLOWERING MAPLES

Flowering maples are old-fashioned favorites for indoor growing. These hibiscus relatives bloom easily year-round in a bright spot; they enjoy spending the summer outdoors.

OTHER COMMON NAMES: Chinese lantern, parlor maples.

DESCRIPTION: These South American shrubs have maple-like, green leaves and papery, 1-inch (2.5 cm), nodding blooms in white, yellow, orange, or red. The bushy or trailing plants can grow to 6 feet (1.8 m) tall.

LIGHT NEEDS: Bright, reflected sun 4–6 hours a day.

BEST TEMPERATURES: Average room temperature during the day; intermediate to cool nights (50°–60°F [10°–16°C]). A 10°F (6°C) difference between day and night temperatures is ideal.

WATER AND HUMIDITY NEEDS: Keep evenly moist while in active growth. Allow the soil to dry out slightly between waterings in winter.

GROWING GUIDELINES: Grow in pots or hanging baskets in all-purpose potting soil. Repot in late winter, if needed. Stake for upright growth. Feed with fish emulsion twice a month. Prune off one-third of the plant in winter.

COMMON PROBLEMS: Spider mites can cause yellowish stippling or browning on the leaves; increase the humidity and treat affected plants (especially the undersides of the leaves) with superior oil.

PROPAGATION: Take tip cuttings at any time or grow plants from seed.

COMMENTS: For best flowering, pinch back new growth once six leaves appear.

Acalypha hispida   Euphorbiaceae

CHENILLE PLANT

Fluffy, red or purplish cattails highlight these fast-growing heirloom plants year-round. The puffed plumes are reminiscent of chenille piling on bedspreads.

OTHER COMMON NAMES: Red hot cattails.

DESCRIPTION: In ideal conditions, chenille plants are rampant growers. They can grow up to 15 feet (4.5 m) tall, although 6 feet (1.8 m) is more likely in containers. Their bright green leaves can reach 9 inches (22.5 cm) long. The 12–18-inch (30–45 cm), dense, pendant flower clusters are typically red or purplish.

LIGHT NEEDS: Full to medium light in winter; medium light (with some shade against direct sun) in summer.

BEST TEMPERATURES: Warm, not below 60°F (16°C).

WATER AND HUMIDITY NEEDS: Keep evenly moist. Provide high humidity and mist daily.

GROWING GUIDELINES: A self-watering pot with all-purpose potting soil works well for chenille plant. Fertilize monthly with a 1-2-1 mix. Prune heavily in spring to promote bushy new growth.

COMMON PROBLEMS: If spider mites cause yellow stippling on leaves, spray the plant thoroughly with superior oil. Dry air and lack of water can cause plants to drop their leaves; increase humidity around the plant and water more often to keep the soil evenly moist.

PROPAGATION: Take tip cuttings in early spring or late summer. If you have trouble getting tip cuttings to root, try taking a piece with a bit of older growth at the base.

Anthurium spp.   Araceae

FLAMINGO FLOWERS

The lacquered-looking, puckered blooms of flamingo flowers often fool people into thinking they must be artificial. Each flower can last for 2–3 months.

DESCRIPTION: This upright, many-stemmed plant can grow to 20 inches (50 cm) tall, with long, graceful, leathery, green leaves. The flowers can be 3–6 inches (7.5–15 cm) long. Each flower has a curved, tail-like spadix and a thick, shiny, heart-shaped spathe. The spathe can range in color from deep red to pink, salmon, white, and speckled. Miniature types are available.

LIGHT NEEDS: Medium indirect light.

BEST TEMPERATURES: Warm year-round. Ideal conditions are 85°F (29°C) days and 65°F (18°C) nights. To encourage plants to bloom, reduce the nighttime temperature to 60°F (16°C) for 6 weeks.

WATER AND HUMIDITY NEEDS: Provide constant moisture and high humidity while plants are actively growing. Let the soil dry out a bit between waterings in winter, but never allow it to get bone dry.

GROWING GUIDELINES: Grow flamingo flower in a mix of equal parts potting soil and sphagnum moss. Repot plants in spring if needed. Fertilize with an all-purpose, organic fertilizer twice a month from early spring to early fall; do not fertilize in winter.

COMMON PROBLEMS: Flamingo flower does not appreciate cold temperatures or hard water. Keep the temperature at least 60°F (16°C).

PROPAGATION: Divide in spring or summer, remove offshoots at the base, or grow new plants from seed.

Begonia spp.	Begoniaceae

FLOWERING BEGONIAS

The thousands of begonia hybrids and species provide a wealth of indoor houseplant choices. Those grown for flowers often have beautiful foliage as well.

OTHER COMMON NAMES: Angelwing (cane) begonias, Reiger begonias, wax begonias.

DESCRIPTION: Angelwing begonias can grow to 6 feet (1.8 m) tall, with thick, sturdy stems and an upright or spreading habit. They have showy flower clusters and relatively narrow, pointed leaves. Reiger begonias offer outstanding huge flowers and medium to dark green leaves on 12–18-inch (30–45 cm) stems. Wax begonias are compact, 6–12-inch (15–30 cm) plants with succulent stems and thick, waxy leaves. The white, pink, or red single or double flowers form in small clusters.

LIGHT NEEDS: Medium; protect from hot summer sun.

BEST TEMPERATURES: Average room temperature; prefers at least 60°F (16°C).

WATER AND HUMIDITY NEEDS: Let dry slightly between waterings.

GROWING GUIDELINES: Grow in humus-rich, soilless mix. Repot in spring as needed. Fertilize lightly twice a month from spring through fall. Pinch off the stem tips every month or so to encourage branching. To reflower, Reiger begonias need a 3-month, cool, dry rest period after bloom.

COMMON PROBLEMS: Lower leaves may drop if plants get too little or too much water; overwatering can also lead to rot and mildew.

PROPAGATION: Begonias generally root easily from tip cuttings. You can also grow plants from seed.

Bougainvillea spp.	Nyctaginaceae

BOUGAINVILLEA

The beautiful papery blooms of this South American vine can be orange, red, yellow, pink, or white. The flowers appear on the new growth. Leaf drop in fall and winter is normal.

OTHER COMMON NAMES: Paper flower.

DESCRIPTION: Bougainvilleas are climbing, woody vines or bushes, usually with large thorns. The foliage can be solid green or mottled with white or yellow. The true flowers are actually small white blooms surrounded by colorful, long-lasting, single or double bracts; they appear in fall and winter.

LIGHT NEEDS: High.

BEST TEMPERATURES: Warm, at least 60°F (16°C); can adapt to 50°F (10°C) nights.

WATER AND HUMIDITY NEEDS: While plants are actively growing, water thoroughly, then let the soil surface dry out before watering again. Reduce watering after bloom until new growth starts again in spring.

GROWING GUIDELINES: Use small pots and all-purpose potting mix enriched with sphagnum moss. Repot in spring as needed. Feed plants twice a month while they are actively growing. Pinch off the shoot tips regularly from spring through mid-summer (stop after July) to encourage a compact, well-branched, 2–3-foot (60–90 cm) plant. Also prune heavily after bloom. Bougainvilleas enjoy spending the summer outdoors in full sun.

COMMON PROBLEMS: If plants are not flowering, increase light and cut back on water.

PROPAGATION: Take stem or root cuttings in late spring and early summer.

Chrysanthemum spp. Compositae

CHRYSANTHEMUMS

Potted chrysanthemums provide a magnificent, if brief, show. Plant spring-blooming kinds outdoors for another set of flowers before frost.

OTHER COMMON NAMES: Florist's chrysanthemum.

DESCRIPTION: These 15-inch (37.5 cm) tall, bushy plants have divided, aromatic, green leaves. They come in a wide array of flower colors and shapes—often daisy-like, button, or pompon—and may bloom for 2–3 weeks. Unlike garden mums, many of the chrysanthemums grown for indoor bloom will not survive the winter outdoors in cold climates.

LIGHT NEEDS: Medium, indirect light.

BEST TEMPERATURES: Flowers last longest in cool 55°F (13°C) temperatures.

WATER AND HUMIDITY NEEDS: Water frequently to keep the soil evenly moist.

GROWING GUIDELINES: Grow in well-drained, all-purpose mix. Discard the fall-flowering potted mums after bloom. To get a late-season garden display from spring bloomers, cut them back by one-half to two-thirds after bloom and plant them in the ground. Pinch off the shoot tips every 2 weeks until mid-July, then stop pinching to allow flower buds to form. Plants may or may not live through the winter.

COMMON PROBLEMS: Aphids may feed on leaves, shoots, and buds, causing distorted growth. Knock them off with a strong spray of water, or spray with insecticidal soap, superior oil, or neem.

PROPAGATION: Take tip cuttings in spring.

Citrus spp. Rutaceae

CITRUS

In return for giving citrus plants lots of light and space, you'll be rewarded with the thrill of picking your own oranges, lemons, limes, and grapefruits.

DESCRIPTION: Citrus are tree-like or shrubby branched plants that can grow to 8 feet (2.4 m) tall indoors. Their glossy, decorative leaves make a beautiful backdrop for the perfumed, white blooms and brightly colored, pulpy fruits. Easy-to-grow calamondin or Panama orange (*Citrofortunella mitis*) produces 2–4-foot (60–120 cm) plants; its sour fruit is good for culinary uses. Spring-blooming, 8-foot (2.4 m) tall key lime (*C. aurantiifolia*) has tart, juicy, greenish yellow fruit.

LIGHT NEEDS: High light. A spot against a window with at least 4 hours of full sun is best.

BEST TEMPERATURES: Average room temperature during the day; approximately 50°F (10°C) nights.

WATER AND HUMIDITY NEEDS: Let the top 1 inch (2.5 cm) of soil dry out between waterings. Provide extra humidity.

GROWING GUIDELINES: Pot in 5-gallon (22 l) tubs with extra drainage in African violet–type mix (or a mixture of sand, peat moss, and fine bark). Spread coffee grounds on the soil to maintain the acidity and add nutrients. Put plants outdoors for the summer. If the stems get leggy, cut them back by one-third in midwinter.

COMMON PROBLEMS: Spider mites can cause yellow stippling on leaves; raise the humidity around the plant and spray with superior oil.

PROPAGATION: Take cuttings in spring or summer.

Clivia miniata   Amaryllidaceae

CLIVIA

Clusters of spectacular, trumpet-shaped blooms and handsome, glossy leaves make this flowering houseplant a favorite of many indoor gardeners. Clivias may take several years to flower.

DESCRIPTION: The strap-like, leathery, green leaves of clivia emerge from a bulbous base. Mature plants can reach 2 feet (60 cm) tall and 3 feet (90 cm) wide. Clusters of 12 to 20 winter blooms are usually orange-red with yellow interiors.

LIGHT NEEDS: Medium to high, indirect light.

BEST TEMPERATURES: Average room temperature in spring and summer; much cooler—to 40°F (4.5°C)—in fall and winter.

WATER AND HUMIDITY NEEDS: Keep the soil evenly moist in spring and summer; allow it to dry a bit between waterings in fall and winter. When you notice a flower stalk forming, water more often.

GROWING GUIDELINES: Start clivias in small clay pots. Use a blend of 3 parts all-purpose potting mix and 1 part sand, with a handful or two of bonemeal. Clivias seem to grow best when crowded, so leave them in their pot for about 3 years before repotting them in late winter. Feed with liquid fertilizer twice a month during spring and summer. Give plants a cool, somewhat dry rest period without fertilizer in winter.

COMMON PROBLEMS: Mealybugs produce cottony white clusters on leaves. Knock them off with a strong spray of water, or spray plants with insecticidal soap, superior oil, or neem.

PROPAGATION: Divide overgrown plants when you repot them, or remove offsets in late winter.

Coffea arabica   Rubiaceae

COFFEE PLANT

While coffee plant won't supply you with enough beans for your morning brew, it's worth growing for its glossy, green leaves and sweetly scented, white flowers.

DESCRIPTION: These shrubby plants grow 3–4 feet (90–120 cm) tall and have shiny, green leaves up to 6 inches (15 cm) long. Clusters of many small, white flowers appear in spring to summer, turning to pulpy, red berries by winter.

LIGHT NEEDS: High indirect light; provide at least 4 hours of filtered sun a day.

BEST TEMPERATURES: Warm; at least 60°F (16°C) at night.

WATER AND HUMIDITY NEEDS: Keep constantly moist and provide high humidity.

GROWING GUIDELINES: Grow coffee plant in a humus-rich all-purpose mix. Repot in spring as needed. Fertilize with fish emulsion and add coffee grinds to the soil twice a month from spring to fall, decreasing to monthly through March.

COMMON PROBLEMS: Set coffee plant where it won't be disturbed; the leaves tend to turn brown when touched. It grows very slowly and must be several years old before it will bloom.

PROPAGATION: Take tip cuttings from soft, upright shoots. Coffee plant is also easy to grow from seeds removed from the fresh berries.

COMMENTS: Coffee plant performs best in humid greenhouses but can adapt to life in the home if you're willing to provide some special care.

| *Cuphea ignea* | Lythraceae | *Cyclamen persicum* | Primulaceae |

CIGAR PLANT

FLORIST'S CYCLAMEN

The summer blooms of this Mexican native look like bright red cigarettes or firecrackers. The plants will bloom generously if you give them plenty of light.

OTHER COMMON NAMES: Firecracker flower.

DESCRIPTION: This pretty little shrub grows 12–24 inches (30–60 cm) tall. The leafy green stems are dotted with slender, tubular, red flowers that are tipped with purple and white. Each flower is about 3 inches (7.5 cm) long.

LIGHT NEEDS: High light.

BEST TEMPERATURES: Average room temperature; cooler in winter.

WATER AND HUMIDITY NEEDS: Allow the soil surface to dry between waterings. Mist regularly.

GROWING GUIDELINES: Grow cigar plant in all-purpose mix in a pot with plenty of drainage holes. Fertilize twice a month in spring through fall, while the plant is actively growing. Water less and hold back on the fertilizer during the winter to give the plant a rest period. If an older plant looks scraggly, take cuttings to start new plants and throw away the old one.

COMMON PROBLEMS: Cottony, white masses on leaves and stems are signs of mealybugs. Knock these pests off with a strong spray of water, or spray the plant with insecticidal soap, superior oil, or neem.

PROPAGATION: Take stem or tip cuttings in fall.

The butterfly-like blooms of florist's cyclamen flutter grace-fully over beautiful silver-marked leaves. The flowers are available in pink, red, lavender, and white.

DESCRIPTION: Florist's cyclamen forms compact, 12-inch (30 cm) tall clumps of heart-shaped, mottled green leaves that grow from a flattened underground tuber. The single-stemmed flowers emerge from leafy clumps from October to April.

LIGHT NEEDS: High indirect light while in bloom; medium light after bloom.

BEST TEMPERATURES: During the day, florist's cyclamen prefers 60°–72°F (16°–22°C); at night, keep temperatures at 40°–60°F (4.5°–16°C).

WATER AND HUMIDITY NEEDS: Keep the soil evenly moist while plants are in bloom. When flowering ends, allow the soil to dry between waterings.

GROWING GUIDELINES: Grow in all-purpose soil-based mix. Repot crowded plants to a slightly larger container only when nights are above 55°F (13°C). Fertilize twice a month from fall to early spring. Plants need a cool, dry rest period in the summer to rebloom. To provide this dormancy, put the plants outdoors in a shaded spot and turn the pots on their side; water occasionally to keep them barely moist until new leaves begin to appear.

COMMON PROBLEMS: Spider mites and cyclamen mites can be a problem, causing distorted growth. Discard infested plants.

PROPAGATION: Sow seed in September and keep it dark until seedlings appear. Put seedlings in a cool, bright spot for the winter; repot them in May.

CROWN OF THORNS

POINSETTIA

Crown of thorns will bloom freely with minimal care as long as it has plenty of bright light. Give it an out-of-the-way spot where you won't have to deal with the thorny stems!

This Mexican native now reigns as the quintessential winter holiday plant. Its showy blooms last for months, with petal-like bracts in red, pink, yellow, or cream.

DESCRIPTION: The spiny, woody stems of crown of thorns sport scattered green leaves, mostly on the young growth. The stems may reach 4 feet (1.2 m) tall. The tiny flowers are surrounded by showy red, yellow, pink, or salmon-colored, petal-like bracts. They bloom mostly in summer but can appear at any time.

LIGHT NEEDS: High light, with some direct sun.

BEST TEMPERATURES: Average room temperature.

WATER AND HUMIDITY NEEDS: Water thoroughly, then let dry before the next watering. In winter, reduce watering somewhat.

GROWING GUIDELINES: Grow crown of thorns in clay pots; use all-purpose potting mix with some added sand. Fertilize twice a month, except in winter. When the plants get leggy, cut the stems back to a pleasing shape in spring.

COMMON PROBLEMS: Crown of thorns will sulk if it's in a drafty spot, so choose its site carefully.

PROPAGATION: Take tip cuttings and allow them to dry for 24 hours before placing the cut ends in moist sand.

COMMENTS: The stems produce an irritating, milky sap when you cut them; apply cold water to stop it from flowing.

DESCRIPTION: These shrubby plants usually grow to about 2 feet (60 cm) tall in containers. The sturdy stems carry broad, green leaves up to 7 inches (17.5 cm) long. In winter, the stems are tipped with tiny flowers surrounded by leafy bracts.

LIGHT NEEDS: High light.

BEST TEMPERATURES: Cool conditions, with days not over 70°F (21°C) and nights around 55°F (13°C).

WATER AND HUMIDITY NEEDS: Allow to dry between waterings.

GROWING GUIDELINES: Poinsettias prefer well-drained, all-purpose mix. If you buy a plant in bloom and plan to discard it when the season's over, it won't need special care. If you want to try getting it to bloom again, repot it and cut the stems back to 6 inches (15 cm). Water as needed and fertilize weekly from Labor Day to Thanksgiving. Give the plant 14 hours of total darkness at night for 8 weeks beginning in mid-September, with temperatures of 75°F (24°C) during the day and 60°F (16°C) at night. Once the plant is in bloom, you can display it as desired. Hold off on fertilizing while the plant is flowering.

COMMON PROBLEMS: Leaves will drop due to low light, drafts, or overwatering.

PROPAGATION: Take tip cuttings in late spring and early summer; allow to dry overnight before rooting in moist sand.

| *Gardenia jasminoides* | Rubiaceae | *Hibiscus rosa-sinensis* | Malvaceae |

GARDENIA

HIBISCUS

For gorgeous fragrance and corsage-worthy flowers, few house-plants can surpass the gardenia. Even when your plant isn't in bloom, you'll still enjoy the glossy foliage and shrubby form.

OTHER COMMON NAMES: Cape jasmine.

DESCRIPTION: This handsome woody shrub bears pointed, 4-inch (10 cm), glossy, dark green leaves on stems that can reach 6 feet (1.8 m) tall in ideal conditions. Creamy, 3-inch (7.5 cm) wide flowers appear in spring to fall.

LIGHT NEEDS: High light, especially in winter, with 4 hours of full sun per day.

BEST TEMPERATURES: Between 65° and 80°F (18° and 26°C) during the day; around 60°F (16°C) at night.

WATER AND HUMIDITY NEEDS: Keep the soil evenly moist. Mist regularly to provide high humidity.

GROWING GUIDELINES: Grow gardenias in all-purpose potting mix with added peat moss and sand. Feed monthly from spring to fall with acid fertilizer. Adding used coffee grounds to the soil several times a year stimulates flower production.

COMMON PROBLEMS: Spider mites can cause yellow stippling on leaves; raise the humidity and spray the plant with superior oil. Drafts and/or low temperatures can cause leaves to yellow and drop; prevent by choosing a warm, sheltered spot. Dry air and/or too little light causes buds to wilt and drop before opening; move the plant to a brighter location and increase the humidity.

PROPAGATION: Take cuttings of ripe (firm but still green) stems with a bit of mature wood at the base.

Fabulous huge flowers in white, pink, rose, red, yellow, and orange are often just a single day, but they bloom successively and almost continuously. Break or snip off faded flowers.

OTHER COMMON NAMES: Rose-of-China.

DESCRIPTION: Tree-like hibiscus can reach 8 feet (2.4 m) tall, with glossy, green, oval leaves to 6 inches (15 cm) long. The dramatic, single or double flowers can be 5–6 inches (12.5–15 cm) wide.

LIGHT NEEDS: High light with some direct sun.

BEST TEMPERATURES: Warm conditions; at least 70°F (21°C) during the day and at least 60°F (16°C) at night.

WATER AND HUMIDITY NEEDS: Keep the soil moist, but don't allow the pot to sit in water.

GROWING GUIDELINES: Grow hibiscus in a well-drained, soil-based mix and a relatively small container. Repot every 2 or 3 years in spring. Fertilize with a 3-1-2 fertilizer twice a month. Pinch new growth to keep plants bushy.

COMMON PROBLEMS: Whiteflies may feed on the underside of leaves. Catch these pests on yellow sticky traps, vacuum them off the leaves, or spray with insecticidal soap, superior oil, or neem. Wash cottony white mealybugs off plants with a strong spray of water, or treat the leaves and stems with insecticidal soap, superior oil, or neem. If leaves turn yellow, use a higher nitrogen fertilizer, such as fish emulsion.

PROPAGATION: Take stem cuttings in spring.

COMMENTS: Rejuvenate leggy plants by cutting the stems down to 4 inches (10 cm) in spring.

| *Hippeastrum* hybrids | Amaryllidaceae | *Hoya carnosa* | Asclepiadaceae |

AMARYLLIS

WAX VINE

Spectacular and astonishingly easy to bring into bloom, amaryllis makes a perfect winter gift plant. Keep the plant cool when it is in bloom so the flowers last longer.

DESCRIPTION: The large bulb of amaryllis sends up a 2-foot (60 cm) tall, hollow bloom stalk, along with or slightly before the long, arching, strap-like leaves. One to 10 trumpet-shaped, single or double flowers bloom atop the stalk for up to a month.

LIGHT NEEDS: Medium light when first planted; increase to a half-day of sun when the flower stalk is 6 inches (15 cm) tall.

BEST TEMPERATURES: Warm conditions: 70°F (21°C) days and 60°F (16°C) nights.

WATER AND HUMIDITY NEEDS: Moisten the soil thoroughly at planting time, then wait until growth starts before watering again. Keep the soil evenly moist while the plant is actively growing.

GROWING GUIDELINES: Set the bulb in well-drained, all-purpose potting mix. Choose a pot that is 1 inch (2.5 cm) wider than the bulb. Position the bulb in the pot so the top quarter is sticking out of the soil. Feed monthly while the plant is growing; stop fertilizing and watering when the leaves turn yellow. Allow the bulb to rest for a month, then repot it or replace the top inch (2.5 cm) of potting soil with fresh mix and 1 teaspoon of bonemeal. Water thoroughly and place the bulb in a warm spot to promote new growth.

COMMON PROBLEMS: If your amaryllis produces lots of leaves but no flowers, its pot may be too large.

PROPAGATION: Remove offsets from the parent bulb.

Wax vine's long stems can climb up trellises or trail around window frames. This milkweed relative produces clusters of very fragrant, starry blooms from May to September.

OTHER COMMON NAMES: Honey plant, porcelain flower.

DESCRIPTION: Wax vine has succulent, 3-inch (7.5 cm), silvery green leaves atop trailing vines that climb to 20 feet (6 m). Clusters of small, pinkish, red-centered flowers dangle from the stems in summer.

LIGHT NEEDS: High light; avoid direct, midday sun.

BEST TEMPERATURES: Intermediate to warm conditions not below 50°F (10°C).

WATER AND HUMIDITY NEEDS: From spring through fall, let the soil dry between waterings. In winter, reduce water drastically, just enough to prevent shriveling. Do not use cold water.

GROWING GUIDELINES: Grow wax vine in a peat-moss-based mix in a pot or in a hanging basket lined with sphagnum moss. Provide potted plants with a trellis or wire hoop; wind the stems counterclockwise around the support. Fertilize once in spring with an all-purpose fertilizer. Once buds form, avoid moving the vine. Wax vine must be 3 feet (90 cm) long to bloom, so avoid pruning, or you'll remove the stubby flowering spurs.

COMMON PROBLEMS: White, cottony growths are signs of mealybugs. Wash them off with a strong spray of water, or spray the plant with insecticidal soap or neem.

PROPAGATION: Take cuttings of the previous year's growth in spring.

| *Jasminum* spp. | Oleaceae | *Kalanchoe blossfeldiana* | Crassulaceae |

JASMINES

KALANCHOE

To get the best from your jasmines, give them lots of light and provide extra humidity. They'll reward you with masses of delicate-looking, fragrant blossoms.

This Madagascar native has beautiful glossy foliage and huge clusters of winter flowers held high above the leaves. Remove the stalks when the flowers fade.

OTHER COMMON NAMES: Jessamine.

DESCRIPTION: Jasmines are shrubby or vining climbers with small, white blooms almost all year long. Poet's or French perfume jasmine (*J. officinale* var. *grandiflorum*) has double, white flowers on twining stems. Let it trail from a hanging basket, train it to climb up a trellis, or shape it into a bush form. Another good basket plant is winter jasmine (*J. polyanthum*). This robust vine bears pink-blushed, white blooms from February on if you keep it cool (40°–55°F [4.5°–13°C]) in fall to early winter. In warmer conditions, try *J. tortuosum* instead.

LIGHT NEEDS: High light, with a half-day of direct sun.

BEST TEMPERATURES: Warm conditions between 60° and 80°F (16° and 26°C).

WATER AND HUMIDITY NEEDS: Keep the soil very moist. Extra humidity is very helpful.

GROWING GUIDELINES: Grow in humus-rich mix in pots or hanging baskets. Fertilize with fish emulsion twice a month in spring through summer. Prune after bloom season to shape the plant.

COMMON PROBLEMS: If spider mites attack, causing yellow stippling on leaves, it usually means that the air is too dry. Spray with superior oil and raise the humidity around the plant.

PROPAGATION: Take cuttings of half-ripe (green but somewhat firm) stem tips.

OTHER COMMON NAMES: Flaming Katy.

DESCRIPTION: Kalanchoe forms clumps of succulent, 3-inch (7.5 cm), deep green leaves. Plants bloom for 2–3 months with clusters of red, pink, yellow, orange, or white flowers on 12-inch (30 cm) stems.

LIGHT NEEDS: High, indirect light.

BEST TEMPERATURES: Provide cool conditions—50°–60°F (10°–16°C)—in fall while buds are forming, then move to average room temperature.

WATER AND HUMIDITY NEEDS: Let the soil dry between waterings. Do not overwater.

GROWING GUIDELINES: Grow kalanchoe in all-purpose potting mix with added sand. Fertilize with fish emulsion once a month from when bloom ends until late summer. Put the plant outdoors for the summer, then give it a cool, drier rest period in fall to encourage bud formation.

COMMON PROBLEMS: Aphids and mealybugs may feed on leaves and stems. Knock the pests off with a strong spray of water, or spray the plant with insecticidal soap or neem.

PROPAGATION: Take stem cuttings in summer, or grow plants from seed.

COMMENTS: Kalanchoe isn't particularly attractive when it's not flowering, and it may be challenging to get it to rebloom. If you just want to enjoy the flowers, treat kalanchoe as a seasonal plant and discard it after flowering.

ORANGE JASMINE

ORCHIDS

This easy-to-grow little shrub blooms on and off year-round. Its white flowers smell strongly of orange blossoms. Give plants plenty of light and water for best growth.

Some 25,000 species and 100,000 hybrids make this the largest flowering plant group on earth, with something for every grower. Many are excellent for windowsills.

OTHER COMMON NAMES: Chinese box.

DESCRIPTION: Orange jasmine is a compact shrub that bears small, bright green, glossy leaves. Waxy, white flowers appear several times per year, followed by bright red berries.

LIGHT NEEDS: High light, with some direct sun.

BEST TEMPERATURES: Warm conditions, at least 60°F (16°C).

WATER AND HUMIDITY NEEDS: Keep the soil very moist.

GROWING GUIDELINES: Grow orange jasmine in all-purpose potting mix. Fertilize twice a month with an all-purpose fertilizer. Clip as desired to shape the plant. It adapts well to training as a topiary or bonsai.

COMMON PROBLEMS: Leaves drop and plants wilt if the soil gets too dry; otherwise, orange jasmine is fairly trouble-free.

PROPAGATION: Grow new plants from seed.

COMMENTS: Do not eat the berries.

RELATED PLANTS:

M. exotica, mock orange, is another easy, fragrant windowsill plant.

DESCRIPTION: Most orchids are tropical epiphytes (plants that grow on the sides of trees instead of in the ground). There are two types of growth habits: sympodial and monopodial. A sympodial orchid grows along a horizontal rhizome, producing new growing points along its length. Monopodial orchids originate from a single growing point, producing leaves from a central rosette or single stem. The flowers have three sepals and three petals, with one petal modified into a showy "lip." Indoor orchids usually bloom in winter.

Cattleyas (*Cattleya* spp. and hybrids) are among the most recognizable orchids, with big, showy, fragrant flowers that are commonly used for corsages. Brightly colored, new "mini-catts" such as 'Hazel Boyd' are better for windowsills. These miniatures grow only 4–10 inches (10–25 cm) tall, as compared to 3 feet (90 cm) for standard types. These sympodial orchids adapt to intermediate temperatures and medium light.

Dendrobiums (*Dendrobium* spp. and hybrids) include a wide range of tropical and subtropical orchids. Two are common houseplant types, both sun-lovers with long, sympodial cane growth and sprays of flowers. Brilliantly bloomed *D. nobile* types (Yamamoto hybrids) are deciduous, needing a cool, dry rest period; evergreen *D. phalaenopsis* prefers warmer conditions.

SWEET OLIVE

Many orchids grow well under a setup of four fluorescent tubes spaced 6 inches (15 cm) above the plants and left on for 14 hours per day.

Moth orchids (*Phalaenopsis* spp. and hybrids) have a monopodial growth habit. They are low-growing, with green or silver-mottled leaves. They produce arching, 3-foot (90 cm) tall sprays of large, long-lasting, striped and spotted blooms in white, pink, yellow, green, and red. Moth orchids are excellent beginner's plants for a warm, low-light spot.

LIGHT NEEDS: Low to high light, depending on the type of orchid.

BEST TEMPERATURES: Cool to warm conditions, depending on the type of orchid. A 10°–15°F (6°–9°C) temperature drop at night is essential, especially in fall, to set buds.

WATER AND HUMIDITY NEEDS: Allow pots to dry between waterings; overwatering is deadly. Extra humidity results in better growth and bloom.

GROWING GUIDELINES: Grow in small pots of a well-drained epiphytic mix: three-quarters fir bark chips to one-quarter perlite. Repot after bloom with fresh mix to maintain good drainage. Fertilize twice a month with a weak solution of fish emulsion, manure tea, or all-purpose fertilizer.

COMMON PROBLEMS: Aphids, mealybugs, and scale may feed on orchid plants; treat with insecticidal soap, superior oil, or neem.

PROPAGATION: Divide sympodial types, leaving three stems on each. Remove rooted offshoots from monopodial types.

Sweet olive is one of the most fragrant houseplants you can grow. The small flowers have a scent reminiscent of ripe apricot. Cool temperatures and high humidity keep plants looking good.

OTHER COMMON NAMES: Fragrant olive, tea olive.

DESCRIPTION: Sweet olive's leathery, elliptical, finely toothed leaves grow on woody, shrubby branches to 6 feet (1.8 m) tall. Clusters of small, creamy white, fragrant flowers appear mainly in fall and winter; they occasionally bloom in spring and summer as well.

LIGHT NEEDS: High, indirect light.

BEST TEMPERATURES: Cool conditions, between 40° and 65°F (4.5° and 15°C).

WATER AND HUMIDITY NEEDS: Keep moist, allowing the soil to dry just slightly between waterings during bloom. Extra humidity is essential.

GROWING GUIDELINES: Grow sweet olive in soil-based container mix well amended with leaf mold or compost. Repot every other year in spring; top-dress with compost during spring in the years you don't repot. Fertilize monthly. Prune in spring after bloom. Put plants outdoors for the summer.

COMMON PROBLEMS: Leaf tip browning indicates that the plant is lacking phosphorus and potash; look for a fertilizer material that contains more of these nutrients than what you're currently using.

PROPAGATION: Take stem cuttings, set them in sand, and keep the humidity very high for good rooting.

COMMENTS: For fragrance, sweet olive cannot be beat.

RELATED PLANTS:

O. fragrans f. *aurantiacus* has orange flowers.

Oxalis spp.   Oxalidaceae   *Passiflora* spp.   Passifloraceae

OXALIS

PASSIONFLOWERS

Oxalis boasts beautiful blooms up to 3 inches (7.5 cm) wide, in just about every color except blue. Some of the new hybrids can flower nearly year-round.

OTHER COMMON NAMES: Wood sorrel.

DESCRIPTION: These bushy, shamrock-leaved plants grow 4–20 inches (10–50 cm) tall. Pink-leaved, lavender-flowered *O. regnellii* var. *atropurpurea* from Brazil is especially easy. It blooms almost continually, even in a low-light, northern window. Pink-flowered *O. rubra* (*O. crassipes*) is also a good choice.

LIGHT NEEDS: High light, with full to part sun.

BEST TEMPERATURES: Intermediate conditions, at or above 50°F (10°C).

WATER AND HUMIDITY NEEDS: Keep evenly moist; reduce water somewhat after bloom.

GROWING GUIDELINES: Add sand and peat moss to all-purpose mix. Repot in fall as needed. Trim everblooming kinds in summer to tidy them up. If your plant flowers only in one season (winter blooming is common), water less after flowering to give the plant a rest period.

COMMON PROBLEMS: Spindly growth results from too little light.

PROPAGATION: Separate offsets from the parent plant and pot them up. You can also divide types that grow from rhizomes.

COMMENTS: Leaves can be poisonous if eaten. Flowers close and leaves fold up at night and on cloudy days.

Passionflowers are coveted for their large, gorgeous, fringed flowers. They often bloom in rare shades of blue, and some are delightfully scented; plants may also produce edible fruit.

DESCRIPTION: Passionflowers have robust vines that grow to 20 feet (6 m) long, with handsome, lobed foliage. Intricate white, purple, red, and blue flowers can bloom almost continuously. Orchid passionflower (*P.* x *alatocaerulea*) is one of the longest bloomers, with 4-inch (10 cm) flowers in a blend of purple, white, and pink. The best edible type is *P. edulis* 'Compact Purple Granadilla'.

LIGHT NEEDS: High light, with at least 4 hours of sun.

BEST TEMPERATURES: 60°F (16°C) or warmer.

WATER AND HUMIDITY NEEDS: Keep the soil moist while plants are actively growing; reduce watering slightly in fall and winter.

GROWING GUIDELINES: Grow in all-purpose mix in a large container. Replace the top 1–2 inches (2.5–5 cm) of soil every year. Fertilize twice a month from spring to late summer with an all-purpose fertilizer.

COMMON PROBLEMS: If plants don't get enough light, their buds will wilt and drop before opening.

PROPAGATION: Take stem cuttings at any time, or grow new plants from seed.

COMMENTS: To produce fruits, most passionflowers must be hand pollinated. Use a small artist's brush to transfer the powdery pollen from the downward-facing, narrow, yellow anthers to the tips of the stigmas. (The stigmas are at the ends of the three-part structure in the very center of the flower.)

| *Pelargonium* spp. | Geraniaceae | *Saintpaulia* hybrids | Gesneriaceae |

GERANIUM

AFRICAN VIOLETS

Geraniums aren't just for outdoor gardens! You can bring some types indoors to enjoy their colorful flowers and scented or patterned leaves all winter long.

The colorful blooms and compact habit of African violets make them the most popular of all flowering houseplants. Grow them on windowsills or under fluorescent lights.

DESCRIPTION: Geraniums are shrubby or trailing plants that can grow to 4 feet (1.2 m) tall. Their leaves may be round, scalloped, or intricately cut; some have pleasant scents or multicolored markings. Flowers generally appear in spring and summer, although some bloom year-round—usually in white, pink, red, or bicolors. Ivy geraniums (*P. peltatum*) have trailing stems that make them ideal for hanging baskets. Regal geraniums, also called Martha Washington geraniums, have large, throat-marked, rhododendron-like blooms.

LIGHT NEEDS: High light, with full sun in winter.

BEST TEMPERATURES: Average room temperature for most geraniums; cooler for ivy and regal types (not over 70°F [21°C]).

WATER AND HUMIDITY NEEDS: Allow to dry between waterings. For best results, use distilled water or rainwater.

GROWING GUIDELINES: Grow geraniums in heavy, sandy mix in small pots. Repot in spring as needed. Fertilize monthly with an all-purpose fertilizer in spring to summer only. After bloom, cut the stems back to 3 inches (7.5 cm), set the plants in a cool, bright spot, and keep them fairly dry until spring.

COMMON PROBLEMS: Low light or too much or too little water can cause leaves to yellow; give the plant more light and try to water more evenly.

PROPAGATION: Take tip cuttings in summer.

DESCRIPTION: African violets have velvety, green or variegated, fleshy leaves that grow between 3 and 12 inches (7.5 and 30 cm) tall. Single or double blooms to 2 inches (5 cm) wide appear just above the leaves on and off year-round. The blooms can be blue, purple, pink, red, white, or green; some are multicolored or marked with a white edge or star.

LIGHT NEEDS: Medium to high indirect light.

BEST TEMPERATURES: Warm conditions, with a steady temperature around 65°F (18°C).

WATER AND HUMIDITY NEEDS: Allow the soil to dry slightly between waterings. Water carefully to avoid wetting the leaves.

GROWING GUIDELINES: Grow in soil-based African violet mix in shallow pots, repotting yearly. Fertilize every 2 weeks in spring and summer with quarter-strength African violet–type fertilizer, or add bonemeal or aged manure each time you repot.

COMMON PROBLEMS: Aphids and mealybugs may feed on leaves and stems. Wash the pests off the plants with tepid water, or dab them with a cotton swab soaked in witch hazel. A lack of flowers may mean that the plant isn't getting enough light, that the temperature is too high, or that the soil is too dry. Cold water can cause spots on leaves.

PROPAGATION: Take leaf cuttings by removing a mature leaf where it joins the stem, then planting the leaf with its stem in a moist but loose medium.

Schlumbergera bridgesii   Cactaceae

CHRISTMAS CACTUS

The showy flowers and distinctive, segmented, trailing stems make Christmas cactus an attractive choice for hanging baskets. Put plants outdoors for the summer.

DESCRIPTION: This shrubby, 12-inch (30 cm) cactus has arching, flat-jointed, thornless green leaves and stems. It blooms abundantly in winter with starry, 3-inch (7.5 cm) flowers. Red is a traditional favorite, although you can also find types with pink, white, or yellow flowers.

LIGHT NEEDS: Medium to high, indirect light.

BEST TEMPERATURES: Average room temperature for most of the year; provide 55°F (13°C) nights in fall to set buds.

WATER AND HUMIDITY NEEDS: Through most of the year, keep the soil evenly moist. Reduce watering in fall until buds form.

GROWING GUIDELINES: Grow in small pots with a well-drained mixture of soil, sand, peat moss, and compost. Repot with fresh mix in spring. Bring indoors before frost in fall, and set in a cool room that is not lighted at night to promote bud formation.

COMMON PROBLEMS: Control aphids by knocking them off with a strong spray of water, spraying plants with insecticidal soap, or spot-treating with isopropyl alcohol on a cotton swab. Too much or too little water or water that is too cold can cause leaves to drop; water more carefully with tepid water. Leaves may turn yellow if the light is too bright; move plants to a spot with less light.

PROPAGATION: Take tip cuttings at any time.

Sinningia hybrids   Gesneriaceae

GLOXINIAS

Gloxinias' velvety leaves make a beautiful background for the showy blooms. The plants grow from firm, rounded tubers and thrive in the same conditions as African violets.

DESCRIPTION: Clusters of hairy, succulent, green leaves range in height from the micro-mini—a scant 1 inch (2.5 cm) tall—to 6-inch (15 cm) miniatures and 12-inch (30 cm) standards. The trumpet-shaped, wavy-edged flowers range from reds, pinks, and white to purples and blues. They bloom primarily in summer but may flower year-round.

LIGHT NEEDS: Medium to high, diffused light. Gloxinias also grow well under fluorescent light.

BEST TEMPERATURES: Warm conditions, around 65°–70°F (18°–21°C); cooler dormancy after bloom.

WATER AND HUMIDITY NEEDS: Keep the soil evenly moist and use tepid water. Provide high humidity.

GROWING GUIDELINES: Pot in African violet mix, positioning tubers with the cupped side up. Repot each year when new growth begins. Fertilize during growth as for African violets (see the African violets entry on page 65). If the leaves start to die down after bloom, give plants a rest period; cut down on watering and reduce temperatures to 50°–60°F (10°–16°C).

COMMON PROBLEMS: Cold water can stain leaves; use tepid water and apply it carefully to avoid getting it on the foliage. If the leaves produce long stems and the leaf edges curl under, the plant isn't getting enough light; move it to a brighter spot.

PROPAGATION: Propagate as for African violets; see the African violets entry.

| *Stephanotis floribunda* | Asclepiadaceae | *Streptocarpus* hybrids | Gesneriaceae |

STEPHANOTIS

Stephanotis has starry, sweet-scented blooms that are traditional favorites for bridal bouquets. Their intoxicating scent can be overwhelming in a small space.

OTHER COMMON NAMES: Bride's flower, Madagascar jasmine.

DESCRIPTION: Stephanotis has waxy, 3-inch (7.5 cm), green leaves along twining vines that can reach 20 feet (6 m). Waxy, white, tubular, 2-inch (5 cm) flowers appear from late spring through fall.

LIGHT NEEDS: High light, with direct sun in winter.

BEST TEMPERATURES: Average to warm conditions—around 70°F (21°C)—in spring and summer; cooler—around 55°F (13°C)—in fall and winter.

WATER AND HUMIDITY NEEDS: During active growth, keep the soil evenly moist; reduce water in winter to keep it barely damp.

GROWING GUIDELINES: Pot in well-drained, all-purpose mix, and provide a trellis for the vine to climb. Fertilize monthly between February and October with an all-purpose fertilizer.

COMMON PROBLEMS: Insufficient light can lead to few or no blooms; move plants to a brighter spot. If spider mites cause yellow stippling on leaves, raise the humidity and spray the plant with superior oil. Leaf yellowing can be a sign of soggy roots; hold off a bit on watering.

PROPAGATION: Take 4-inch (10 cm) stem cuttings of half-matured (still green but somewhat firm) stems in spring and early summer. To promote rooting, set potted cuttings on a heating mat (the kind sold for seed starting) to provide bottom heat.

CAPE PRIMROSE

These African violet relatives boast a long period of colorful bloom; try them in a north window or under fluorescent lights. Pinch off faded flowers before the seedpods form.

DESCRIPTION: The compact, hairy-leaved rosettes of cape primrose grow up to 12 inches (30 cm) tall. They freely produce 2-inch (5 cm) wide trumpets of red, pink, blue, or purple blooms atop 6-inch (15 cm) stalks nearly all year.

LIGHT NEEDS: Medium, indirect light.

BEST TEMPERATURES: Intermediate conditions, with a 5°F (3°C) drop at night; adapts to average room temperature.

WATER AND HUMIDITY NEEDS: Keep the soil moist but not soggy. After bloom, allow it to dry somewhat between waterings.

GROWING GUIDELINES: Grow cape primrose in shallow pots in African violet mix, repotting only when absolutely necessary. Fertilize twice a month with African violet fertilizer, or add bonemeal or aged manure to the growing mix when you repot. Provide a drier rest period after bloom.

COMMON PROBLEMS: Limp stems and leaves indicate too little light; move plants to a brighter spot. Wilted, yellowed leaves may also indicate root rot from overwatering; plants may recover if you let the soil dry out a bit between waterings.

PROPAGATION: Take leaf cuttings by slicing a leaf into three or four parts crossways; stand the pieces upright in a moist growing medium, and keep them warm until they produce roots and new growth. You can also divide plants in spring.

Agave spp.   Agavaceae

CENTURY PLANTS

This succulent plant seems to take a century to bloom, hence its name; actually, though, 15 years is more typical. Give it plenty of light, but water sparingly.

DESCRIPTION: Century plant grows in a rosette of sharp, long, upright foliage. The blue-gray or silvery leaves are narrow, with spiny edges. Some types can reach 4 feet (1.2 m) across. The most popular species for indoor growing is *A. victoriae-reginae,* with thick, blue-green leaves edged and lined in white; it grows to 10 inches (25 cm) wide. *A. desmettiana* grows to 2 feet (60 cm) wide, with dark green to blue-green leaves.

LIGHT NEEDS: High light, with full sun.

BEST TEMPERATURES: Average room temperature.

WATER AND HUMIDITY NEEDS: Allow to dry somewhat between waterings, especially in winter.

GROWING GUIDELINES: Century plants grow well in a mix of sand and soil; add a pinch or two of ground limestone to the mix, too. Plants like being potbound, so move them to a bigger container only when they've completely outgrown their pot. Fertilize just once yearly, in spring, with an all-purpose fertilizer.

COMMON PROBLEMS: Too much water will cause rot. If the plant is getting too big for its pot, keep it in the same pot and cut back on its food and water.

PROPAGATION: Remove offsets from the base of the plant and pot them up to root. You can also grow plants from seed. (Flowers will produce seed if you hand-pollinate them with a fine brush.)

Aglaeonema spp.   Araceae   *Aloe* spp.   Liliaceae

CHINESE EVERGREENS

MEDICINE PLANTS

Chinese evergreen offers gorgeous foliage marked with a mixture of green, pewter, silver, cream, and white; some kinds may even show a bit of pink. Few houseplants adapt as well to a dark corner.

DESCRIPTION: These shrubby, many-stemmed plants can reach 3 feet (90 cm) tall. They are notable for their patterned, elliptic foliage, which grows up to 12 inches (30 cm) long and 4 inches (10 cm) wide. *A. commutatum* is source of many cultivars: The 10-inch (25 cm) tall *A. costatum* has dark green leaves marked with creamy blotches. *A. roebellinii* produces elongated, oval, green leaves and has an upright habit.

LIGHT NEEDS: Low (even dark).

BEST TEMPERATURES: Warm, 65°F (18°C) nights to 85°F (29°C) days.

WATER AND HUMIDITY NEEDS: Keep just moist. Use unchlorinated water, allowing tap water to stand overnight before use for best results.

GROWING GUIDELINES: Pot in a peat-based mix, repotting when the plant looks tired. Fertilize three times a year, or less if in low light. Periodic showers will clean leaves.

COMMON PROBLEMS: Brown leaf edges indicate dry air, bad drainage, or too much minerals or salts from tap water. Leaf variegation fades in too much light. Mealybugs hide at leaf bases. Wash off with a sharp stream of water or drench with insecticidal soap or horticultural oil or neem.

PROPAGATION: Take stem cuttings, divide the stalks, or air layer at any time.

These handsome, succulent, cactus-like houseplants can live for years on benign neglect. Water thoroughly when you think of it, then let the soil dry out before you water again.

OTHER COMMON NAMES: Aloe, burn plant.

DESCRIPTION: Medicine plants grow in a rosette of serrated, soft, sword-like leaves filled with clear, gel-like juice. The leaves may be plain green or variegated or spotted with white or gray. Plants range in size from 1 inch (2.5 cm) to several feet tall. If they get plenty of light, medicine plants may produce spikes of orange, yellow, or red flowers in fall to winter. Burn plant (*A. barbadensis*, also known as *A. vera*) has sword-like leaves that grow to 2 feet (60 cm) long. The bright green foliage has pale cream spots. This species is a popular choice for growing on a kitchen windowsill, since the juicy sap inside the leaves can relieve the pain of burns and cuts. Tiger aloe (*A. variegata*) grows to 9 inches (22.5 cm) tall, with attractive clumps of lance-like, green leaves that have wavy, ivory striping.

LIGHT NEEDS: High light, with a half-day of sun, is best; adapts to less.

BEST TEMPERATURES: Intermediate conditions; approximately 70°F (21°C) days and 50°F (10°C) nights.

WATER AND HUMIDITY NEEDS: Allow to dry between waterings.

GROWING GUIDELINES: Grow medicine plants in clay pots and all-purpose mix with added sand for best drainage. Fertilize lightly once a year, in fall.

COMMON PROBLEMS: Overwatering causes rotting.

PROPAGATION: Remove the offsets at any time.

Aphelandra squarossa   Acanthaceae

ZEBRA PLANT

For dramatic foliage, it's hard to beat the highly striped leaves of zebra plant. It can also produce bright yellow flowers in late summer and fall.

OTHER COMMON NAMES: Saffron spike.

DESCRIPTION: Zebra plant produces dark stems and oval, glossy, green leaves with cream-colored veins. Individual leaves can reach 1 foot (30 cm) long. The shrubby plants grow to 3 feet (90 cm) tall, although compact cultivars are more popular.

LIGHT NEEDS: High, indirect light.

BEST TEMPERATURES: Warm conditions, at least 65°F (18°C).

WATER AND HUMIDITY NEEDS: Provide abundant water in spring through fall; allow to dry somewhat during winter rest. Provide high humidity.

GROWING GUIDELINES: Grow zebra plant in all-purpose potting mix, and fertilize twice a month from spring through fall. After flowering, cut the stem back drastically to just above the lowest node (where the lowest pair of leaves join the stem). Pinch out the tips of new growth when it reaches 6 inches (15 cm) to encourage bushiness.

COMMON PROBLEMS: Spider mites can cause stippling on leaves; raise the humidity and spray the plant with superior oil. If you notice the cottony white bodies of mealybugs, knock them off with a strong spray of water, or spray the plant with insecticidal soap, superior oil, or neem. It is normal for leaves to fall after the plant blooms.

PROPAGATION: Take tip cuttings in late winter to early summer.

Araucaria heterophylla   Araucariaceae

NORFOLK ISLAND PINE

Norfolk Island pine's graceful habit makes it a winning houseplant. Purchase full, dense plants, since sparse-looking specimens will stay that way when you get them home.

DESCRIPTION: This pyramidal, tiered tree has bright green, soft needles. It can grow up to 200 feet (60 m) tall in nature. Fortunately for indoor gardeners, it usually only reaches about 7 feet (2.1 m) tall as a houseplant. The branches have resinous sap.

LIGHT NEEDS: High light, with full sun, is best, but plants can live with less.

BEST TEMPERATURES: Ideal conditions are 70°F (21°C) during the day and 50°–55°F (10°–13°C) at night (particularly in winter). Norfolk Island pine can, however, adapt to a range of temperatures from 45°–85°F (7°–29°C).

WATER AND HUMIDITY NEEDS: Keep evenly moist.

GROWING GUIDELINES: Grow Norfolk Island pine in African violet mix. Repot every 3 years. Fertilize four times a year.

COMMON PROBLEMS: Needles drop if the air is too hot and dry; move the plant to a cooler spot and increase the humidity. Lower branches fall as the plant ages.

PROPAGATION: Buy new plants or start them from seed. Taking cuttings will ruin the shape of your plant.

COMMENTS: Many gardeners enjoy using their Norfolk Island pine as a small Christmas tree during the holiday season.

| *Asparagus densiflorus* | Liliaceae | *Aspidistra elatior* | Liliaceae |

ASPARAGUS FERN

CAST-IRON PLANT

Show off asparagus fern's arching stems by displaying the plant in a hanging basket. The needle-like leaves are actually flattened stems; they are soft when young.

Known since the Victorian age, this Chinese native is renowned for its "cast-iron" constitution. It's suitable for even the most black-thumbed gardener.

OTHER COMMON NAMES: Emerald feather.

DESCRIPTION: This plant has delicate, feathery, arching, green plumes on distinctive, woody, spiny stems to 3 feet (90 cm) long. Tiny, pink flowers may form, followed by small berries that turn successively from white to green to red to black.

LIGHT NEEDS: High, indirect light.

BEST TEMPERATURES: Average to cool conditions (55°–70°F [13°–21°C]).

WATER AND HUMIDITY NEEDS: Keep the soil just moist.

GROWING GUIDELINES: Grow asparagus fern in a humus-rich mix. Fertilize four times a year. Repot whenever the fast-growing roots start creeping out of the pot.

COMMON PROBLEMS: Yellowed foliage means too much light or a lack of nitrogen; reduce the light slightly and fertilize with fish emulsion. Brittle stems and dropping leaves usually indicate that the plant has outgrown its pot and depleted the available nutrients; move the plant to a larger pot with fresh mix.

PROPAGATION: Divide large plants by cutting all the stems down to the soil, then slicing the root ball into 4-inch (10 cm) wide wedges; plant the wedges in individual pots. You can also grow asparagus ferns from seed.

OTHER COMMON NAMES: Barbershop plant.

DESCRIPTION: Usually between 18 and 24 inches (45 and 60 cm) tall, cast-iron plant has an upright growth habit. Its leaves grow to 30 inches (75 cm) long and 4 inches (10 cm) wide. The foliage is generally dark green, although you can occasionally find variegated forms. Small, bell-shaped, purple blooms may form at the base of the plant.

LIGHT NEEDS: Tolerates low light, even very dim corners.

BEST TEMPERATURES: Average room temperature during the day; around 50°F (10°C) at night.

WATER AND HUMIDITY NEEDS: Keep evenly moist.

GROWING GUIDELINES: Repot this slow grower in all-purpose potting mix only every 5 years. Fertilize once in spring (and again in fall if the plant gets medium light).

COMMON PROBLEMS: Spider mites occasionally attack the foliage. Control these pests by washing the leaves monthly with plain water or with a solution of insecticidal soap.

PROPAGATION Divide the roots in early spring and replant in fresh mix; plant two or three pieces together in each pot.

CULTIVARS: 'Variegata' has long creamy or white stripes: the color is best when the plant gets more light and no fertilizer.

Beaucarnea recurvata   Agavaceae

PONYTAIL PALM

Native to the deserts of Mexico, ponytail palm has a thick, swollen base that can store up to a year's supply of water. It's a good choice if you tend to forget to water regularly!

OTHER COMMON NAMES: Elephant foot palm.

DESCRIPTION: When young, ponytail palm is just a grassy clump of narrow leaves growing from a swollen, enlarged base. As it ages, the base expands, and the plant develops a greenish brown trunk topped with a tuft of thin, leathery, strap-like, green leaves. Mature plants can reach 3 feet (90 cm) tall.

LIGHT NEEDS: High or medium light.

BEST TEMPERATURES: Average room temperature but cooler than 75°F (24°C) in winter.

WATER AND HUMIDITY NEEDS: Water thoroughly, then allow the soil to dry before you water again.

GROWING GUIDELINES: Grow ponytail palm in a well-drained cactus mix. Wait several years between repottings. Fertilize annually in early spring.

COMMON PROBLEMS: Too little sun causes limp, pale leaves; move the plant to a brighter location. Otherwise, ponytail palm is generally easy.

PROPAGATION: Separate and repot offsets.

COMMENTS: Ponytail palm produces only one flush of growth a year in spring.

Begonia spp.   Begoniaceae

FOLIAGE BEGONIAS

Who needs flowers when you can have leaves like these? Actually, some foliage begonias do produce flowers, but the blooms tend to be inconspicuous.

OTHER COMMON NAMES: Painted begonia.

DESCRIPTION: Foliage begonias mostly grow from rhizomes (creeping underground stems) to a height of about 16 inches (40 cm). The leaves are often hairy and heart-shaped, with bold or subtle markings in the form of marbling, mottling, spots, or zones. Leaf colors range from green to silver, bronze, purple, red, pink, and black; a silvery overlay is common. Iron cross begonia (_B. masoniana_) has a chocolate-colored cross in the center of each leaf.

LIGHT NEEDS: Medium to high, indirect light; protect from direct sun. Foliage begonias also grow well under fluorescent lights.

BEST TEMPERATURES: Warm—75°F (24°C) during the day and at least 60°F (16°C) at night—for most of the year; slightly cooler in winter.

WATER AND HUMIDITY NEEDS: Allow the soil surface to dry between waterings, especially in winter. Provide extra humidity.

GROWING GUIDELINES: Grow in all-purpose mix in shallow pots. Repot only when the plant outgrows its container. Fertilize monthly from spring to fall, allowing a slight dormancy in winter.

COMMON PROBLEMS: Leaf drop in winter is not unusual during the plant's winter rest period. If leaf colors fade, move the plant to a brighter spot.

PROPAGATION: Take stem or leaf cuttings at any time. Divide the rhizomes in spring.

Brassaia actinophylla Araliaceae	Various genera Bromeliaceae

SCHEFFLERA

BROMELIADS

This elegant indoor tree is very popular and with just cause: It has handsome foliage and can adapt to a range of growing conditions. Prune frequently to keep plants bushy.

OTHER COMMON NAMES: Umbrella tree; Australian umbrella tree.

DESCRIPTION: Scheffleras are shrubby plants with large, compound leaves. Each leaf is composed of seven or more glossy, green leaflets combined in an umbrella-like cluster. Scheffleras can grow to 40 feet (12 m) tall in their native home of Australia and Java; when they're grown indoors in pots, 8 feet (2.4 m) tall is more likely.

LIGHT NEEDS: High light, with a little direct sun.

BEST TEMPERATURES: Average to warm conditions, around 60°–70°F (16°–21°C).

WATER AND HUMIDITY NEEDS: Allow the soil to dry between waterings.

GROWING GUIDELINES: These fast growers need big pots and all-purpose mix; repot at any time. Fertilize monthly in spring and summer, while plants are actively growing.

COMMON PROBLEMS: Spider mites may cause stippling on leaves. Control problems by increasing the humidity around the plant and washing the leaves monthly with water; spray serious infestations with insecticidal soap.

PROPAGATION: Take cuttings, air layer the stems, or grow new plants from seed.

RELATED PLANTS:

    B. arboricola, Hawaiian elf, is a more compact species.

Bromeliads include a variety of striking, slow-growing tropical plants. They may take several years to bloom; in the meantime, enjoy their colorful, beautifully marked leaves.

OTHER COMMON NAMES: Air plants, living vase plants.

DESCRIPTION: Bromeliads produce rosettes of stiff leaves that range in height from 1 inch (2.5 cm) to 3 feet (90 cm) tall. Flowers may arise from the center of a rosette, with showy spikes of red, yellow, pink, and green.

    Air plant (*Tillandsia cyanea*) has long, narrow, arching, green leaves and flat plumes of deep pink or red bracts and violet-blue flowers.

    Flaming sword (*Vriesia splendens*) has vases of brown-banded, green leaves and gorgeous, long, red flower spikes that can grow to 3 feet (90 cm) tall.

    Guzmanias (*Guzmania* spp. and hybrids) grow in a vase shape with strap-like, arching, green leaves to 18 inches (45 cm). *G. musaica* has mottled foliage and orange-yellow spires of flowers.

    Living vases (*Aechmea* spp. and hybrids) include some of the most well-known houseplant bromeliads. They often have strap-shaped, blue-green leaves marked with silvery bands. The spiny-edged, silvery-green urn plant (*A. fasciata*) grows to 3 feet (90 cm), with fat spikes of blue flowers and showy, pink, petal-like bracts.

    Neoregelias (*Neoregelia* spp. and hybrids) form somewhat flattened rosettes of green leaves. As the flowers appear, the center of the plant takes on a colorful blush.

BROMELIADS—CONTINUED

CACTI

The green leaves of Neoregelia carolinae 'Tricolor' are striped with ivory and rose. After blooming, the flowering rosette will be replaced by offsets from the base.

Cacti are generally rugged enough for even black-thumbed gardeners. Their brilliant flowers are often surprisingly large compared to the size of the plant.

Pineapple (*Ananas comosus*) has a vase-shaped habit and narrow, toothed, gray-green leaves. The flower stalk that eventually emerges from the center of the plant is topped with a miniature pineapple.

LIGHT NEEDS: High light with some direct sun; protect from midday sun.

BEST TEMPERATURES: 60°F (16°C) or warmer.

WATER AND HUMIDITY NEEDS: Keep the center cups of vase-shaped types filled with rainwater; drain and refill the cups every week or two. Let other types dry between waterings. Provide extra humidity.

GROWING GUIDELINES: Most bromeliads grow best in clay pots and an epiphytic wood chip mix (as you would use for orchids). Pineapples can grow in well-drained cactus potting soil. Provide liquid fertilizer twice a month in spring and summer and once a month during the rest of the year. Put plants outdoors for the summer.

COMMON PROBLEMS: Too much light can sunburn leaves; move plants outdoors or to high light areas gradually. If you have hard water or if you allow the leaf cups to dry out, you may notice white stains (salt or lime buildup) on leaves; flush the cups weekly with rainwater to remove the stains.

PROPAGATION: Remove and pot up offsets, or grow plants from seed.

DESCRIPTION: Cacti have no leaves to speak of, just thickened, water-storing, spiny stems. They come in a wide variety of shapes and sizes.

Barrel cacti (*Echinocactus* spp.) are spiny, clumping, and barrel-shaped, with showy, bell-shaped flowers that are often yellow. The plants are particularly pretty and colorful while young and are fun to grow from seed.

Chin cactus (*Gymnocalycium mihanovichii*) is globe-shaped with prominent ribs and long-lasting blooms. You may see red or yellow forms of this cactus grafted atop a green stem.

Cob cactus (*Lobivia leucomalla*) has huge flowers on compact, 1-inch (25 mm) plants.

Mammillarias (*Mammillaria* spp.) include many species of easy-to-grow, clustering cacti with showy hairs or spines. They tend to have a ring of small flowers around the top.

Old man cactus (*Cephalocereus senilis*) looks like a hunched man covered with long, white "hair." It blooms at night with rose-pink flowers.

Peanut cactus (*Chamaecereus silvestri*) forms 6-inch (15 cm) long clusters of green branches with soft, white spines. It produces orange-red flowers.

Prickly pear cacti (*Opuntia* spp.) are among the most recognized cactus groups, with their flat "pads" and glossy flowers.

Rabbit ears (*O. microdasys*) reaches 1 foot (30 cm)

SPIDER PLANT

Repot every few years in early spring. Protect your hands while repotting by wearing sturdy gloves or by wrapping newspaper around the thorny plants.

tall, with green pads dotted with small clusters of tiny, spine-like glochids.

Rattail cactus (*Aporocactus flagelliformis*) is good for hanging baskets, with 3-foot (90 cm) long stems and bright red blooms.

LIGHT NEEDS: High light, with direct sun.

BEST TEMPERATURES: Average room temperature for most of the year; cool conditions—approximately 65°F (18°C) days and 40°F (4.5°C) nights—in winter.

WATER AND HUMIDITY NEEDS: In late March and April, water thoroughly and wait until the soil surface feels dry before watering again. Begin decreasing water steadily from May through December; give almost no water in winter.

GROWING GUIDELINES: Keep cacti potbound in well-drained clay pots of all-purpose mix with added sand. Fertilize once a year in early spring. Put plants outdoors for the summer. Provide a cool, dry winter rest period.

COMMON PROBLEMS: Plants that do not get a winter rest period may produce weak, spindly growth. Overwatering can lead to wilting and root rot.

PROPAGATION: Take stem or leaf cuttings, remove and repot offsets, or grow new plants from seed. Any cactus can be grafted to another by placing the cut bottom of one atop a cut tip of another and tying them firmly until they unite.

One of the most common plants for a hanging basket, spider plant is beloved for its graceful habit. It produces baby plants at the ends of long, arching stems.

OTHER COMMON NAMES: Ribbon plant, spider ivy.

DESCRIPTION: Spider plant grows from rhizomes (creeping underground stems) to produce arching, narrow, 12–18-inch (30–45 cm) long, green leaves. It also sends out long, pale yellow stems, with small white flowers along their length.

LIGHT NEEDS: Medium light; avoid strong, direct sun.

BEST TEMPERATURES: Average room temperature during the day; approximately 50°F (10°C) at night.

WATER AND HUMIDITY NEEDS: Allow the soil surface to dry between waterings. Plants can take dry conditions but prefer extra humidity and rainwater.

GROWING GUIDELINES: Use all-purpose mix in small hanging baskets, leaving 1 inch (2.5 cm) between the rim of the pot and the top of the soil. Fertilize twice a month in spring and summer.

COMMON PROBLEMS: High temperatures and over-drying can cause brown leaves; move the plant to a cooler spot and water more regularly to keep the soil evenly moist. Some kinds of tap water can cause brown leaf tips; if this is a problem, snip off the damaged tips and try using rainwater to water your plants.

PROPAGATION: Divide the parent plant or grow new plants from seed. You can also make new plants by removing plantlets from the end of the dangling stems. Set the base of the plantlet in water until roots begin to form, then move it to a pot.

Cissus spp.　　　　　　　　　　　　Vitaceae

GRAPE IVY

Grape ivies make splendid foliage vines, adapting to low light and dry air without too much fuss. Provide some kind of trellis so vines can climb.

OTHER COMMON NAMES: Kangaroo vine.

DESCRIPTION: These tendril-climbing vines can grow to 10 feet (3 m). The fleshy, green leaves grow to 4 inches (10 cm) long; they are sometimes fuzzy underneath. Grape ivy (*C. rhombifolia*), from tropical America, has large, metallic green, lobed leaves; it is easy to grow. Kangaroo vine (*C. antarctica*) is a vigorous grower with shiny, leathery leaves; it hails from Australia. Dwarf grape ivy (*C. striata*), from Chile, is a compact climber with small, five-lobed leaves.

LIGHT NEEDS: Medium to high light, but keep the plant out of direct sun.

BEST TEMPERATURES: Warm conditions but cooler than 75°F (24°C).

WATER AND HUMIDITY NEEDS: Keep evenly moist, but don't let the plant sit in water. Tolerates low humidity.

GROWING GUIDELINES: Provide all-purpose mix in very well-drained baskets. Repot as needed. Fertilize twice a month in spring and summer. Pinch sideshoots back frequently to encourage dense growth.

COMMON PROBLEMS: Grape ivies are generally problem-free.

PROPAGATION: Take stem cuttings at any time, or grow new plants from seed.

Codiaeum variegatum var. *pictum*　　　Euphorbiaceae

CROTON

These tropical Indian and Malaysian plants provide some of the most gorgeous, brilliantly colored houseplant foliage. Their colors often change as the plants age.

OTHER COMMON NAMES: Variegated laurel.

DESCRIPTION: These shrubby, 4-foot (1.2 m) plants boast spectacular, oak-leaf-shaped to oval-shaped leaves. The foliage color ranges through yellow, red, pink, orange, green, and brown, with markings often different from leaf to leaf on the same plant.

LIGHT NEEDS: High light, with some direct sun.

BEST TEMPERATURES: Warm conditions between 65° and 80°F (18° and 26°C).

WATER AND HUMIDITY NEEDS: Keep evenly moist for most of the year; allow the surface to dry between waterings in winter. Provide extra humidity.

GROWING GUIDELINES: Repot in spring into soil-based mix. Fertilize twice a month except in winter. Set crotons outside for the summer. If plants get leggy, cut the stems back to about 6 inches (15 cm) above the soil, just above a node (the slightly swollen point where the lowest leaf was attached to the stem).

COMMON PROBLEMS: If spider mites cause stippling on leaves, raise the humidity and spray with superior oil. Knock cottony white mealybugs off the plant with a strong spray of water, or spray with insecticidal soap, superior oil, or neem. Lack of light can cause leaf colors to fade. Cold temperatures can cause leaf drop.

PROPAGATION: Air layer the stems, or take cuttings from half-ripe (green but somewhat firm) sideshoots.

JADE PLANT   # DUMBCANE

This slow-growing, easy-care succulent is one of the most widely grown houseplants. Its fleshy, emerald green leaves branch off of thick, trunk-like stems.

Bold, fancy leaves are the trademark of this popular plant. It gets the name dumbcane due to its irritating sap, which causes swelling and pain of the tongue if eaten.

OTHER COMMON NAMES: Baby jade.

DESCRIPTION: Jade plant grows slowly to 4 feet (1.2 m) tall, with thick branches and a shrubby form. The smooth, oval, 2-inch (5 cm) long leaves are usually bright green. The plant seldom blooms when grown indoors.

LIGHT NEEDS: Medium to high light.

BEST TEMPERATURES: Intermediate; 50°–80°F (10°–26°C).

WATER AND HUMIDITY NEEDS: Allow to dry between waterings; don't overwater.

GROWING GUIDELINES: Grow jade plant in a blend of half perlite and half all-purpose potting mix. Fertilize every 3 months, except in winter. Pinch new growth to encourage bushiness. If you keep it cool and allow it to get potbound, the plant may flower in winter.

COMMON PROBLEMS: Mealybugs like to hide along stems and under leaves. Knock them off the plant with a strong spray of water, or spray with insecticidal soap, superior oil, or neem. Weak or leggy growth tells you the plant isn't getting enough light; move it to a brighter spot.

PROPAGATION: Take stem or leaf cuttings.

COMMENTS: Leaf margins take on a reddish tinge when the plant is getting the ideal amount of light.

OTHER COMMON NAMES: Mother-in-law's tongue

DESCRIPTION: The upright stems of dumbcane grow to 6 feet (1.8 m) tall, with elliptical leaves that can reach 18 inches (45 cm) long by 12 inches (30 cm) wide. The green foliage is marked and spotted in various shades of green, cream, and yellow.

LIGHT NEEDS: High, indirect light is best, although the plant can adapt to less.

BEST TEMPERATURES: Warm conditions (at least 60°F [16°C]). Keep the plant out of drafts.

WATER AND HUMIDITY NEEDS: Allow the soil to dry a bit between waterings. Provide extra humidity.

GROWING GUIDELINES: Grow dumbcane in all-purpose mix, and keep it potbound. Fertilize lightly with fish emulsion twice a month in warm seasons. Rinse dust off of the leaves several times a year.

COMMON PROBLEMS: As they age, plants tend to drop their lower foliage, leaving you with a bare stem topped with a tuft of leaves. To rejuvenate the plant, cut the stem to about 6 inches (15 cm) tall. Control spider mites by raising the humidity and spraying with superior oil. Knock mealybugs off the plant with a strong spray of water, or treat the plant with insecticidal soap, superior oil, or neem. Overwatering and lack of light can produce thin stems and widely spaced leaves.

PROPAGATION: Air layer the stems, or take tip or stem cuttings.

| *Dizygotheca elegantissima* | Araliaceae | *Dracaena* spp. | Agavaceae |

FALSE ARALIA

False aralia sports upright stems clad in lacy leaves. This South Pacific native is a good choice for warm, shaded, humid spots with low to medium light.

DESCRIPTION: This elegant, shrubby tree grows to 6 feet (1.8 m) tall, with serrated, fern-like, palmate leaves. The young foliage is coppery bronze, sometimes mottled with cream; the leaves change to dark greenish black as they age.

LIGHT NEEDS: Low to medium, indirect light.

BEST TEMPERATURES: Warm conditions; at least 60°F (16°C) in winter.

WATER AND HUMIDITY NEEDS: Allow the soil surface to dry between waterings. Provide extra humidity.

GROWING GUIDELINES: Grow false aralia in all-purpose potting mix. Repot every few years as needed. Fertilize twice a month in spring and summer.

COMMON PROBLEMS: If spider mites cause light-colored stippling on leaves, control the pests by raising the humidity and spraying the plant with superior oil. Leaves may drop as the plant ages or because of overwatering or moving the plant from place to place. Age, cold, and lack of humidity can cause the plant to get scraggly; take cuttings to rejuvenate the plant and keep in a warm, humid location.

PROPAGATION: Take stem cuttings in warm seasons.

COMMENTS: If you always want the best-looking false aralias, treat them as short-lived specimens and replace them when they start looking shabby.

DRACAENA

Dracaenas are tough, adaptable plants that are easy to find and easy to grow. With age, they produce a thick trunk and lose their bottom leaves.

DESCRIPTION: Dracaenas are tree-like plants that can grow anywhere from 18 inches (45 cm) to 8 feet (2.4 m) tall. They are noted for their distinctively marked, bold, often sword-like foliage. Corn plant (*D. fragrans*) has green, corn-like foliage. Dragon tree (*D. marginata*)—also known as red-margined dracaena—has narrow, dark green leaves that are edged in maroon. Slow-growing golddust dracaena (*D. godseffiana*) has gold-and-white spotted leaves. Striped dracaena (*D. deremensis*) can reach 15 feet (4.5 m), with green leaves usually striped with white and gray.

LIGHT NEEDS: High, indirect light is best, but dracaena tolerates less.

BEST TEMPERATURES: Warm conditions (65°–70°F [18°–21°C]).

WATER AND HUMIDITY NEEDS: Keep evenly moist most of the year; allow it to dry somewhat between waterings in winter. Provide extra humidity.

GROWING GUIDELINES: Grow dracaenas in all-purpose potting mix. Fertilize twice a month in warm seasons.

COMMON PROBLEMS: Low light causes thin stems and faded leaves. Browned leaf edges indicate overdrying and/or salt buildup.

PROPAGATION: Take tip or stem cuttings, or air layer the trunk.

| *Fatsia japonica* | Araliaceae | Various genera | Polypodiaceae |

ARALIA

This ivy relative is a fast-growing houseplant that's ideal for cool spots. Wipe the broad leaves with a damp cloth several times a year to keep them clean and glossy.

OTHER COMMON NAMES: Formosa rice tree, Japanese aralia.

DESCRIPTION: Aralia's large, green, lobed leaves can grow up to 1 foot (30 cm) across. The shrubby plant may reach 5 feet (1.5 m) tall.

LIGHT NEEDS: High light.

BEST TEMPERATURES: Cool conditions, with days around 65°F (18°C) and nights around 50°F (10°C).

WATER AND HUMIDITY NEEDS: Keep the soil just moist in spring and summer; reduce watering in fall and winter, but don't let the soil dry out. Provide extra humidity in warm temperatures.

GROWING GUIDELINES: Grow aralia in large pots in all-purpose mix. Repot as needed in spring. Fertilize twice a year—in early spring and early summer. Set plants outdoors for the summer. Keep them bushy by trimming stems lightly in spring.

COMMON PROBLEMS: If the stems get leggy, cut them back by half in spring.

PROPAGATION: Take cuttings in late winter and spring, or grow new plants from seed.

RELATED PLANTS:

Fatshedera lizei, tree ivy, was produced by crossing aralia (*Fatsia japonica*) with English ivy (*Hedera helix* var. *hibernica*). It has five-lobed leaves and aralia's shrubby form. Its upright stems grow to 3 feet (90 cm) tall. Tree ivy appreciates the same growing conditions as its parents.

FERNS

Beloved for their gracefully arching, often feathery fronds, ferns are a mainstay for houseplant growers. These flowerless plants grow from rhizomes and reproduce via spores.

DESCRIPTION: Ferns are a broad group of plants that includes many different genera.

Boston fern (*Nephrolepis exaltata* 'Bostoniensis') has been grown in cultivation for over 100 years for its graceful, arching fronds.

Maidenhair ferns (*Adiantum* spp.) produce thin, dark stems and lacy, light green fronds. Australian maidenhair (*A. hispidulum*) is the most rugged species for indoor growing.

Rabbit's foot fern (*Davallia fejeensis*) is an unfussy, feathery fern with "furry-footed" rhizomes.

LIGHT NEEDS: Medium to high, indirect light.

BEST TEMPERATURES: Average conditions, with day temperatures up to 75°F (24°C) and nights between 55° and 65°F (13° and 18°C).

WATER AND HUMIDITY NEEDS: Keep evenly moist water daily if necessary. Extra humidity is a plus

GROWING GUIDELINES: Grow ferns in small pots in light, well-drained, all-purpose mix with added peat moss and perlite. Repot in spring as needed. Fertilize twice a year—in early spring and early summer—with fish emulsion.

COMMON PROBLEMS: Scales may produce small, irregularly spaced spots on the fronds; scrape them off with your fingernail or with a cotton swab.

PROPAGATION: Divide clump-forming ferns, grow new plants from spores, or pin the runners to the soil and repot them when they are rooted.

FIGS

This large group of tropical plants has produced some of our best-known and easiest-to-grow houseplants. All of these plants produce a harmless milky sap when cut.

OTHER COMMON NAMES: Ficus, rubber plant.

DESCRIPTION: Figs can be trees, shrubs, or woody vines, with milky sap and usually thick leaves. Many species make good houseplants.

Creeping fig (*F. pumila*) is a fast-growing, dark, oval-leaved vine suitable for baskets. The tiniest types, such as quilted creeping fig (*F. pumila* var. *minima*), are excellent growing on moss-stuffed topiary forms.

Edible fig (*F. carica*) grows to 8 feet (2.4 m) tall in big tubs, producing large leaves and edible fruits. It drops its leaves in winter, when it needs a cool, dry rest period.

Mistletoe fig (*F. deltoidea*) has flat, green leaves that are oval at the tips and pointed at the base. It produces small, yellowish fruits on plants shorter than 6 feet (1.8 m).

Rubber plant (*F. elastica*), with its large, elliptical, dark green leaves, is a common sight in houseplant collections. It normally reaches about 6 feet (1.8 m) tall indoors. 'Burgundy' is the purple rubber tree.

Weeping or java fig (*F. benjamina*) is one of the best species for indoor gardens. It grows in a tree-like form to 8 feet (2.4 m) tall, with dainty, 2–5-inch (5–12.5 cm), oval leaves and cinnamon-colored bark. It is easy to grow even in low light, although the more light it gets, the more leaves it produces.

Rubber plant has large, bold leaves. It was the original source of latex rubber. Air layer the stems if rubber plants are leggy or too bare at the bottom.

LIGHT NEEDS: Medium to high light.

BEST TEMPERATURES: Average room temperature; avoid moving plants from high to low light.

WATER AND HUMIDITY NEEDS: Allow the soil of most figs to dry somewhat between waterings. Keep creeping types evenly damp.

GROWING GUIDELINES: Grow figs in all-purpose mix that's been enriched with compost. Keep them potbound to prevent overwatering; repot only every 3–4 years. Feed twice a year, occasionally providing a very dilute vinegar solution. Wipe large-leaved types periodically with a damp sponge. Fresh air is very beneficial.

COMMON PROBLEMS: Spider mites and scale can attack if the air is hot and dry; control them by raising the humidity and decreasing the temperature. Treat scale by spraying with insecticidal soap or superior oil or by dabbing them with a cotton swab dipped in isopropyl alcohol. Treat spider mites by spraying with superior oil. Lower leaves may drop due to temperature or light changes, drafts, or too much or too little water. If the bottom of a weeping fig becomes too bare, cut it back to 5 inches (12.5 cm) above the soil and withhold water until new growth begins.

PROPAGATION: Air layer the stems of upright types. Root creeping types from tip cuttings or divide the rooting stems.

FITTONIA

The green leaves of fittonia are etched in an intricate mosaic pattern with rosy white veins. This plant is beautiful but can be finicky, especially with regard to humidity.

OTHER COMMON NAMES: Mosaic plant, red-nerved plant.

DESCRIPTION: These low, creeping or trailing plants have olive green, oval leaves veined in rose, cream, or red, depending on the cultivar.

LIGHT NEEDS: Low light. Fittonia grows well under fluorescent lights.

BEST TEMPERATURES: Warm conditions, with both day and night temperatures at least 65°F (18°C).

WATER AND HUMIDITY NEEDS: Keep the soil evenly moist. High humidity is essential; mist often.

GROWING GUIDELINES: Grow fittonias in African violet mix. Feed monthly with a half-strength, all-purpose fertilizer. Pinch the stem tips often to keep the plant dense.

COMMON PROBLEMS: Plants get scraggly with age; take cuttings and discard old plants.

PROPAGATION: Root stem or tip cuttings in sand.

COMMENTS: Fittonias thrive in terrariums.

RELATED PLANTS:

F. verschaffeltii argyroneura 'Stripes Forever', silver-nerved fittonia, has bright white veins on tiny, light green leaves.

PEARL PLANT

This small, easy-to-grow, African native has spiky rosettes of upright, spotted or striped, succulent leaves. It's a great choice for a beginner, since it's practically indestructible.

DESCRIPTION: Pearl plant forms 4-inch (10 cm) tall rosettes of fat, green leaves that are decorated with small, white, raised spots. You may occasionally see the plant produce slender stems topped with small, white blooms.

LIGHT NEEDS: Medium light, without direct sun. Pearl plant grows well under fluorescent lights.

BEST TEMPERATURES: Average room temperature.

WATER AND HUMIDITY NEEDS: Allow the soil to dry a bit between waterings. Water less often in winter, but don't let the soil get completely dry.

GROWING GUIDELINES: Grow pearl plant in cactus soil in shallow pots. Do not fertilize.

COMMON PROBLEMS: This plant is virtually trouble-free and tough to kill.

PROPAGATION: Separate offsets and pot them up.

RELATED PLANTS:

H. fasciata, zebra plant, has 2-inch (5 cm) leaves that are wonderfully striped in dark green and black.

H. retusa, cathedral window cactus, has flat, spade-shaped leaf tips windowed with pale lines.

Hedera helix   Araliaceae

ENGLISH IVY

English ivy leaves come in just about any shape and markings you can imagine. Train them to climb trellises or let them cascade from hanging baskets.

DESCRIPTION: These woody vines bear green or mottled, lobed leaves in a variety of oval, pointed, and heart shapes. The young leaves tend to have the most attractive forms and colors; older leaves often lose their lobes and revert to solid color forms. The stems can climb by means of clinging roots.

LIGHT NEEDS: Medium to high, indirect light is best, although English ivy can adapt to a range of light conditions.

BEST TEMPERATURES: Keep plants around 65°F (18°C) during the day and 50°F (10°C) at night; they can tolerate lower temperatures.

WATER AND HUMIDITY NEEDS: Allow the soil surface to dry somewhat between waterings. English ivy appreciates misting.

GROWING GUIDELINES: Grow in all-purpose mix in pots or hanging baskets or provide a trellis for climbing. Fertilize twice a year (spring and summer). Pinch off the tips of new growth to keep the plant bushy.

COMMON PROBLEMS: Spider mites can be a real nuisance in hot, dry conditions; raise the humidity and rinse the plant off in the shower every few weeks to discourage them.

PROPAGATION: Take tip cuttings at any time.

CULTIVARS: 'Filigran', filigree ivy, has green leaves with fluted edges. 'Sagittaefolia Variegata', bird's foot ivy, forms mounds of white-frosted leaves.

Hypoestes phyllostachya   Acanthaceae

POLKA DOT PLANT

Who could believe that something this colorful is actually real? Polka dot plant is a striking and unique addition to bright indoor gardens; it also grows well outdoors.

OTHER COMMON NAMES: Freckleface.

DESCRIPTION: Polka dot plant is a woody-based shrub that can grow up to 3 feet (90 cm) tall, although it is normally smaller when grown indoors. Its 2½-inch (7 cm) long, pointed, dark green leaves are liberally spotted in lavender-rose or white.

LIGHT NEEDS: High light.

BEST TEMPERATURES: Average room temperature.

WATER AND HUMIDITY NEEDS: Allow the soil surface to dry just slightly between waterings.

GROWING GUIDELINES: Grow in all-purpose, soil-based mix. Fertilize twice a month in spring and summer. Pinch off the shoot tips to promote bushy growth; the plant is best at about 18 inches (45 cm) tall.

COMMON PROBLEMS: The colorful leaf spots tend to fade if the plant isn't getting enough light; move it to a brighter location. Plants get leggy with age; replace them with new plants or cut the old ones back to 1 inch (2.5 cm) tall and repot them.

PROPAGATION: Take tip cuttings, or grow new plants from seed.

COMMENTS: *H. phyllostachya* is often sold as *H. sanguinolenta*.

PRAYER PLANT

This showy foliage houseplant has two special features: the unique markings that look as though a rabbit left tracks down the leaves and the way the leaves fold upward at night.

OTHER COMMON NAMES: Rabbit tracks.

DESCRIPTION: Prayer plant's branching stems form clumps to 12 inches (30 cm) tall, with 5-inch (12.5 cm) long, oval leaves. The bright green, satiny foliage is very distinctively marked with brownish purple "rabbit tracks" on either side of the midrib. Each leaf has large, rosy pink veins and a red-purple underside.

LIGHT NEEDS: Medium, indirect or artificial light.

BEST TEMPERATURES: Warm conditions, between 60° and 70°F (16° and 21°C).

WATER AND HUMIDITY NEEDS: Keep the soil evenly moist through most of the year and somewhat drier in winter. Mist often.

GROWING GUIDELINES: Grow prayer plant in soil-less mix. Repot into fresh mix each year in early spring. Fertilize twice a month from spring to fall; do not fertilize in winter.

COMMON PROBLEMS: Prayer plant likes fresh air, but cold drafts can lead to poor growth and a gradual decline in health.

PROPAGATION: Divide in spring.

CULTIVARS: The variety *kerchoveana* is deep green and chocolate without rosy veins; 'Variegata' adds yellow and pink spots.

SPLIT-LEAVED PHILODENDRON

These sometime enormous and always very popular houseplant vines offer spectacularly notched, perforated leaves. Sponge leaves often to keep them clean.

OTHER COMMON NAMES: Hurricane plant.

DESCRIPTION: This semi-shrubby vine grows to 30 feet (9 m) in the jungle, although it usually stops at about 6 feet (1.8 m) indoors. The dark green leaves can reach 3 feet (90 cm) wide, with many indented notchings.

LIGHT NEEDS: Medium to high, indirect or artificial light.

BEST TEMPERATURES: Warm conditions, with daytime temperatures to 85°F (29°C) and nights from 65°–70°F (18°–21°C).

WATER AND HUMIDITY NEEDS: Keep barely moist.

GROWING GUIDELINES: Grow split-leaved philodendron in all-purpose mix, and provide a wood slab or trellis for support. Repot as needed. Fertilize twice a year (early spring and mid-summer). Pinch back regularly to encourage side branching. To rejuvenate overgrown plants, air layer the tops and drastically cut back the remaining stems.

COMMON PROBLEMS: Split-leaved philodendron will not grow if the temperature is too cold. Weak growth, sparse foliage, or solid, unsplit leaves tell you that your plant is not getting enough light. It's natural for bottom leaves to drop as the plant ages.

PROPAGATION: Take leaf bud cuttings by slicing the stem into sections, each with one leaf, and placing the stem pieces into soil; or air layer stems.

MYRTLE

PALMS

Myrtle's aromatic leaves are great for flavoring roasted meats. But even if they weren't useful, you'd enjoy growing myrtles for their glossy, dark green foliage and shrubby form.

Palms appreciate a summer vacation outdoors; just make sure they're sheltered from direct sun. If you notice brown leaf tips, you can trim them off with scissors.

OTHER COMMON NAMES: Greek myrtle.

DESCRIPTION: Myrtles produce dense, upright, shrubby mounds from woody trunks. They grow to 16 feet (4.8 m) tall in nature, although 3 feet (90 cm) is about the limit as a houseplant. The stems carry many small, boxwood-like, dark green, fragrant leaves. Dainty, orange-blossom-scented, white flowers may appear from spring to summer, then turn to blue-black berries.

LIGHT NEEDS: High to medium light.

BEST TEMPERATURES: Average room temperature in spring and summer; cooler (around 45°–50°F [7°–10°C]) in fall and winter.

WATER AND HUMIDITY NEEDS: Keep evenly moist.

GROWING GUIDELINES: Grow in a soil-based mix. Repot as needed in spring. Fertilize monthly in spring and summer; do not fertilize in fall or winter.

COMMON PROBLEMS: Mealybugs and scale may attack. Myrtle responds badly to soaps; use neem.

PROPAGATION: Take cuttings from firm or part-ripe wood at any time or from seed.

COMMENTS: It's easy to train myrtle into geometric or fanciful topiary shapes, since it tolerates regular pruning and responds with bushy growth.

DESCRIPTION: Indoor palms range in size from 3–15 feet (0.9–4.5 m) tall, with stiff trunks and fan-like or feathery, compound leaves.

Chamaedoreas (*Chamaedorea* spp.) are small palms. The popular parlor palm (*C. elegans,* also known as *Neanthe bella* or *Collinia elegans*) is a true dwarf, with 2-foot (60 cm) long, medium to light green leaves and a single, 3–4-foot (90–120 cm), dark green, ringed trunk.

Kentia palm (*Howea forsterana*) is the easiest and most popular indoor palm, enduring drought and low light. It produces gorgeous, arching, dark green fronds to a height of about 7 feet (2.1 m).

LIGHT NEEDS: Medium, indirect light.

BEST TEMPERATURES: Average room temperature, not below 55°F (13°C).

WATER AND HUMIDITY NEEDS: Water abundantly while the plant is in active growth; allow the soil surface to dry just slightly between waterings.

GROWING GUIDELINES: Grow in a mixture of equal parts all-purpose potting soil and sandy, organic topsoil. Provide fish emulsion from late spring to early fall. Repot as needed in spring or summer. Put plants outdoors for the summer. Wash foliage frequently with a hose or in the shower.

COMMON PROBLEMS: If spider mites attack, raise the humidity and spray with superior oil.

PROPAGATION: Grow new palms from seed.

PEPEROMIAS

Peperomias thrive in warm, bright spots with extra humidity. These compact plants come in a wide range of leaf textures and patterns; sometimes they also produce flower spikes.

DESCRIPTION: Most peperomias have vining or bushy stems that usually grow to about 6 inches (15 cm) tall. Their fleshy, oval leaves may be flat and smooth or puckered and wrinkled. Some species have plain green leaves; others may be edged or veined with cream, gray, or silver. The plants occasionally produce thin pink stems topped with narrow, creamy white flower spikes.

LIGHT NEEDS: High light, with some full sun (especially for variegated types); peperomias also grow well under fluorescent lights.

BEST TEMPERATURES: Average room temperature.

WATER AND HUMIDITY NEEDS: Keep evenly moist in spring and summer; allow to dry slightly between waterings in fall and winter. Extra humidity is necessary.

GROWING GUIDELINES: Grow peperomias in clay pots in light, well-drained mix. Repot with fresh mix each spring. Give dilute fertilizer monthly in spring and fall.

COMMON PROBLEMS: Peperomias rot easily if you overwater them or if water stands on the leaves; water carefully to prevent this problem. Tan patches on leaves are a sign of sunburn; pinch off damaged leaves and move the plant to a spot out of direct sun.

PROPAGATION: Divide clump-forming types; take leaf or stem cuttings from upright or vining types.

PHILODENDRON

If you're nervous about growing houseplants, start with philodendrons—they're durable plants that don't take much fussing to stay green and look good.

DESCRIPTION: Philodendrons produce climbing or bushy growth that can eventually reach 9 feet (2.7 m) tall. Their stems carry thin aerial roots and usually lobed green leaves that can be marked with gold, red, or white. The young leaves are often not as distinctively shaped or colored as the older ones. Bushy, self-heading types of philodendron grow from a single crown near the ground. Heart-leaved philodendron (*P. scandens* subsp. *oxycardium,* also known as *P. cordatum*) is a small-leaved, silky, green vine that can trail or be trained upright. Of the bushy, self-heading types, slow-growing *P. selloum* is best. The species has green leaves and can grow to 8 feet (2.4 m) tall; miniature cultivars are available.

LIGHT NEEDS: Medium to high, indirect light; bushy types tolerate lower light.

BEST TEMPERATURES: Warm conditions, with nights around 65°–70°F (18°–21°C).

WATER AND HUMIDITY NEEDS: Keep just moist.

GROWING GUIDELINES: Philodendron grows fine in almost any mix; it will even root and grow in water! Repot at any time. Fertilize every 3 months.

COMMON PROBLEMS: Direct sun can produce tan patches of sunburn on leaves; move the plant out of the sun to prevent further damage.

PROPAGATION: Take tip or stem cuttings from vining types at any time. Grow self-heading (bushy) types from seed, or separate and pot up the offsets.

Pilea spp.   Urticaceae

PILEAS

Pileas are excellent terrarium plants. To keep them looking good, take cuttings each year to start new plants, then dispose of the old, scraggly ones.

OTHER COMMON NAMES: Aluminum plant.

DESCRIPTION: These low-growing, tropical, shrubby plants are distinguished by their textured and sometimes puckered leaves. Ferny, bright green, 12-inch (30 cm) artillery plant (*P. microphylla*) is so named because it releases its pollen in puffs. Cat's tongue (*P. mollis*) has green-and-brown, puckered leaves. The Pan-American friendship plant (*P. involucrata*) from Peru grows 6–8 inches (15–20 cm) tall. It offers wonderful oval, quilted, chocolate-veined, hairy leaves, as well as tiny creamy or greenish flowers on occasion. Trailing creeping Charlie (*P. nummulariifolia*) is a lovely little rooting groundcover. Aluminum plant (*P. cadieri*) is the most popular species, growing to 12 inches (30 cm) tall with silver-painted, green, oval leaves.

LIGHT NEEDS: Medium to high, indirect light.

BEST TEMPERATURES: Warm conditions, with 65°–70°F (18°–21°C) nights.

WATER AND HUMIDITY NEEDS: Water to moisten the soil, then let the surface dry before you water again. Provide extra humidity.

GROWING GUIDELINES: Grow pileas in all-purpose potting mix with added peat moss. Fertilize twice a month in spring and summer.

COMMON PROBLEMS: Plants get leggy with age. Discard plants each year after taking cuttings.

PROPAGATION: Take tip cuttings or divide in spring.

Plectranthus australis   Labiatae

SWEDISH IVY

Swedish ivy's trailing stems make it a perfect choice for hanging baskets. Pinch off the stem tips frequently to promote full growth, then use the pieces to start new plants.

DESCRIPTION: The scalloped, round, green, fleshy leaves of Swedish ivy grow along trailing stems that can reach 8 inches (20 cm) long. Occasionally, small, light purple flowers will appear.

LIGHT NEEDS: Medium to high light.

BEST TEMPERATURES: Average room temperature.

WATER AND HUMIDITY NEEDS: Keep the soil evenly moist.

GROWING GUIDELINES: Grow Swedish ivy in hanging pots in all-purpose mix. Repot yearly. Fertilize twice a month from spring to fall (or less often if you don't want your plant to grow quite so fast). Pinch off the tips of new growth often.

COMMON PROBLEMS: Wash the cottony white bodies of mealybugs off plants with a strong spray of water; you could also spray with insecticidal soap, superior oil, or neem. Strong sun can cause tan patches on leaves; move the plant out of direct sun to prevent further damage. Swedish ivy tends to get scraggly with age; root new plants from young stem pieces and discard the old plants.

PROPAGATION: Take tip cuttings and stick them in all-purpose potting mix to root.

RELATED PLANTS:

P. oertendahlii, candle plant, has dark green, silver-veined leaves that are red underneath. It may also produce lacy white flowers.

POTHOS

Pothos is a trailing or climbing houseplant that's often confused with philodendron. It's a real survivor that can take some neglect.

OTHER COMMON NAMES: Devil's ivy.

DESCRIPTION: This vining plant produces long stems that can climb to 40 feet (12 m) if left unpruned. The stems will trail out of a hanging basket or climb a support, clinging with aerial roots. The leathery, heart-shaped leaves grow to 4 inches (10 cm) long. The foliage and stems are bright green and richly splashed with yellow and/or white.

LIGHT NEEDS: High, indirect light is best, although the plant adapts to less.

BEST TEMPERATURES: Average room temperature.

WATER AND HUMIDITY NEEDS: Let the soil dry somewhat between waterings, especially for plants growing in low light. Avoid keeping the soil very wet or very dry.

GROWING GUIDELINES: Grow pothos in a soil-based potting mix in hanging baskets or trained on wire wreath forms. Fertilize twice a year, while the plant is producing new growth. Cut the stems back if they get leggy. Wash the leaves occasionally to keep them clean.

COMMON PROBLEMS: Pothos is generally pest-free. If you notice the leaf and stem markings are fading, move the plant to a brighter spot.

PROPAGATION: Take tip cuttings at any time.

CULTIVARS: 'Marble Queen' has ivory-and-white variegated leaves and stems. 'Orange Moon' has apricot markings.

MOSES-IN-A-BOAT

This plant's curious common name refers to the small flowers, which are cradled in boat- or basket-like bracts. But the real highlight of this Mexican native is the colorful, two-toned foliage.

OTHER COMMON NAMES: Moses-in-the-cradle.

DESCRIPTION: Upright, lance-shaped, 8-inch (20 cm) long leaves grow from a mounded rosette to 1 foot (30 cm) tall. The foliage is dark green on the upper sides and iridescent purple underneath. At the base of the plant, small, white flowers are cradled in cupped, purple bracts.

LIGHT NEEDS: High light with some direct sun; adapts to less light.

BEST TEMPERATURES: Average conditions but not over 70°F (21°C).

WATER AND HUMIDITY NEEDS: Water often to keep the soil evenly moist while the plant is in active growth; allow to dry between waterings in winter. Provide extra humidity.

GROWING GUIDELINES: Grow Moses-in-a-boat in all-purpose potting mix. Repot only when the plant is really crowded in its current container. Fertilize twice a month in spring and summer.

COMMON PROBLEMS: Too little light will make the plant lanky and not as colorful; move it to a brighter spot. Older plants tend to look shabby; start new plants and discard the old ones.

PROPAGATION: Take offsets or divide at any time, or remove and repot seedlings that appear in the pot.

COMMENTS: *R. spathacea* is also known as *R. bermudensis.*

CULTIVARS: The leaves of 'Variegata' are striped with pale yellow

SNAKE PLANT

Extraordinarily striped, stiff leaf swords have made snake plants very popular. They often look dreadful when neglected but are very handsome if you give them just a little care.

DESCRIPTION: Snake plant's tall, upright, stemless, spear-like leaves can grow to 4 feet (1.2 m) tall. The green foliage is crossbanded in darker green, yellow, white, and/or black. Plants sometimes produce tall sprays of green-white, fragrant flowers.

LIGHT NEEDS: High light is best, although plants can tolerate almost any level of light.

BEST TEMPERATURES: Average conditions, with 65°F (18°C) nights.

WATER AND HUMIDITY NEEDS: Allow the soil surface to dry between waterings in spring to fall. In winter, water only enough to prevent shriveling. Snake plant endures drought well.

GROWING GUIDELINES: Grow snake plant in cactus or all-purpose mix in a well-drained pot. This slow-growing plant can wait 3–4 years between repottings. Fertilize infrequently, perhaps once a year.

COMMON PROBLEMS: Cold temperatures can cause leaf edges to turn brown; move the plant to a warmer spot to prevent further damage.

PROPAGATION: Divide plants at any time, or separate and pot up offsets. Propagate green-leaved types by leaf cuttings: Remove a leaf, slice it crosswise into 3-inch (7.5 cm) sections, and insert the bottom side of each section into moist sand. (Leaf cuttings from yellow-edged types will root, but the plants they produce will be all green.)

STRAWBERRY BEGONIA

Show off strawberry begonia's trailing habit by growing it in a hanging basket. 'Tricolor' has green leaves marked with cream, pink, rose, or white; it can be difficult to grow.

OTHER COMMON NAMES: Mother-of-thousands, strawberry geranium.

DESCRIPTION: This creeping plant grows in compact rosettes to about 4 inches (10 cm) tall. The round leaves are silver-veined, dark green above and pinkish purple underneath. Clusters of small, white flowers appear on 9-inch (22.5 cm) stalks. The thread-like stolons, reminiscent of strawberry-plant runners, carry baby plantlets.

LIGHT NEEDS: Medium light.

BEST TEMPERATURES: Cool conditions, around 50°–60°F (10°–16°C); can take temperatures to 72°F (27°C).

WATER AND HUMIDITY NEEDS: Provide abundant water to keep the soil evenly moist from spring through fall; in winter, allow the soil surface to dry between waterings.

GROWING GUIDELINES: Grow strawberry begonia in all-purpose mix with added compost. Fertilize monthly from spring to fall.

COMMON PROBLEMS: Plants tend to get scraggly as they age; repot plantlets and discard the old plants.

PROPAGATION: Pot plantlets in a mix of peat moss and sand; repot them into all-purpose mix when they've rooted.

COMMENTS: Strawberry begonia is most commonly sold as a houseplant, but it can also grow outdoors to form a groundcover as far north as Zone 5.

Sedum morganianum   Crassulaceae

BURRO'S TAIL

A basket of burro's tail adds a unique accent to a sunny window. To keep the trailing stems full, hang the plant where it won't be disturbed.

OTHER COMMON NAMES: Donkey tail.

DESCRIPTION: Burro's tail offers succulent, grayish blue-green, 1-inch (2.5 cm) leaves densely strung on hanging stems to 4 feet (1.2 m) long. Coral to red flowers sometimes appear.

LIGHT NEEDS: High light, with some direct sun.

BEST TEMPERATURES: Average room temperature.

WATER AND HUMIDITY NEEDS: Keep moderately moist in spring to fall; in winter, water only to prevent shriveling.

GROWING GUIDELINES: Grow burro's tail in all-purpose mix with sand added for better drainage. Repot only when absolutely necessary, since the leaves break easily when the plant is handled. Fertilize three times a year: in early spring, late spring, and late summer.

COMMON PROBLEMS: Roots rot if you provide too much water; otherwise, these plants are fairly trouble-free.

PROPAGATION: Tip or leaf cuttings root easily in damp sand.

COMMENTS: An easy, slow-growing conversation piece.

Soleirolia soleirolii   Urticaceae

BABY'S TEARS

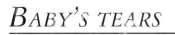

The tiny, oval leaves of this little creeper are delicate enough to have inspired the name "baby's tears." It's an excellent ground-cover for terrariums or for growing around the base of ferns.

OTHER COMMON NAMES: Irish moss.

DESCRIPTION: Baby's tears grows in creeping, dense mats to 4 inches (10 cm) tall. The tiny, juicy, green stems and leaves can become nicely mounded.

LIGHT NEEDS: Medium light, with no direct sun.

BEST TEMPERATURES: Average room temperature.

WATER AND HUMIDITY NEEDS: Water often to keep the soil evenly moist. Extra humidity is a must; mist plants often.

GROWING GUIDELINES: Grow baby's tears in a mix of peat moss and soil, with no lime. Rainwater is beneficial. Fertilize infrequently, perhaps once a year. Trimming plants with scissors will encourage new growth

COMMON PROBLEMS: The center of the plant will turn brown if the soil dries out or if the plant gets direct sun.

PROPAGATION: It's easy to divide the clumps. You can also grow baby's tears from cuttings.

COMMENTS: Also known as *Helxine soleirolii.*

| *Spathiphyllum* hybrids | Araceae | *Syngonium podophyllum* | Araceae |

PEACE LILY

SYNGONIUM

Peace lily is popular for its graceful, shiny, green leaves, as well as its curious, hooded flower spikes. This tolerant plant adjusts to many conditions and is generally problem-free.

OTHER COMMON NAMES: Spathe flower.

DESCRIPTION: Peace lily grows to 2 feet (60 cm) tall, with sword-like, long leaves. The many-stemmed plant blooms occasionally throughout the year, first in white, then turning green. The flowers can last for 6 weeks.

LIGHT NEEDS: Low to medium, indirect light.

BEST TEMPERATURES: Warm to average conditions (around 65°–70°F [18°–21°C]).

WATER AND HUMIDITY NEEDS: Keep the soil evenly moist.

GROWING GUIDELINES: This easy grower thrives in all-purpose potting mix enriched with compost or other organic material. Fertilize twice a month. Repot in early spring as needed. Provide monthly showers to keep the leaves clean.

COMMON PROBLEMS: Too much light actually inhibits bloom. If you want flowers but none are appearing, try moving your plant to a slightly darker spot. Too much fertilizer or too little water can cause brown leaf tips; keep the soil evenly moist and try fertilizing only every other month.

PROPAGATION: Remove and repot offsets, or divide the clumps in spring.

RELATED PLANTS:
S. wallisii, at 12 inches (30 cm), is a more compact, spring to late-summer bloomer.

Syngonium has lovely, arrow-shaped leaves on climbing or trailing stems. The species has plain green foliage, but there are several variegated cultivars.

OTHER COMMON NAMES: Nephthytis.

DESCRIPTION: Syngonium's long-stalked, green leaves grow to 1 foot (30 cm) long and are arrow-shaped when young. They can climb or trail, with vining stems up to 15 feet (4.5 m) long.

LIGHT NEEDS: Medium light.

BEST TEMPERATURES: Average room temperature (60°–70°F [16°–21°C]).

WATER AND HUMIDITY NEEDS: Water green-leaved types often so the soil stays evenly moist. Keep variegated forms slightly dry for best coloration.

GROWING GUIDELINES: Grow syngonium in all-purpose potting mix in a hanging basket, or give it a wooden slab to climb. Prune frequently to promote the growth of young, arrow-shaped leaves.

COMMON PROBLEMS: Mealybugs may be a problem; look for their cottony white bodies clustered on stems and leaves. If the plant is badly infested, cut the whole thing back to 1 inch (2.5 cm); otherwise, knock the pests off with a strong spray of water, or spray the plant with insecticidal soap, superior oil, or neem. If new growth is spindly, give the plant more light. Leaf markings tend to fade as the plant gets older or if it gets too much fertilizer; remove green reverted leaves.

PROPAGATION: Grow new plants from cuttings.

| *Tolmeia menziesii* | Saxifragaceae | *Zebrina pendula* | Commelinaceae |

PIGGYBACK PLANT

WANDERING JEW

Native to the American Pacific Coast, piggyback plant is a favorite for its unique growth habit. Try it in a hanging basket to show off the baby plantlets that form at the base of older leaves.

OTHER COMMON NAMES: Pickaback.

DESCRIPTION: Piggyback plant grows in rosettes to 12 inches (30 cm) tall and 18 inches (45 cm) wide. Its hairy, scalloped, green leaves grow to 5 inches (12.5 cm) wide. New plantlets form where the leaf stalk meets the blade.

LIGHT NEEDS: Medium to low, indirect light.

BEST TEMPERATURES: Prefers cool conditions (50°–60°F [10°–16°C]) but will take average room temperature.

WATER AND HUMIDITY NEEDS: Water and mist frequently in spring to fall; keep slightly drier in winter.

GROWING GUIDELINES: Grow in hanging baskets in all-purpose potting mix. Repot in spring. Fertilize twice a month in spring and summer. Wash the plant off in the shower every month or two.

COMMON PROBLEMS: If you spot the cottony white bodies of mealybugs, knock them off the plant with a strong spray of water, or spray the plant with insecticidal soap or neem. Warm, dry conditions may encourage spider mites, which cause yellow stippling on leaves; move the plant to a cooler spot and raise the humidity. Older plants tend to look scraggly; discard them and start with new ones.

PROPAGATION: Root plantlets by pinning the parent leaf to the soil; when rooted, dig up the plantlet and pot it up separately.

Wandering Jew's green and purple iridescence, along with its ability to root quickly from cuttings, has long made this Mexican vine a favorite "pass-along" plant.

OTHER COMMON NAMES: Inch plant.

DESCRIPTION: This trailing vine has 2-inch (5 cm), green leaves colored or striped with red, purple, yellow, pink, and/or silver.

LIGHT NEEDS: Medium to high, indirect light.

BEST TEMPERATURES: Average conditions during the day with cool nights (50°–60°F [10°–16°C]).

WATER AND HUMIDITY NEEDS: Allow the soil surface to dry a bit between waterings.

GROWING GUIDELINES: Grow wandering Jew in all-purpose potting mix. Provide dilute fertilizer twice a month. Pinch back new growth often to keep the plant full.

COMMON PROBLEMS: If your plant's leaves are fading, try moving it to a brighter spot. Older plants tend to get scraggly; take cuttings to start new plants and discard the old ones.

PROPAGATION: Cuttings root easily. Pot several together, arranging them around the rim and also in the center of the container, to create a bushy new plant.

COMMENTS Wandering Jew is very easy to grow. Variegated types will need higher light.

CULTIVARS: 'Purpusii' has dark, greenish red leaves.

GARDENING IN CONTAINERS

The great thing about gardening in containers is the flexibility you get: Since the plants aren't rooted in the ground, you can place them exactly where you want them. You can create a miniature landscape filled with your favorite plants right around your deck or patio, where you get to relax and really enjoy their beauty and fragrance. If you live in a high-rise apartment building or condo where you have no ground for a garden, you can create a lush green oasis on a tiny balcony or outdoor stairway. City dwellers can grow large gardens entirely in containers on building rooftops. Even if you have nothing but a wall and windows to call your own, you can fill hanging baskets with trailing plants and pack window boxes full of flowers, herbs, and vegetables. In this chapter, you'll learn about all of the creative and exciting ways you can use container plants to liven up your living spaces.

With plants in containers, you can rearrange and replace each pot as needed, maintaining a garden that always looks picture-perfect. While the plants are flowering, you can place the container where you'll see it best and enjoy it most. Then, as the blooms fade, you can retire the pot to the basement or garage until next year. Or, if your season permits, you can redo it with fresh plants and enjoy it all over again. For more ideas on displaying containers creatively, see "Designing Your Container Garden" on page 94.

In Northern areas, container growing has another big advantage—it allows you to grow all sorts of perennial plants that are not cold-hardy enough to live outdoors year-round. Camellias, for instance, are hardy outside only to Zone 3, where winter minimum temperatures average 10° to 20°F (–12° to –7°C). As container plants, however, you can grow them anywhere by moving them outside in the summer and indoors to a bright, cool sunroom or breezeway in winter. (Plus, they can bloom from November to April—a time when their splendid flowers will be especially welcome.) Fragrant orange and lemon trees are other tender plants Northerners can enjoy if grown in containers.

The fact is, you can grow practically any plant you want in a container—all kinds of flowers, bulbs, vegetables, and even small trees and shrubs. "Flowers for Pots and Planters" on page 95 is full of tips on choosing annuals and perennials for colorful containers all season long. "Wonderful Window Boxes" on page 98 and "Beautiful Hanging Baskets" on page 99 offer other ideas for displaying your container plantings. If you have room for a large pot, you may want to try adding a few trees or shrubs to give height and year-round interest to your collection; see "Trees, Shrubs, and Vines for Containers" on page 100 for details. Fragrant and culinary herbs like lavender, lemon verbena, and basil adapt well to life in containers; so do many compact cultivars of peppers, zucchini, tomatoes, and other favorite fruits and vegetables. For more information on choosing productive crops, see "Easy Edibles for Containers" on page 102.

Annuals are traditional favorites for filling containers, but you don't have to stop there! Increase your enjoyment by trying bulbs for early bloom, perennials for seasonal interest, and edibles for a handy harvest.

With a little planning, you can put together eye-catching container combinations that change with the season.

A pot packed full of grape hyacinths (*Muscari* sp.) adds a touch of spring to any part of the garden.

Designing Your Container Garden

A container planting can be as simple as a single pot of flowers or as lush and full as any garden border. You'll get the most enjoyment from your potted plants when you choose and group them to match your setting.

Choose the Right Size

Plants in single, small containers can look puny and out of place all alone on a deck or patio. To get the best effect, you want your container plants to be in proper scale with the great outdoors. Whenever possible, opt for larger containers, at least 10 inches (25 cm) in diameter; generally the bigger, the better. (Large planters get very heavy, so be sure to place them where you want them before you fill them with potting soil.) Using larger containers will cost a little more up front, but the plants will definitely grow better, you'll have to water

less often, and the overall effect of the container garden will be more dramatic.

If you prefer to grow your plants in smaller containers, group them together to create an eye-catching effect. It also makes the regular watering and maintenance much easier, since all the plants are in the same place. For extra interest, it's a good idea to vary the heights of plants in a group of pots. You can use short plants in smaller pots for the front and taller plants in the back. Or use bricks, plastic milk crates, or upside-down pots to vary the height of individual pots in a grouping.

Consider the Colors

To get the most enjoyment out of your container gardens, don't forget to think about color combinations when you're buying the plants. Groupings usually look best when one or two colors dominate. For example, a yellow accent (maybe dwarf marigolds) works well with a group of blue flowers, such as ageratum. White is also a good accent color—it looks good with every color. Sweet alyssum (*Lobularia maritima*) is an excellent white trailing plant that always looks nice as it spills loosely over the sides of the pots. (It also has an outstanding sweet fragrance.)

A mixture of many different colors can look too "busy," but you can create an attractive grouping with several shades of the same color. You might, for instance, try red pansies with pink primroses or try light blue petunias with deep blue lobelia (*Lobelia erinus*). Plants with attractive silvery or green foliage, such as dusty miller (*Senecio cineraria*) or parsley, make great accents for these kinds of plantings.

For extra color, plant flowers around the base of container-grown trees, shrubs, and vines.

A special, large planter filled with annual flowers can become a focal point for a whole garden.

Flowers for Pots and Planters

Nothing says summer like pots and planters filled to overflowing with lush foliage and beautiful blooms. Create your own colorful container gardens with a bounty of easy annuals and dependable, long-blooming perennials for all-season interest.

Annuals

The easiest and longest-flowering plants you can grow in containers are the many kinds of flowering annuals. Most annuals do extremely well in containers; the many compact cultivars of marigolds, petunias, impatiens, begonias, and ageratum are especially good. These annuals begin blooming early and put on a non-stop show of color all season long.

When planting groups of annual flowers in containers, one factor you must consider is the light requirements of the plants you choose. Most flowering annuals prefer plenty of sun. If you're planting a container for a shady spot, take special care to select plants that can thrive in the shade. Be sure you don't plant sun-lovers, such as marigolds, in the same container with shade-loving annuals, like coleus.

Each cell pack or seed packet will come with a label that tells you if the plants prefer sun or part shade. (Be a little skeptical of those sun/shade ratings; labels sometimes say a particular

Mixing plants with different heights, colors, and textures will give your containers added interest.

For full, lush-looking hanging baskets, use a mixture of plants with bushy and trailing habits.

If you have a special container that you want to show off, look for plants that bloom in a complementary color.

Start the spring season early with cold-tolerant flowers, such as bulbs, pansies, and primroses.

plant can take part shade when it really requires full sun to grow well. To confirm plants' light needs, check their individual entries in the "Guide to Container Plants," starting on page 116.) If you're looking for plants for a shady location, some of the best choices include flowering tobaccos (*Nicotiana* spp.), coleus (*Coleus* x *hybridus*), wishbone flower (*Torenia fournieri*), impatiens (*Impatiens* spp.), and wax begonias (*Begonia*

Semperflorens-cultorum hybrids).

Spring is when garden centers have the largest selection of annual flowers (and again in the fall for those of you in milder climates), and that's when you'll probably want to fill most of your containers. Most annuals aren't frost-tolerant, so you should put them out after the danger of frost has passed. One major exception to this rule is the pansy. Pansies (and their lovely little cousins, Johnny-jump-ups [*Viola tricolor*]) are very fond of cool spring (and fall) weather; plant them outside just as soon as the garden centers get them in.

If you didn't get around to setting up your

Start Your Own Annuals

For an "instant" effect, you can buy and plant annuals that are already blooming. If you're not in a real hurry, however, you can start your own plants; many kinds are easy to grow from seed. Growing your own annuals is also a good way to save money if you need many plants.

Some kinds of annuals, such as marigolds, mature quickly, so you can sow them directly into outdoor pots. Other annuals that are easy from direct-sown seed include sweet alyssum (*Lobularia maritima*), nasturtiums (*Tropaeolum majus*), morning glories (*Ipomoea* spp.), and zinnias. Sweet alyssum is cold-tolerant, so you can

plant the seed in early spring; for the rest, wait until after the danger of frost has passed.

Other annuals have very tiny seed or take a little longer before they start flowering, so they are best started indoors under lights. Check the instructions on the seed packets, and start the seeds the recommended number of weeks before your last spring frost so they'll start flowering shortly after you move them outside. If you're blessed with a long growing season, start another batch of plants in early summer; use these to replace tired container plantings in late summer or early fall to have an all-season display.

Don't forget to include bulbs and other perennials in container gardens for seasonal color.

Compact selections of daylilies and other durable perennials can adapt easily to life in containers.

containers in spring, or if your pansy plantings are looking tired by midsummer, don't assume you're stuck with no flowers for the rest of the season. Grocery and discount stores often sell annuals only in the spring, but you can usually find some nice annuals at local garden centers later in the season.

Perennials

Some perennials work very well in containers, too. Top choices include those with a long season of bloom, such as compact, golden orange 'Stella d'Oro' daylily. Other perennials that look especially nice in containers are those with interesting foliage, such as hostas, ornamental grasses, and lady's mantle (*Alchemilla mollis*). Try using some of these plants in large containers, mixed with annual flowers to provide constant color.

Perennials need a little more care than annuals, since you don't just pull them out at the end of the season. Because they are growing in containers, they are much more susceptible to winter damage than plants growing in the ground. In the North, you'll want to move container perennials to an unheated garage or cold basement to protect them from the alternate freezing and thawing cycles, which can damage or kill them. You'll need to water the pots lightly during the winter months.

Container Water Gardens

A small water garden adds a special sparkle to any collection of container plants. As an added bonus, the open water will attract birds and even frogs and toads. You can use any large container—an old bathtub, half-whiskey barrel, or a special plastic tub sold complete with a filter and small fountain. Set the container on your patio or deck, or sink it into the ground for a natural pool effect.

A filter usually isn't necessary for a small water garden if you make sure you include a few oxygenating plants—such as *Elodea canadensis*—to help keep the water clear. Specialty nurseries sell these oxygenators, along with pygmy (dwarf) water lilies and other water plants suitable for a tub garden. Grow the plants in individual containers set down into the tub so that you can replace them as needed or dismantle the garden for the winter in the North.

Always include a few fish in the container to control mosquito larvae. Goldfish work great, and they're easy to overwinter indoors in a goldfish bowl or small aquarium.

Window boxes attract lots of attention, so make sure you can reach them for regular grooming and watering.

A window box lets you add some color in small spaces where in-ground planting room is limited.

Wonderful Window Boxes

Well-planned window boxes can add a special touch to any home. Besides brightening up otherwise plain windows, boxes can also dress up a deck or porch railing.

Choosing the Container

Many garden centers sell already-made boxes of plastic, wood, or metal, with special brackets that screw to the wall below the window to hold the box. Usually these boxes are not very large, so try not to overplant them; allow enough space for the plants to fill out through the growing season.

If you build your own boxes, make them a little bigger than the typical garden-center sizes. A box about 8 inches (20 cm) wide and deep will give you enough additional soil for a range of plants to grow well. Before you install them, fill one with soil and water it well. Then lift it (carefully!) so you realize how heavy it is: You need to use really sturdy supports to hold all that weight. Be sure to put the box together with galvanized screws. Don't use nails—they won't hold as well as screws. It's also a good idea to reinforce the corners of the box to help them stay together.

Whether you buy your boxes or make your own, be sure there are holes in the bottom so excess water can drain out.

Picking the Plants

Top plant choices for window boxes include all of the low and medium-sized annuals, along with plenty of trailing plants, such as large periwinkle (*Vinca major*) and cascading petunias. And if the window above the box will be open to let in the summer breezes, be sure to include some fragrant plants; see "Fragrant Favorites for Window Boxes" for planting ideas.

Choose compact plants that won't block your view.

Fragrant Favorites for Window Boxes

If you want some powerful nighttime fragrance wafting into your bedroom from your window boxes, pick up a packet of evening-scented stock (*Matthiola longipetala* subsp. *bicornis*) seeds and plant some in a corner of each box. The stock isn't a showy flower, but it has a strong, sweet scent that fills the air at night. Other good choices for fragrance include petunias, sweet alyssum (*Lobularia maritima*), 'Lemon Gem' marigold (*Tagetes tenuifolia* 'Lemon Gem'), scented geraniums (*Pelargonium* spp.), mignonette (*Reseda odorata*), stock (*Matthiola incana*), and night phlox (*Zaluzianskya capensis*).

Beautiful Hanging Baskets

Bring your container gardens to new heights with hanging baskets. Baskets look terrific on porches, beside a doorway, or hanging on an arbor over a patio. You can buy hanging baskets already planted and ready to hang, or you can easily plant them yourself (and probably save a bit of money).

Picking Plants for Baskets

Baskets look best with a combination of low, bushy plants to fill the top and trailing plants to spill over the sides. Good bushy plants include tuberous begonias (*Begonia* Tuberhybrida hybrids), browallia (*Browallia* spp.), and vinca (*Catharanthus roseus*), just to name a few. Around the edge of the basket, include cascading plants such as petunias, ivy, annual lobelia (*Lobelia erinus*), sweet alyssum (*Lobularia maritima*), nasturtium (*Tropaeolum majus*), and mints (*Mentha* spp.). Plants that are both bushy and trailing, such as ivy geranium (*Pelargonium peltatum*) and fuchsia (*Fuchsia* x *hybrida*), look good when planted by themselves to fill a hanging basket.

Planting and Caring for Hanging Baskets

Most hanging basket containers look like regular pots, and you plant them in basically the same way. Baskets dry out even faster than other container plants, however, so it's a good idea to use a potting mix that holds plenty of water. Adding extra vermiculite will help. It also helps to use larger baskets—at least 12 inches (30 cm) in diameter, which will dry out more slowly.

To keep hanging baskets looking lush through the season, water them regularly, fertilize often, and pinch off spent flowers.

Garden centers sell special brackets that let you hang baskets anywhere you choose on a wall or post. Make sure you choose sturdy brackets and fasten them securely; they have to hold a lot of weight.

You won't need to water too much at first, when the plants are small. But as the plants grow, the basket may require watering at least once and possibly twice a day, especially during the hottest part of the season. If you're going to be gone even for one night, move your baskets to a shady spot until you return, or ask a neighbor to water them for you.

Great Balls of Flowers

If you want your hanging baskets to be a solid ball of color, plant the sides of the containers as well as the tops. You can buy special baskets that have holes around the sides, or use wire baskets with fiber or moss liners, which allow you to cut holes for planting all around the sides.

To plant into the holes in the sides of a hanging basket, first fill the basket with potting mix to just below where the holes begin. Then remove a plant from its cell pack, and wrap it loosely inside a little cylinder of newspaper. From the inside of the basket, slip the top part of the cylinder out through a hole, so the leafy top of the plant is on the outside and the roots are on the inside. Slip off the newspaper, then settle the roots in the soil. When you have all the holes filled, add more soil to within 1 inch (2.5 cm) of the rim, then set in more plants on top. Water thoroughly to settle the soil around the roots.

Trees, Shrubs, and Vines for Containers

Trees and shrubs are top choices for containers if you need a large plant for a certain spot. If you select a potted tree or shrub that's evergreen or has attractive bark even when its leaves are gone, you'll get extra year-round enjoyment. Container vines have the plus of providing quick shade or privacy for an exposed porch or patio.

Special Container Considerations

During the growing season, container trees, shrubs, and vines need basically the same attention you give to your other potted plants. In the winter, however, they'll require a little special care.

Roots of plants growing in containers are exposed to more cold than if they were growing in the ground, so a plant that is normally winter-hardy in the garden in your area might not survive a cold winter in a container. To ensure success, there are several things you can do.

First, if you want to leave the plants outside year-round, choose species and cultivars that are rated to be hardy to at least one zone colder than your area. If, for example, you live in Zone 6, choose plants that are hardy to at least Zone 5. (If you're not sure which hardiness zone you live in, see the USDA Plant Hardiness Zone map on page 154.)

If you suspect that a shrub or tree may not be cold-hardy, move it to a protected place for the winter.

Next, give the plants a well-blended, well-drained soil mix to keep the roots healthy. Start with a mix that contains some real soil (not just a soil-less mix). Then add compost (for long-term nutrients) and composted bark pieces (to help maintain good drainage). If you can't get composted bark, use some perlite in the largest particle size you can find. (Some nursery centers carry large bags of ready-made potting mix designed specifically for this kind of long-term container planting, but you may need to ask around to find it.)

If you have plants that you know won't survive in your climate's winters, or if you have some that you really don't want to risk outdoors, move them indoors

Annual Vines for Summer Screens

If you have a location where you need some fast summer shade or a screen for privacy, try growing annual vines in your containers.

Brilliant 'Heavenly Blue' morning glory (*Ipomoea tricolor* 'Heavenly Blue') will quickly grow to 10 feet (3 m) or more. Sweet peas (*Lathyrus odoratus*) won't grow quite as tall, but they'll produce loads of lusciously fragrant flowers for cutting. Or try an edible and ornamental bean like scarlet runner bean (*Phaseolus coccineus*). These annual vines don't need much to climb on—just get them started up some stakes, string, or twine, and they'll do the rest.

Evergreen shrubs, such as boxwoods (*Buxus* spp.), offer garden interest all year long.

for the coldest months. If they are deciduous plants like fruit trees or roses, which go dormant in winter, you can put them in a cold, dark garage. Evergreen plants prefer cold but bright spots in a sunroom or breezeway, but in a pinch, they can spend a couple of months in a cold, dark location.

Indoors or outdoors, your plants will still need some water during the winter. They aren't growing much, so they only need enough water to keep the soil from drying out completely.

Maintaining Container Trees, Shrubs, and Vines

These larger container plants will need some pruning to control their size and keep a pleasing shape. Non-flowering shrubs can usually be trimmed any time from late winter to midsummer. If you are growing a flowering shrub or vine, you'll need to determine whether it flowers on new wood each year (in which case you should prune it back hard right after it flowers) or if it flowers on older wood (avoid heavy pruning and just remove some of the very oldest wood every spring). Not sure how

Container-grown vines, such as sweet peas, can add an exciting movable accent to garden beds and borders.

your plant blooms? Check the individual entries in the "Guide to Container Plants," starting on page 116, ask at your local garden center, or just make a point of watching where the flower buds appear in spring.

Support Your Vines

Vining plants also make great additions to container gardens. To keep them from sprawling, however, you'll need to provide some kind of support for them to climb on.

You can buy trellises or make your own. Since wood or bamboo stakes may rot and break off after a year or two, plastic supports are a better choice for perennial vines. If you buy a ready-made wooden trellis, insert plastic or metal poles in the container soil, then attach the wooden trellis to this permanent support.

If your vines don't cling to the support on their own, you may need to help them out. Use string or plastic-coated wire ties to attach the vine stems to the support. Be careful not to fasten the stems too tight, and check the ties several times during the season; you don't want them to cut into the stems.

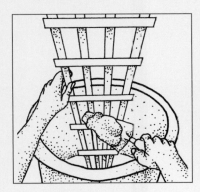

Set the base of the trellis into the pot, then fill in around it with growing mix.

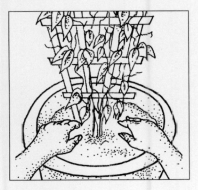

Put the new vine next to the trellis at the same level it was growing in its original pot.

Fill in around the vine with growing mix, then water well to settle the soil around the roots.

Easy Edibles for Containers

Containers are a great way to grow vegetables, herbs, and fruit crops without putting a lot of work into a full-scale garden. You can have a steady supply of fresh produce right outside your door, within easy reach for a finishing touch to any meal. Containers also offer ideal growing conditions for carrots, which can grow short and stunted if your garden soil isn't deep, loose, and rock-free. Mix some flowers in with your edibles, and you can have a container garden that's pretty as well as productive.

Container Crop Basics

Growing vegetables, fruits, and herbs in containers is much like growing flowers, but there are a few special things you'll need to think about.

Choose Compact Crops Most herbs adapt quite well to life in containers, but standard selections of some vegetables and fruits can get too big for successful container culture. Fortunately, plant breeders have worked with many crops to develop compact cultivars specifically suited for container growing. For specific cultivar suggestions, check out the individual vegetable entries in the "Guide to Container Plants," starting on page 116. Also read the descriptions in your favorite seed and nursery catalogs to find cultivars that are recommended for container growing.

Consider the Container You'll get better yields if you use a good-sized container—one that can hold at least 2 gallons (9 l) of potting mix. If you're more

Sweet and hot peppers add a colorful touch to container gardens. You can overwinter your favorites indoors.

interested in good production than how beautiful your containers are, 5-gallon (23 l) plastic buckets make excellent inexpensive and effective containers. (You may be able to find some used buckets you can recycle from a restaurant or delicatessen. Be sure to drill plenty of drainage holes in the bottom.)

Vegetables for Containers

Looking for some ideas of crops to start with? Here are some surefire favorites.

Tomatoes Tomatoes come in all sizes, from giant vining types that may grow to 6 feet (1.8 m) or more (they're called "indeterminate" types) to tiny, compact, cherry tomato cultivars that are perfect for growing in hanging baskets.

Peppers Hot and sweet peppers are excellent plants to grow in containers. Because they are perennials, you can cut them back at the end of each season, move them inside for the winter, and then move them back outside again next spring. (See "Inside Out and Outside In" on page 48 for tips on helping plants adapt to the moves.)

Lettuce Lettuce is easy to grow in containers and looks as great as it tastes. Try a packet of a "cutting mix," which contains several kinds of lettuce, along with other spicy salad greens such as mustard, mizuna, and arugula. With these cutting mixes, you just plant the seed rather thickly, then cut handfuls with scissors as the lettuce grows.

Fruits for Containers

If you enjoy growing edible plants, there's no need to stop with vegetables and herbs. Here are several other food plants that will do very well in containers.

Create a Container Salad Garden

A container garden can be perfect for one-stop salad harvesting. Plant your salad greens in a container or window box outside the kitchen, and add some chives and basil. Hang a basket of cherry tomatoes above the pot or box, and you'll have salads literally at your fingertips!

Lettuce and spinach do best in cooler temperatures, so start some in early spring. Plant again in late summer, and you'll enjoy months of delicious salads. If your greens are still going strong when hard frosts arrive, just move them inside—they'll grow nicely in a bright south window.

Mixing potted herbs and flowers can give you a container garden that's both pretty and practical.

Patio-type tomatoes, such as 'Pixie', can give you a welcome harvest from a very small space.

Strawberries Who doesn't love the taste of fresh strawberries? You can buy strawberry plants from your local garden center in the spring and pop them into pots and planters for luscious, full-sized fruit. Or you might want to try the super-flavorful alpine types like 'Mignonette', which can be grown from seed. Their great taste more than makes up for the smaller size of the berries. Strawberries look good in almost any container or hanging basket. There are even special planters called strawberry barrels, with holes all around the sides so you can cover the barrel with berry plants.

Blueberries Another top container choice is blueberries. They're small shrubs that grow only a few feet high, so they don't need a lot of pruning. Even if you have room for them in the garden, you may choose to grow your blueberries in containers; it's easier to meet the plants' need for acid soil by blending a special container growing mix. Use a soil mix that's at least one-quarter to one-half acidic peat moss and never add any lime, and you'll have blueberries before you know it.

Citrus How about your very own lemons, limes, and oranges? Citrus trees can't tolerate frost, but they grow nicely in containers, especially if you buy plants that have been grafted onto a special dwarfing rootstock to keep them small. The plants need plenty of sun and fertilizer in the summer and a bright window in winter (except in very mild climates, where they can stay outside year-round). Not only will they give you fruit but the flowers are also wonderfully fragrant.

Dwarf Fruit Trees You can enjoy harvesting full-sized apples, peaches, and cherries from container-sized dwarf fruit trees. Provide rooting room by choosing a container at least 30 inches (75 cm) wide and deep. In cold climates (Zone 5 or colder), move the pots to an unheated garage during the coldest part of the winter. In warmer zones, potted fruit trees can stay outside through the winter. Some fruits—including apples and peaches—need a certain amount of cold to set fruit properly, so if you live in Zone 8 or warmer, be sure you get "low-chill" cultivars that will grow well in your climate. For more tips on getting container trees through the winter, see "Special Container Considerations" on page 100.

Dwarf fruit trees can also be great additions to container gardens, but they need fairly large pots.

CARING FOR CONTAINER GARDENS

In many ways, caring for container gardens is basically the same as for houseplants. They all need good soil, periodic fertilizing, and regular watering. The main difference, however, is that outdoor containers are exposed to more light and more wind, so they'll need more water and more fertilizer to stay in top shape. And since they can't spread their roots to search out water and nutrients, container plantings are completely at your mercy for their needs.

To keep your container plants healthy, you'll probably have to pay attention to them at least every other day—and maybe even every day in midsummer. But if you set everything up carefully from the beginning, your plant care chores won't amount to more than a few minutes a day. This chapter will explain the techniques you can use to make your container plantings as low maintenance as possible.

Starting with large containers and using a rich, moisture-retentive potting mix are the two key steps to success. Large containers will look better than smaller pots, and they won't need to be watered as often. Plastic pots tend to lose water more slowly than

clay pots, so they're a good choice for reducing watering chores. You'll find everything you need to know about selecting the right container size and material in "Choosing Containers" on page 106.

Rich, organic soil is the foundation of any good garden. "Selecting Potting Soils" on page 108 will tell you how to choose a commercial potting mix to provide good rooting conditions for your container plants. You'll also learn how to blend your own potting mixes to create a growing medium that's perfectly suited to your plants and less expensive as well!

Once your container gardens are established, routine grooming, fertilizing, and watering will keep them growing strong. The "Container Care Primer" on page 110 offers pointers on planting, pinching, and preventing pest problems to keep your container gardens in peak condition. You'll also want to check out the growing guidelines you'll find in 'Watering Container Gardens" on page 112 and "Fertilizing Container Gardens" on page 114 for the basics on when, how, and how much to feed and water your plants for healthy, vigorous growth.

When planning container plantings, make sure you consider how they'll look through the whole season. Bulbs are great for spring, for instance, but you'll need to replace them with annuals for later color.

Choosing Containers

Picking the right containers can go a long way toward creating a good-looking, easy-care container garden. When you're shopping for a new pot or planter, consider the size, the material that it's made from, and its drainage.

Select the Right Size

The container size that's right for your needs mostly depends on what plants you want to grow. For herbs, small to medium-sized vegetables, and flowering annuals and perennials, containers that hold about 2 to 4 gallons (9 to 18 l) of growing medium will work best. Small trees or shrubs can start out in 2- to 4-gallon (9 to 18 l) pots, but you'll probably need to move them to larger containers after the first season. Large vegetable plants, such as tomatoes and peppers, will be more productive if you give them plenty of room. Five-gallon (23 l) pots are a good size for peppers; full-sized tomatoes should have at least 10-gallon (45 l) pots.

If there's one general rule to follow when deciding what size pots to use, it's bigger is usually better. Small pots can really look out of scale and get lost when you set them down in the great outdoors. The bigger the pot, the better it will look in your overall garden design. Plus, the larger pots don't dry out nearly as fast as little ones, so you won't have to water them as often. Large pots do get very heavy, though, so use

Colorful containers add a whimsical touch to the garden. Just make sure all pots have drainage holes.

them sparingly if you're gardening on a balcony or rooftop. (In fact, you may want to have a structural engineer check out the stability of these areas before you set up any containers.)

Consider the Materials

The material that a container is made out of can be just as important as its size. Each kind of material has advantages and disadvantages, depending on what you're growing and where you're growing it.

Containers made of clay or terracotta look very attractive, and they have the advantage of providing extra bottom weight so that taller plants won't blow over in the wind. Concrete is a good choice for the same reasons, and it's generally more durable for year-round growing than clay, which is easily damaged by freezing temperatures. The main disadvantage of unglazed clay pots is that they are porous, so they can dry out quickly on hot summer days. Large clay and concrete containers can also be quite heavy to move.

For plants that you need to move inside in winter and outside in summer, a plastic or fiberglass container will be much lighter than clay, concrete, or wood. Plastic containers also won't dry out as fast as those made of clay, and plastic is usually much less expensive. If you need to buy several large pots, this cost advantage may well be the main factor you'll need to consider. The main disadvantage of plastic and fiberglass containers is that they are more likely to blow over in windy areas.

Wood falls in between plastic and clay in weight and porosity. It has the advantage of insulating the roots from overheating when the summer sun strikes the

Clay pots are a good choice for succulents, since these plants prefer to stay on the dry side.

Small containers need more frequent watering, but they give you more design flexibility; you can move or replace individual pots as needed.

Large containers offer enough root room for a variety of plants.

planter. Wood can rot, however, so you'll probably need to replace wooden planters every few years. If you like the look and insulating value of wooden planters but want to help them last longer, you could use plastic liners or set already-potted plants inside them.

Whatever kind of container material you choose, look for pots and planters that are light-colored, especially if you live in a very hot climate. Light-colored pots help to reflect the heat and keep the roots cool. Black pots are the worst choice in hot climates, since they can absorb enough heat to damage tender roots. (Metal is usually a poor container choice for the same reason.)

Broad, shallow containers work well for displaying daffodils and other spring bulbs.

Don't Forget Drainage

The third key thing to look for when choosing a container is to make sure that it has drainage holes. Many gardeners used to place coarse rocks or broken pot shards in the bottom of pots thinking it improved the drainage, but this doesn't really help. Adequate drainage holes are the critical thing for healthy root growth and topgrowth. Most commercially available pots and planters already have holes in them. If you are creating your own containers from wood or recycled plastic buckets, make the holes at least 1/2 inch (12 mm) in diameter. Drill at least six holes in medium-sized containers and more in larger ones.

What if you have a great-looking container that doesn't have drainage holes? You can use it for outdoor growing if you're willing to give it a little extra attention. First, put a few blocks of wood in the base. Next, set in an already-potted plant so it rests on the wood blocks. The blocks will keep the plant roots from sitting in the water that collects in the base of the outer pot. Over time—and especially after heavy rains—however, the water level may rise to the level of the inner pot. During wet weather, lift out the inner pot every day or two and dump out any water that has collected; otherwise, your plants may suffer or even die

Selecting Potting Soils

Once you've picked the perfect container, it's time to fill it with the best possible growing medium. The ideal potting soil for most plants will hold enough water for good root growth but allow excess water to drain out freely. It also contains a balance of nutrients that will steadily nourish your plants for normal, healthy growth. You can buy a commercially blended potting soil or make your own to match the particular needs of your plants.

Using Commercial Potting Mixes

For annual plants, which will only live in their pots for one growing season, you can use virtually any well-drained, commercial potting mix. Most such mixes don't have any compost or soil in them—they are primarily composed of peat and usually some vermiculite (to absorb and hold water) and perlite (to improve drainage). If you use these soil-less mixes straight from the bag, you'll need to fertilize regularly.

To improve a commercial soil-less mix for growing perennials, shrubs, and trees, you can add up to 20 percent compost or a combination of 10 percent compost and 10 percent garden soil. Both the compost and the soil provide slow-release nutrients and generally improve the ability of the mix to hold moisture and nutrients. And there's another big bonus when you add compost to your potting mix—microorganisms in

Good drainage is important for healthy container plants, so look for a mix that contains perlite or bark.

the compost, which actually help prevent diseases and keep your plants healthy! Composted bark chips are also an excellent addition to keep the mix loose for good root growth.

If you need to keep your soil mix as light as possible—for a large window box, for example—add the 20 percent compost but no soil. Instead, add some extra perlite (about 10 percent). Or, if you need the mix to be heavier to help prevent a taller shrub from blowing over in the wind, add some extra soil or sand to the mix.

Making Your Own Potting Mix

Blending your own potting soil from scratch is also a possibility for creating the perfect mix. It allows you to custom blend a variety of different ingredients to match the needs of your particular plants. Your main goal is to combine ingredients that have a variety of particle sizes so the mix is not too fine. You'll also always need to add some compost to provide slow-release nutrition and to help prevent diseases.

Making good potting soil is an art, not a science. There are many different recipes that will give great results. The recipes given here are just general guidelines, and your plants will still grow well if you need to use more or less of any ingredients.

To get top performance from large containers, add compost and organic fertilizers to the potting mix.

For temporary plantings, such as spring bulbs, you can get fine results with a basic soil-less mix.

Basic Container Mix This simple blend will work well for a wide variety of container plantings.

4 parts peat moss (mixed thoroughly with 1/2 ounce (15 g) dolomitic limestone per gallon of peat)

1 part compost (or 1/2 part compost and 1/2 part garden soil)

1 part perlite or vermiculite

Pile these materials in a large tub and mix them thoroughly. These materials can be very dusty, so wear a dust mask during the mixing process.

Deluxe Container Mix This blend is especially good for long-term plantings (including trees, shrubs, and perennials) in larger containers.

4 parts sphagnum peat

2 parts compost (or 1 part compost and 1 part garden soil)

1 part small bark chips (composted)

1 part perlite

Combine the materials as you would for the basic mix. To each cubic foot (0.03 cubic meters) (or 7 1/2 gallons [34 l]) of this deluxe mix, add the following slow-release organic fertilizers:

4 ounces (110 g) of dolomitic limestone

4 ounces (110 g) of bonemeal (or 1 pound [500 g] of rock phosphate or colloidal phosphate)

1 pound (500 g) of greensand

2 ounces (55 g) of bloodmeal

2 ounces (55 g) of kelp meal

With this deluxe mix, your plants will have plenty of nutrients to get off to a great start, and you shouldn't need to begin supplemental fertilizing until at least a month after you plant.

How Much Do You Need?

If you need to fill more than a few small containers, it can be hard to decide how much potting mix to buy or blend. You need to do a little calculating to figure it out, but that's a whole lot easier than lugging home more mix than you need or having to go back to the store for more.

- Some containers are labeled by volume, usually given in gallons. In this case, most of your work is done, especially if your potting mix is measured in gallons. (If the mix is measured in cubic feet, divide the number of cubic feet by 7.5 to get the number of gallons of mix.)

- To find the volume of a square or rectangular pot, simply multiply the length and width by the height. For example, if you have a window box that's 24 inches long, 8 inches wide, and 8 inches deep, it can hold 1,536 cubic inches of soil. Divide the number of cubic inches by 1,728 to get the number of cubic feet of soil you need. (In this case, 0.88 cubic feet.) If your potting soil is measured in gallons, multiply the number of gallons by 7.5 to find the number of cubic feet.

- To find the volume of a round pot, you first need to figure out the area of the top circle of the pot. Lay a ruler across the top of the pot to measure the diameter (how far it is from side to side). Now, divide that number by 2, multiply it by itself, and then multiply it by 3.14. Take that answer and multiply it by the height of the pot to find the number of cubic inches of mix the pot can hold. Divide the number of cubic inches by 1,728 to get the number of cubic feet of potting mix you need. If your potting mix is measured in gallons, multiply the number of gallons by 7.5 to find the number of cubic feet.

Container Care Primer

You've got the pot, and you've got the soil—now it's time to get your container garden started! Planting containers is easy, and it's a fun chance to try out new flower and foliage combinations to create pleasing groupings. Once you have your potted plants settled in, you'll want to groom them occasionally to keep them looking their best through the season. You'll also want to keep an eye out for pest and disease problems, and apply control measures so you can catch them before they get out of hand.

Planting

There's no special trick to planting containers; simply do it just as you would garden beds, spacing transplants according to the instructions on the seed packets or the transplant labels. You can space them a little closer in containers if you want, but don't overdo it and try to put too many plants into one container. Remember, the container won't look full and lush immediately, but the little transplants will grow up quickly. It's more likely that you'll need to trim them back than worry about them looking too sparse.

Grooming

Through the season, a little regular pruning will keep all of your container plants looking first-rate. Once a week

Use small stakes to keep weak-stemmed plants from sprawling.

Avoid the urge to overplant your containers in spring. The small plants will fill out quickly!

or so, grab a bucket and your garden shears and take a few minutes to visit each of your container plantings. Snipping back long shoot tips on annuals and removing spent flowers on perennials will stimulate bushy growth and more flowering. Removing any damaged or dead leaves or branches will keep the plants looking fresh and healthy. Collect the clippings in the bucket for later composting.

If you've included taller plants in your containers, you may need to stake them to support their upright growth. You can buy bamboo stakes in various heights, or just use small branches pruned from shrubs in your yard. (If you save a little pile of branches when you prune in late winter, you'll have a perfect source of free material for staking. And the branches actually work better than the bamboo stakes because all of the side twigs help to support the plants better.)

Coping with Container Problems

Keeping your container gardens well watered and fertilized will go a long way toward keeping the plants healthy and vigorous. Insects tend to attack plants that are weak or stressed, so if you prevent the stress, you protect the plants.

Occasionally, though, conditions may be right for insects or diseases to attack even healthy-looking plants. Once a week or so, take a few minutes to really look at your plants and see if you notice any problems developing. Turn over a few leaves, and check the shoot tips for

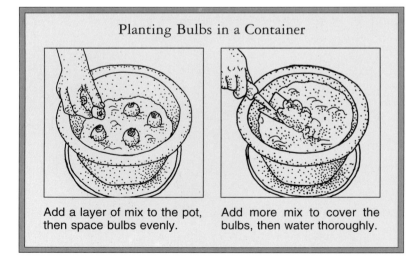

Planting Bulbs in a Container

Add a layer of mix to the pot, then space bulbs evenly.

Add more mix to cover the bulbs, then water thoroughly.

To keep annuals blooming as long as possible, pinch off spent flowers at least once a week.

Container plantings of perennials are fairly trouble-free; just water regularly and remove dead flowers.

any indications of pests. For details on what to look for, refer back to "Common Houseplant Pests" on page 31.

If bugs do show up, the same sprays that protect your houseplants will also work well outside. Spraying plants thoroughly with water will keep aphids and spider mite levels down. Insecticidal soap is generally recommended primarily to control soft-bodied insects (such as aphids), although it also works against tough customers like Japanese beetles. Just be sure you spray plants thoroughly, hitting both the tops and bottoms of all leaves. Soap sprays must hit the insects directly to be effective. Handpicking or flicking pests into a tub of soapy water also works well for larger insects, such as caterpillars and beetles. But be sure you know what you're killing—some very nasty-looking bugs are actually beneficial insects that prey on plant-eating pests.

If you have trouble with slug or snail damage (usual symptoms are large holes in the leaves), sprinkle finely crushed eggshells over the surface of the soil in the pots. The slugs won't crawl over the rough edges of the eggshells. (As a bonus, the shells will provide a slow-release source of calcium, an important plant nutrient.)

Diseases are seldom a problem on container plants. As long as there are holes in the bottom of the container, root

rots due to poor drainage aren't too common. If you let the plants dry out often, leaf tips may turn brown; make more effort to water regularly to prevent further damage. Pinch off and discard plant parts that show fuzzy, white or gray patches—signs of powdery mildew—or off-color spots. Brown or white scorched spots on indoor plants that you've recently moved outside for the summer indicate sunburn. Plants generally grow out of this damage, although they will be somewhat weakened for a while. To avoid this problem, follow the guidelines covered in "Inside Out and Outside In" on page 48.

If you tend to forget about watering, group all of your containers in one place to make maintenance easy.

Watering Container Gardens

For indoor container plants, your biggest concern is providing enough light; outdoors, watering is usually the most critical factor. Plants growing in outdoor containers will need more water as the season grows warmer and as they grow larger in relation to their pots. You must water them when they are dry. Unlike plants growing in the ground, container plants' roots have only a limited space in which to absorb water and nutrients. Plants growing in the ground may be stressed if they aren't watered during a drought, but they usually recover. When the potting soil in a container gets too dry, however, the plants may die.

Knowing How Much to Water

The rule for watering established container plants is to always wet the soil thoroughly, until water runs out the bottom of the pot. The exception to this is when your plants are very young and haven't yet grown roots out into the container. In this case, water sparingly and/or less often until the topgrowth begins to be about the same size as the container. Once the plant is established, water it as you would your other plants.

It's generally not wise to keep saucers under pots, but they can help on certain pots that dry out quickly.

Choosing Equipment for Easier Watering

There are several pieces of equipment that are quite helpful in making container watering as easy and efficient as possible. A watering can will be fine if you have only one or two pots to water. But if you have a collection of many containers, you'll save a lot of time and energy by using a hose with a special attachment called a water breaker. The breaker provides a soft, steady flow that won't wash the soil out of the pots as you water. You can buy the breaker alone or attached to a long-handled watering wand that lets you reach all of your pots and hanging baskets easily. Wands usually come with a shut-off valve so you don't have to leave the hose running when you go to turn it on or shut it off—a very handy feature.

If you live in an apartment and don't have access to an outside faucet connection, you can buy special attachments for your kitchen faucet and special lightweight hoses that you can run from your kitchen out to your balcony or rooftop garden.

Reducing Watering Chores

Besides having the right equipment for the job, there are also several things you can do to keep your watering chores to a minimum.

A watering can may be all you need to water just a few pots.

Save Time with Self-watering Pots

When you're out shopping for containers, you may find some labeled "self-watering." While these containers aren't totally self-watering—you do have to add water from time to time—they have a reservoir area built into the bottom to hold a supply of water. Some of these containers have a wick running down from the soil to the reservoir; others are designed so that a small column of soil extends down into the reservoir to soak up water as needed. There's usually a small hole in the side of the container where you can fill the reservoir and check the water level.

These pots tend to be a bit expensive, but they definitely help to reduce the frequency of watering. If you want to place a container planting in a spot where it's difficult for you to check it daily, by all means consider using a self-watering pot.

Large pots tend to dry out more slowly than small pots, so they'll need watering less often.

If plants wilt, water immediately. Misting may help, too.

• **Use large pots.** The bigger the pots you use, the less often you will have to water (and the better your container garden will look).

• **Choose plastic or wood over clay.** Clay pots dry out much faster than plastic or wood, so you may want to avoid using clay containers if you live in a hot, dry climate.

• **Cover the soil with mulch.** Mulching plants with shredded bark or grass clippings will help to reduce evaporation and keep moisture in the soil.

• **Amend your soil mix.** Adding extra compost or vermiculite to potting soil will help it hold more moisture. Or you may want to try the new synthetic water-absorbing polymers now on the market. These polymers aren't organic, but they are apparently nontoxic. You just mix the polymer granules into the potting mix before planting, and they work by absorbing large amounts of water and holding it until the plant's roots need it.

If you follow all of these tips and your plants are drying out so fast that they need watering twice a day, either move them to larger pots or prune them back to bring the topgrowth into better balance with the roots. (Pruning off older growth also helps to stimulate fresh new flowers on annuals and many perennials.)

In general, you should not keep saucers under outdoor plants because they will fill up with water during rainstorms and could cause the soil to become

waterlogged and the roots to rot. If you are concerned about pots possibly leaving stains where they sit on your deck or patio, just set them up on small scraps of wood. (This is especially a good idea for large containers to ensure that water drains well from the bottom holes.)

There are two instances where it can be all right to put saucers under your outdoor plants. The first is when a plant should be moved to a bigger pot and needs a little extra water until you have time to repot it. The other time you may want to use saucers is when you are going away for a day or two and want your plants to get by without extra watering. Water as normal and add some extra water to the saucers to sustain the plants; remove the saucers when you return.

Covering exposed soil with mulch while plants are young can keep it from drying out as quickly.

Fertilizing Container Gardens

To keep your container plantings in great shape from spring through fall, you'll need to supply extra nutrients sometime during the growing season. You can choose from a variety of solid or liquid materials to fertilize your plants and flowers. Whichever form you choose, make sure it's an organic nutrient source. Chemical fertilizers generally dissolve quickly in water, releasing large amounts of chemical salts if you apply them too liberally. A buildup of these salts can harm roots and seriously damage your container plants. Organic fertilizers are generally in a form that breaks down slowly and gradually, steadily feeding the plants the nutrients they need without any danger of overfeeding.

There's another reason why organic fertilizers are better for container plants than soluble chemical plant foods. Plants in containers must be watered often, and the chemical fertilizers may be quickly washed away as water runs through the soil. But organic fertilizers are slow-release, which means that each day only a small amount of the total nutrients is converted into a soluble form that your plants can use. The rest of the organic fertilizer remains in the soil, resistant to leaching and slowly being converted to soluble nutrients, so your plants get a steadier, more reliable food supply.

Finding Organic Fertilizers

You can buy organic fertilizers, such as fish emulsion, bloodmeal, and bonemeal, at most local garden centers. Or you can combine these ingredients with wood ashes, coffee grounds, and other recyclable organic "wastes" to make your own organic fertilizer blends. For complete details on selecting and blending various organic fertilizers, see "Understanding Organic Fertilizers" on page 25.

Using Organic Fertilizers

Meeting the nutrient needs of your container plants starts at planting time. Adding compost to commercial or homemade potting mixes is one of the best things you can do to promote good root growth. Compost provides millions of live microorganisms, which

Regular feedings with liquid fertilizer will keep annuals vigorous and blooming through the season.

feed on other organic fertilizers and make the nutrients available to your plants. (Organic fertilizers will still work in soils without compost, but they are much more effective with it.)

If you're growing annual flowers, herbs, and vegetables, mixing additional organic fertilizers into the compost-enriched soil is not really necessary. However, for long-term container plantings,

Acid compost to perennials, shrubs, and trees each spring.

Organic fertilizers release nutrients slowly, promoting steady, healthy plant growth.

To keep long-term plantings vigorous, mix compost and organic fertilizers into the container soil.

such as perennials, shrubs, and trees, supplementing the soil with kelp (seaweed) meal, greensand, and other organic nutrients will help ensure a steady supply of nutrients for the developing root systems. "Making Your Own Potting Mixes" on page 108 offers a recipe for a well-balanced, nutrient-enriched, deluxe growing medium that's great for meeting the needs of these "permanent" plantings.

Once your plants are established (after a few weeks), it's time to start adding a supply of additional nutrients. Begin feeding with a liquid fish product, using it at half the recommended strength every 2 weeks. Most fish fertilizers are higher in nitrogen than in potassium or phosphorus, and this is fine until it's time for flowering plants to begin blooming. Then you may want to treat flowering plants to a small handful of bonemeal (for extra phosphorus) and kelp (seaweed) meal or wood ashes (for plenty of potassium). Mix these materials with a little compost and scratch them into the soil surface.

You can keep feeding most container plants through late summer; after that, the cooler temperatures of fall will naturally slow their growth. For outdoor potted trees and shrubs, stop fertilizing by mid-summer to give the new growth a chance to "harden up" before frost.

Successful Containers Start with Compost

There's just nothing quite like compost for keeping container plants healthy and happy. Besides helping your organic fertilizers work harder, the beneficial microorganisms the compost supplies can also suppress the development of disease problems.

Hopefully, you have enough space to maintain at least a small compost pile. You just need an area that's at least 3 feet (90 cm) long, wide, and high. You can buy a commercial compost bin, build your own out of old pallets or chicken wire, or just heap the material in a pile. Good compost ingredients include most organic garden and kitchen wastes. Avoid oils, fats, and bones—all of which break down slowly and attract scavengers—and human and pet wastes, which can carry diseases. Also avoid adding diseased or insect-infested materials.

Mix a balance of dry materials, such as leaves or shredded newspaper, with moist materials, such as grass clippings or vegetable peelings. The pile should feel damp but not soggy. If it's dry, add water; if it's too wet, mix in some more dry material. Keep adding more materials as you gather them until the pile fills its space or bin. About once a week, use a pitchfork to turn over, or at least stir up, the mix. Eventually—after a few weeks or months—the original ingredients will break down into dark, crumbly compost. Before using the finished compost, sift it through ½-inch (12 mm) wire mesh to screen out any lumps that are left.

If you don't have the space for outdoor composting, try worm composting. You can keep worms in an indoor bin and feed them your food scraps to make an especially rich compost. Several garden-supply catalogs now offer bins, instructions, and even the worms themselves.

Of course if you just need a little compost now and then, or if you need more than you can make, you can buy it in bags at your garden center. If your community has a composting program, you may also be able to get it at no charge from your local yard waste composting site.

GUIDE TO CONTAINER PLANTS

Gardening in containers doesn't have to mean that your plant choices are limited. Just about any plant that you could enjoy in the garden will also grow just fine in a container. Annual flowers are traditional favorites for pots, planters, window boxes, and hanging baskets. But you can also get multi-season interest from carefully chosen perennials, vines, shrubs, and small trees. Planters can be both pretty *and* productive if you include a variety of vegetables, herbs, and fruits. With container plantings, you can enjoy a whole garden's worth of plants in just a small area.

The key to success is providing the right growing conditions: a container big enough to support the root system, the right growing mix to encourage good root growth, and adequate light for leaf and flower production. Plants growing in containers also need careful watering and fertilizing, since their roots can't spread as far as they would in the soil for moisture and nutrients. For this bit of extra attention, your container plants will reward you with a bounty of lovely leaves, colorful flowers, and possibly even a tasty harvest!

To get you started, we've included this guide to over 60 great plants for containers. "Flowers," starting on page 118, is the place to look if you're thinking about colorful annual and perennial plants. "Trees, Shrubs, and Vines," starting on page 137, covers some of the best bushy and vining plants for more permanent container plantings. And if you're considering growing vegetables, fruits, or herbs, check out "Edible Plants," starting on page 144.

Because ornamental plants (such as flowers, shrubs, and trees) can have many common names, these entries are arranged alphabetically by the botanical names. (If you aren't sure of the botanical name, look up the name you know in the index, and it will tell you where to find the entry.) Edible plants (vegetables, herbs, and fruits) generally only have one common name, so those entries are alphabetized by the common name.

In each entry, you'll find a color photograph of the plant, along with an informative caption and a description of the plant's special features. You'll also find the information you need to grow the plant successfully, including its water, fertilizer, soil, and light needs. Depending on the type of plant, you may also find suggested uses and companions or harvesting tips. Refer to these encyclopedia entries when you're choosing your plants, and again through the season to make sure you're giving them the best care possible, and you'll enjoy great results with your container gardens.

Containers gardens give you the freedom to change your displays with the season. This colorful grouping of marigolds, calendulas, cabbage, and kale makes an eye-catching combination for early fall

F
L
O
W
E
R
S

Ageratum houstonianum   Compositae

AGERATUM

This Mexican native combines rare blue colors with a neat, compact, edging habit. The name "ageratum" is from the Greek for "not growing old," a testament to its staying power.

OTHER COMMON NAMES: Flossflower.

DESCRIPTION: This annual plant forms small, 3–6-inch (7.5–15 cm) tall mounds, bearing soft, green, hairy leaves. Fuzzy, tassel-like, 1/2-inch (12 mm) flowers bloom above the leaves in lavender, blue, pink, and white.

LIGHT NEEDS: Full or half-day of sun; protect from hot midday sun.

WATER NEEDS: Keep the soil evenly moist.

GROWING GUIDELINES: Plant ageratums in all-purpose container mix that's enriched with compost. Set plants 6–8 inches (15–20 cm) apart. Regularly pinch off spent blossoms.

COMMON PROBLEMS: Plants can look ragged by midsummer. Shear them to 2 inches (5 cm) tall to promote new growth, or replace them with new plants.

PROPAGATION: Start ageratums from seed sown indoors 6–8 weeks before the last frost. Grow them in separate pots to prevent root disturbance at transplant time. Take cuttings of young growth at any time.

COMMENTS: Grow ageratums in pots, hanging baskets, or window boxes.

COMPATIBLE COMPANIONS: Ageratum looks best combined with other plants, since it tends to fade in hot weather. Try it with dwarf yellow marigolds, pink petunias, white lobelia, large periwinkle (*Vinca major*), English ivy, wax begonias, sweet alyssum, chives, and eggplant.

| *Alchemilla mollis* | Rosaceae | *Begonia* Semperflorens-Cultorum hybrids | Begoniaceae |

LADY'S-MANTLE

WAX BEGONIA

Grow lady's-mantle for its soft, rounded leaves and tall-stalked clusters of chartreuse blooms. It is especially pretty growing in a cool, moist, partly shady spot.

Wax begonias are among the most popular and dependable bedding plants. In containers, these rugged heat-resistant annuals flower nonstop from late spring until frost.

DESCRIPTION: Lady's-mantle's grayish, rounded, lobed, hairy leaves grow on long stems in a clump 6–18 inches (15–45 cm) tall. Each clump produces starry, 2–3-inch (5–7.5 cm) wide clusters of greenish yellow flowers in late spring. This perennial is hardy in Zones 3–9.

LIGHT NEEDS: Part shade.

WATER NEEDS: Keep the soil evenly moist, especially during hot weather.

GROWING GUIDELINES: Plant in spring in all-purpose container mix with added compost. Set plants 8 inches (20 cm) apart; three clumps together make a nice show. Remove the flowers before they go to seed to prevent rampant spreading.

COMMON PROBLEMS: Plants are basically trouble-free, except that they may suffer during hot weather; it's especially important to keep the soil moist then.

PROPAGATION: Divide the clumps as needed in early winter or early spring. Lady's-mantle also self-sows if you don't remove the flowers.

COMMENTS: This is an easy-to-grow, long-lived plant. You can cut the flower stems and hang them upside down to dry for arrangements.

COMPATIBLE COMPANIONS: Grow lady's-mantle under a Japanese maple (*Acer palmatum*), or combine it with other perennials, such as hardy geraniums (*Geranium* spp.) and hostas.

DESCRIPTION: Wax begonias produce small, mounded, fibrous-rooted plants that normally grow 6–9 inches (15–22.5 cm) tall. Their rounded, shiny leaves may be green, reddish, bronze, or variegated. Small flowers in white, pink, or red bloom among the leaves all summer.

LIGHT NEEDS: A half-day of sun is best, although plants can take full sun if they're shaded at midday.

WATER NEEDS: Keep the soil evenly moist, especially if the plants are growing in sun.

GROWING GUIDELINES: Wax begonias appreciate all-purpose container mix that's been amended with compost and/or peat moss. Set plants 6–8 inches (15–20 cm) apart.

COMMON PROBLEMS: Wax begonias are relatively trouble-free.

PROPAGATION: Start the fine seed indoors 8–12 weeks before the last frost; leave the seed uncovered. Take cuttings of young growth at any time.

COMMENTS: Begonias make good winter houseplants if you bring them indoors before frost.

COMPATIBLE COMPANIONS: Grow wax begonias alone, or combine them with ageratum, large periwinkle (*Vinca major*), or clematis.

CULTIVARS: The very sun-resistant Cocktail series (including pink 'Brandy', rose-pink 'Gin', and white 'Whiskey') has bronzy leaves and grows to 5 inches (12.5 cm) tall.

Begonia Tuberhybrida hybrids   Begoniaceae

HYBRID TUBEROUS BEGONIAS

Hybrid tuberous begonias produce their spectacular large flowers from summer until frost. Both the upright and pendulous types make a sensational show in containers.

DESCRIPTION: These showy plants grow from frost-tender tubers to produce lush, bushy plants from 12–18 inches (30–45 cm) tall. The succulent stems may be upright or trailing, with green or bronze leaves. The flowers come in all shades except blue.

LIGHT NEEDS: A half-day of sun or filtered sun; tolerates shade.

WATER NEEDS: Keep the soil evenly moist.

GROWING GUIDELINES: Buy the largest available tubers in spring. Plant them rounded side down in all-purpose container mix. Plant two or three tubers per 8–10-inch (20–25 cm) pot. To keep the tubers over winter, reduce watering in fall and bring the pot indoors before or just after the first frost. Cut back the remaining topgrowth, then store the pot in a frost-free place. Replant the tubers in fresh soil the following spring.

COMMON PROBLEMS: Powdery mildew can cause gray or white patches on leaves. Spray affected leaves with sulfur or a baking soda solution (1 teaspoon of baking soda in 1 quart [1 l] of water). Yellowed leaves indicate overwatering.

PROPAGATION: In late winter, divide tubers into pieces with one eye each.

COMPATIBLE COMPANIONS: Try hybrid tuberous begonias with coleus or large periwinkle (*Vinca major*). They are also very effective alone in masses.

Bergenia cordifolia   Saxifragaceae

HEART-LEAVED BERGENIA

If you want to add year-round interest to a container planting, it's hard to beat heart-leaved bergenia. This rugged perennial has glossy evergreen leaves that turn red in fall.

DESCRIPTION: Heart-leaved bergenia bears thick, waxy, wavy-edged leaves in dense, 12–20-inch (30–50 cm) tall clumps. The leaves are shiny green for much of the year, turning scarlet red in fall. In spring, the clumps are accented by sturdy, 1-foot (30 cm) stems topped with pink, rose, or white flowers. This perennial is hardy in Zones 3–9.

LIGHT NEEDS: Partial shade is best, although plants can adapt to nearly full sun or full shade.

WATER NEEDS: Keep the soil evenly moist.

GROWING GUIDELINES: Heart-leaved bergenia prefers rich, cool, moisture-retentive mix. To keep plants neat and compact, you can shear all of the leaves to the ground in early spring. Divide when crowded.

COMMON PROBLEMS: Snails and slugs love to feed on bergenia leaves. Keep damage to a minimum by putting the container up high—perhaps on a table or pedestal.

PROPAGATION: Divide plants after bloom.

COMMENTS: Heart-leaved bergenia grows quickly. You may need to divide the plants every year or two to keep them from getting overcrowded.

COMPATIBLE COMPANIONS: Combine heart-leaved bergenia with other shade-lovers, such as ferns, hostas, rhododendrons, common periwinkle (*Vinca minor*), edging lobelia (*Lobelia erinus*), and forget-me-not (*Myosotis sylvatica*).

Brachycome iberidifolia Compositae	*Browallia speciosa* Solanaceae
# SWAN RIVER DAISY	# BROWALLIA

In full sun and cool temperatures, this Australian native blooms freely for months and produces a sweet scent as a bonus. It is an excellent annual for hanging baskets.

DESCRIPTION: Swan River daisy has finely divided, 3-inch (7.5 cm) foliage on many-branched mounds that trail to 18 inches (45 cm) wide. Exquisite little daisy-like, 1-inch (2.5 cm) wide, blue, white, or rose flowers bloom from spring through summer.

LIGHT NEEDS: Full sun.

WATER NEEDS: Keep the soil evenly moist.

GROWING GUIDELINES: Grow Swan River daisy in all-purpose container mix. Set plants 6 inches (15 cm) apart. If you're not growing this plant as a hanging basket, stick some short, twiggy prunings into the pot to support the floppy stems.

COMMON PROBLEMS: Swan River daisy tends to stop blooming in hot weather. Shearing the plants back by half and watering them well can encourage new growth and a second flush of bloom.

PROPAGATION: Sow seed indoors 6–8 weeks before the last frost, or plant it directly into the container in late spring.

COMMENTS: Swan River daisy is generally easy to grow, although it dislikes hot weather. Its sprawling habit makes it a good edging plant.

COMPATIBLE COMPANIONS: Pair this pretty daisy with zonal geraniums, sweet alyssum, clematis, or jasmine (*Jasminum officinale*).

CULTIVARS: The starry flowers of 'Blue Star' have curled petals in varying shades of blue on 8-inch (20 cm) plants.

Browallia adds a cool blue accent to window boxes and baskets in partial shade. Before the first frost, cut the plants back and bring them indoors to enjoy in winter.

OTHER COMMON NAMES: Amethyst flower.

DESCRIPTION: This easy annual has a graceful, sprawling habit, growing to 14 inches (35 cm) tall and 15 inches (37.5 cm) wide. Five-petaled flowers to 2 inches (5 cm) wide bloom just above the emerald green foliage in white or many shades of blue or lilac.

LIGHT NEEDS: A half-day of sun is best. Plants tolerate full to filtered sunlight, although the flower color may fade in too much sun.

WATER NEEDS: Water often to keep the soil evenly moist.

GROWING GUIDELINES: Grow browallia in all-purpose container mix with added compost. Space plants 10 inches (25 cm) apart. Pinch off the stem tips of young plants once or twice to promote branching.

COMMON PROBLEMS: Plants may look tired by midsummer; cut them back by half in midsummer to promote new growth and more flowers.

PROPAGATION: Sow seed indoors 8–10 weeks before the last frost; leave it uncovered. Take cuttings any time during the season.

COMMENTS: Browallia makes a nice winter houseplant.

COMPATIBLE COMPANIONS: Don't plant browallia alone, since it tends to look a bit ragged by midsummer. Good companions include marigolds, sweet alyssum, dahlias, petunias, and large periwinkle (*Vinca major*).

Chrysanthemum frutescens   Compositae

MARGUERITE

Marguerites offer ferny foliage covered with dainty, daisy-like blooms practically all summer. They are perennial in warm climates; grow them as annuals north of Zone 9.

OTHER COMMON NAMES: Paris daisy.

DESCRIPTION: This shallow-rooted, shrubby plant grows to about 3 feet (90 cm) tall. It has bright green or bluish leaves and abundant, daisy-like, 2-inch (5 cm) blooms in white, pink, or yellow.

LIGHT NEEDS: Full sun.

WATER NEEDS: Keep the soil evenly moist.

GROWING GUIDELINES: Plant marguerites in light, well-drained mix. Fertilize twice a month. Prune plants lightly every month or two for best flowering.

COMMON PROBLEMS: Leafminers can tunnel through leaves, causing unsightly patches. Control these pests by removing and destroying infested leaves and spraying with insecticidal soap.

PROPAGATION: Take cuttings any time.

COMMENTS: Large-flowered types are not as prolific as those with small blooms. You can bring marguerites indoors for the winter and move them back outdoors the following spring.

COMPATIBLE COMPANIONS: Marguerites combine well with many other sun-loving annuals, including zonal geraniums, verbenas, and dusty millers.

CULTIVARS: 'Chyrsaster', with yellow flowers, is known as Boston yellow daisy.

RELATED PLANTS:
  C. pacificum, gold-and-silver chrysanthemum, has silver-edged green leaves and gold fall flowers. It looks great trailing over the rim of a pot.

Coleus x *hybridus*   Labiatae

COLEUS

Coleus is unsurpassed for foliage interest in shady gardens. Pinch off the stem tips frequently to remove the dull-looking flower spikes and promote bushy new growth.

OTHER COMMON NAMES: Painted leaves.

DESCRIPTION: This easy-to-grow plant has been bred for over a century to create laced, fringed, oak-leaved, and filigreed shapes in astonishing colors and variegations. The plants form bushy mounds from 6–24 inches (15–60 cm) tall.

LIGHT NEEDS: High, indirect light is best, although coleus can take quite a bit of shade.

WATER NEEDS: Keep the soil evenly moist.

GROWING GUIDELINES: Plant coleus in loose, average to rich, well-drained mix. Space plants 6–9 inches (15–22.5 cm) apart. Fertilize every 2–3 weeks with fish emulsion.

COMMON PROBLEMS: Leaf colors fade in low light; move the container to a brighter spot. Too much light promotes flower spikes instead of leaves; move the container to a shadier location.

PROPAGATION: Sow seed indoors 8–10 weeks before the last frost; leave it uncovered but keep it warm. Take cuttings from overwintered plants in spring.

COMMENTS: Although commonly grown as an annual, coleus is actually a perennial in frost-free areas. In other climates, bring coleus plants indoors before frost to enjoy them as winter houseplants.

COMPATIBLE COMPANIONS: Grow coleus by itself, with green ferns, or with single-colored flowers, such as tuberous begonias. Dwarf types are best for window boxes.

| *Convolvulus tricolor* | Convolvulaceae | *Dahlia* hybrids | Compositae |

DWARF MORNING GLORY

DAHLIAS

This easy annual looks much like the common vining morning glory, but it is a clumper rather than a climber. Another difference is that dwarf morning glory flowers stay open all day.

OTHER COMMON NAMES: Bush morning glory.

DESCRIPTION: Dwarf morning glory produces bushy plants with small, narrow, green leaves. The plants grow 1 foot (30 cm) tall and 2 feet (60 cm) wide. Funnel-shaped, 2-inch (5 cm) flowers appear all summer. They are generally blue with a yellow throat and white central band, although rainbow mixes are now available.

LIGHT NEEDS: Full sun.

WATER NEEDS: Allow to dry a bit between waterings.

GROWING GUIDELINES: Plant in all-purpose container mix in a warm spot. Space plants 12 inches (30 cm) apart. Pinch off spent flowers.

COMMON PROBLEMS: Plants may grow slowly or even die if the roots are damaged during transplanting.

PROPAGATION: Sow seed indoors in large containers 6 weeks before the last frost. You can also sow directly into the planter after the last frost date. Either way, nick the tough seed coat with a knife or nail file before planting.

COMMENTS: Dwarf morning glory is a super hanging basket plant. It's also wonderful for edging pots and planters. The seeds are poisonous if eaten.

COMPATIBLE COMPANIONS: Use dwarf morning glories to add color to potted junipers or false cypress (*Chamaecyparis* spp.). Or combine them with other sun-loving annuals, such as yellow nasturtiums and silvery dusty miller.

Dahlias come in two types: tall border selections and dwarf bedding types. The dwarf types are usually best for container gardening. Remove spent flowers to prolong the bloom season.

DESCRIPTION: Dahlias grow from frost-tender, tuberous roots. They produce single or branched stems that range in size from 8-inch (20 cm) dwarfs to 6-foot (1.8 m) giants. The single or double flowers bloom from midsummer through fall in a range of shapes and in all shades but blue.

LIGHT NEEDS: Partial to full sun.

WATER NEEDS: Keep evenly moist after growth begins.

GROWING GUIDELINES: Grow dahlias in a well-drained, peat moss-and-sand-based mix. If you're growing full-sized types, plant one tuber per 10-inch (25 cm) pot. Set the crown—the end where the roots join—1 inch (2.5 cm) below the surface. If you're using dwarf, bedding dahlia plants, space them about 10 inches (25 cm) apart. North of Zone 9, bring the roots indoors for winter storage in dry peat moss in a cool, dry spot.

COMMON PROBLEMS: Scraggly growth means not enough light; move the container to a sunnier location. Too much fertilizer encourages leaves instead of flowers; avoid high-nitrogen fertilizers.

PROPAGATION: Divide the root clumps in fall or spring, keeping one eye (bud) on each. You can grow bedding types from seed; sow indoors 6–8 weeks before the last frost.

COMPATIBLE COMPANIONS: Try dahlias with large periwinkle (*Vinca major*), coleus, petunias, zonal geraniums, impatiens, or boxwood (*Buxus* spp.).

Fuchsia x *hybrida*   Onagraceae

FUCHSIA

Fuchsias make splendid hanging baskets for shady, cool spots; protect them from midday sun. The dramatic blooms always attract attention (and they may attract hummingbirds, too).

OTHER COMMON NAMES: Lady's eardrops.

DESCRIPTION: Fuchsias are shrubby plants with an upright or trailing habit. Upright forms can grow as much as 6 feet (1.8 m) tall. Both types bloom all summer, with pendant, single or double flowers up to 3 inches (7.5 cm) long. The flower colors are generally white, red, or pink with violet, blue, purple, or red. Some kinds are hardy as far north as Zone 7.

LIGHT NEEDS: Filtered light is best.

WATER NEEDS: Water often to keep evenly moist.

GROWING GUIDELINES: Plant in well-drained, compost-enriched container mix. Feed frequently (every 10 days or so). Pinch off the shoot tips every few weeks to keep the plants bushy, or train a single stem upward to form a trunk, then let the top bush out to produce a standard (tree) form. Remove spent flowers regularly. In cold areas, bring the plants indoors before frost, but first cut them back by half, divide them, and repot. Keep in a bright, cool but frost-free spot.

COMMON PROBLEMS: Direct sun can produce tan patches on leaves; move the plant to a shadier spot. The plant may turn yellow and wither if you let the soil dry out. Flowering may stop in hot weather.

PROPAGATION: Take tip cuttings of soft green growth at any time.

COMPATIBLE COMPANIONS: These showy specimens are best planted alone in hanging baskets.

Helichrysum petiolatum   Compositae

LICORICE PLANT

Licorice plant has soft, silvery leaves that complement both pale pastels and bold, bright hues. It's a perfect choice for cascading over the edges of pots, planters, hanging baskets, and window boxes.

DESCRIPTION: Licorice plant has a shrubby form that's partly upright and partly trailing. A single plant can grow to 2 feet (60 cm) tall and 4 feet (1.2 m) wide; container plants are generally smaller. The woody stems carry oval, felted, white-green-gray foliage. Small, yellow-white blooms may appear. Licorice plant is generally grown as an annual, since it is winter-hardy only south of Zone 9.

LIGHT NEEDS: Full sun.

WATER NEEDS: Allow the soil to dry somewhat between waterings.

GROWING GUIDELINES: Grow licorice plant in sandy, well-drained mix. Space plants about 1 foot (30 cm) apart. Pinch off the shoot tips every few weeks to encourage bushy growth. Bring the plant indoors to a cool sunroom or greenhouse for overwintering.

COMMON PROBLEMS: The stems can get leggy if you don't pinch them regularly.

PROPAGATION: Sow seed indoors or outdoors in late spring or early summer. Take cuttings during the growing season.

COMPATIBLE COMPANIONS: Licorice plant combines well with almost any colorful companion. It's especially good with dark-leaved plants, such as 'Purple Ruffles' basil, 'Palace Purple' heuchera (*Heuchera micrantha* var. *diversifolia*), or purple-leaved bush beans.

Hemerocallis hybrids   Liliaceae

DAYLILIES

Daylilies make excellent container plants, since they have attractive, arching foliage as well as showy flowers. They adapt to a range of conditions and don't require much care.

DESCRIPTION: Daylilies grow in clumps of 1–2-foot (30–60 cm), arching, sword-like, green leaves. In summer, these leafy mounds are accented by 2–8-inch (5–20 cm) wide blooms on 12–42-inch (30–95 cm) stalks. Some cultivars rebloom later in the season. The funnel-shaped flowers may be orange, yellow, red, pink, buff, apricot, or green, sometimes with a contrasting band or throat. Daylilies are generally hardy in Zones 4–9.

LIGHT NEEDS: Full sun to partial shade.

WATER NEEDS: Keep the soil evenly moist, especially during bloom.

GROWING GUIDELINES: Grow each daylily plant in its own 5-gallon (22 l) tub of well-drained, all-purpose container mix. Pinch off spent flowers every day or two. Also pull or cut off dead or discolored leaves. Remove the flower stalks once all of the buds on that stalk have bloomed.

COMMON PROBLEMS: Flower color tends to fade in full sun. If this is a problem, you may want to move your plant to a slightly shadier spot.

PROPAGATION: Divide plants in spring or late fall.

COMMENTS: "Mini" classifications often refer to flower size; the actual plant may still be large.

COMPATIBLE COMPANIONS: To extend the season of interest, combine daylilies with spring bulbs or pansies. As the spring flowers fade, the emerging daylily foliage will cover the yellowing plants.

Heuchera spp.   Saxifragaceae

CORAL BELLS

Some coral bells have green leaves and colorful flowers; others have dull blooms but strikingly colored foliage. Both kinds are heat-tolerant and adapt well to container growing.

OTHER COMMON NAMES: Alumroot.

DESCRIPTION: Coral bells produce neat, compact, 1–2-foot (30–60 cm) tall clumps of rounded, scalloped leaves. The clumps are topped by airy spires of small, bell-shaped blooms in red, rose, green, or white through summer. Common coral bells (*H. sanguinea*) is the best-known species, with green leaves and red, pink, or white blooms. 'Palace Purple' heuchera (*H. micrantha* var. *diversifolia* 'Palace Purple') has maple-like, purplish leaves and pinkish white flowers on 20-inch (50 cm) stems. Most coral bells are hardy in Zones 3–8.

LIGHT NEEDS: Full sun to light shade.

WATER NEEDS: Keep the soil evenly moist.

GROWING GUIDELINES: Grow coral bells in very well-drained, compost-enriched container mix, setting plants 6 inches (15 cm) apart. When the flowers fade, pinch off the flower stalk at the base.

COMMON PROBLEMS: Mealybugs may cluster and feed on plant parts. Knock them off with a strong spray of water, or spray with insecticidal soap.

PROPAGATION: Divide clumps in fall or spring, or sow seed indoors in spring.

COMPATIBLE COMPANIONS: Pink- or white-flowered coral bells look especially pretty edged with pink or white sweet alyssum (*Lobularia maritima*). The colored-foliage selections can provide all-season interest to any container planting.

HOSTAS

NEW GUINEA IMPATIENS

Hostas are one of the most popular perennials for shady containers. Some hostas produce beautiful flowers, but most gardeners grow them for their strikingly colored and textured leaves.

New Guinea impatiens do not bloom as abundantly as their shade-loving relatives. But this isn't a drawback, since it allows you to see the beautiful foliage more easily.

OTHER COMMON NAMES: Plantain lily.

DESCRIPTION: Hostas grow in leafy mounds anywhere from 6 inches (15 cm) to 3 feet (90 cm) tall, in shades and markings of green, blue, gold, and/or white. The leaves can be rounded, heart-shaped, or lance-shaped. Spires of sometimes fragrant, purplish or white flowers appear in summer. Hostas are generally hardy in Zones 4–9.

LIGHT NEEDS: Light to moderate shade is best, although some can tolerate full sun.

WATER NEEDS: During the growing season, keep the soil evenly moist. Water less in winter, so the soil is just barely moist.

GROWING GUIDELINES: Grow hostas in all-purpose container mix with added compost to help hold moisture. Fertilize once in spring with fish emulsion. Mulch the container in winter to protect the crown and roots; remove the mulch in spring.

COMMON PROBLEMS: Hungry slugs and snails can quickly turn hosta leaves into lacy skeletons. Minimize problems by putting the container up on a table or pedestal. Or catch the pests in beer traps.

PROPAGATION: Divide in spring or fall.

COMPATIBLE COMPANIONS: Grow hostas with ferns, forget-me-not (*Myosotis sylvatica*), purple-leaved oxalis (*Oxalis hedysaroides*), lady's-mantles (*Alchemilla* spp.), and wishbone flower (*Torenia fournieri*).

DESCRIPTION: New Guinea impatiens are upright, mounded spreaders that grow 8–24 inches (20–60 cm) tall. Their pointed, green leaves can be brilliantly variegated in red, cream, or bronze. The 2-inch (5 cm) wide, flat flowers appear all summer in shades of orange, red, purple, pink, and lavender. New Guinea impatiens are perennial in frost-free areas; elsewhere, grow them as annuals.

LIGHT NEEDS: Full sun to filtered light.

WATER NEEDS: Water often to keep the soil evenly moist.

GROWING GUIDELINES: Grow New Guinea impatiens in all-purpose container mix. Space plants about 12 inches (30 cm) apart. Fertilize twice a month.

COMMON PROBLEMS: Dry winds can cause plants to wilt, particularly in full sun. Water often to keep the soil moist, and move the container to a more sheltered location if necessary.

PROPAGATION: Sow seed indoors 6–8 weeks before the last frost date. Take cuttings at any time.

COMMENTS: You may be able to hold over favorite plants by bringing their pots into a sunny room for the winter.

COMPATIBLE COMPANIONS: New Guinea impatiens are so colorful that they tend to look best planted alone. If you really need a filler, try the rich green foliage of parsley.

IMPATIENS

LANTANA

Impatiens are justifiably popular for pots, planters, window boxes, and hanging baskets. They add plenty of color to shady spots and don't demand much care in return.

This fast-growing shrub is rugged enough to withstand heat and drought but not cold winters. Display it in a hanging basket, or train it to grow upright into a standard (tree) form.

OTHER COMMON NAMES: Busy Lizzie.

DESCRIPTION: Impatiens grow into bushy mounds that are usually 4–12 inches (10–30 cm) tall and 12–15 inches (30–37.5 cm) wide. They have glossy, dark green, 2-inch (5 cm) long leaves and juicy stems. The 1–2-inch (2.5–5 cm) flowers come in a range of colors, from bright hues to soft pastels and white. Impatiens are perennial in frost-free areas; elsewhere, grow them as annuals.

LIGHT NEEDS: Partial shade.

WATER NEEDS: Keep the soil evenly moist.

GROWING GUIDELINES: Grow impatiens in all-purpose container mix with added compost. Set plants 12 inches (30 cm) apart. Do not fertilize.

COMMON PROBLEMS: Too little light can lead to leggy growth; move the container to a brighter spot. Plants wilt dramatically if they dry out but usually spring back if you water them right away.

PROPAGATION: Sow seed indoors (leave it uncovered) 8–10 weeks before your last frost date. In fall, take cuttings to grow indoors for next year's plants.

COMMENTS: Double-flowered, rosebud types are beautiful, but they tend to bloom sparsely and can be disappointing.

COMPATIBLE COMPANIONS: Impatiens look wonderful when planted alone in a container. If you want to soften the edge of the pot, add some large periwinkle (*Vinca major*).

OTHER COMMON NAMES: Yellow sage.

DESCRIPTION: Lantana is a coarse, upright shrub that grows to 3 feet (90 cm) tall. It has stiff branches and dark green foliage that is aromatic when crushed. During the warmth of summer, small yellow, orange, red, or bicolored flowers bloom in 1–2-inch (2.5–5 cm) wide heads. The flowers are followed by black berries. Lantana can survive winters outdoors south of Zone 8; elsewhere, grow it as an annual or bring it inside for the winter.

LIGHT NEEDS: Full sun.

WATER NEEDS: Allow the soil to dry somewhat between waterings.

GROWING GUIDELINES: Grow lantana in all-purpose container mix. Set plants 18 inches (45 cm) apart. Prune lantana back by one-half to two-thirds in spring and remove dead wood.

COMMON PROBLEMS: Mildew may produce gray patches on leaves. Move the pot to a spot with more light and better air circulation. Pinch off severely infected leaves; spray the rest with a solution of 1 teaspoon of baking soda in 1 quart (1 l) of water.

PROPAGATION: Sow seed indoors in midwinter; it may take 8 weeks to germinate. Take cuttings of young growth in late summer.

COMPATIBLE COMPANIONS: Since lantana grows so quickly, it is often best in its own container.

| *Lobelia erinus* | Lobeliaceae | *Lobularia maritima* | Cruciferae |

EDGING LOBELIA

The tiny blue flowers of edging lobelia add sparkle to spring and early-summer containers. Use them to fill in until summer-blooming plants get settled and start to flower.

DESCRIPTION: Edging lobelia grows to about 6 inches (15 cm) tall and 9 inches (22.5 cm) wide, with a bushy or trailing habit. The delicate, $^3/_4$-inch (18 mm), tubular flowers bloom in blue, violet, pink, or white, with a yellow or white throat.

LIGHT NEEDS: Partial to full sun. Partial shade is best in hot weather.

WATER NEEDS: Keep the soil evenly moist, especially if the plants are growing in full sun.

GROWING GUIDELINES: Grow in all-purpose container mix with added compost and/or peat moss. Space plants 4–6 inches (10–15 cm) apart.

COMMON PROBLEMS: Edging lobelia tends to look ragged by midsummer; shear the plants back by half to promote rebloom.

PROPAGATION: Sow seed indoors 6 weeks before the last frost; leave it uncovered.

COMMENTS: An especially effective way to display edging lobelia is in strawberry-jar planters, with two or three plants tucked into each hole.

COMPATIBLE COMPANIONS: If you need a whole season of bloom from a container, combine edging lobelia with bushier plants, such as dusty miller, geraniums, pansies, petunias, and clematis. For a blue-and-yellow planting, try it with torenia (*Torenia fournieri*) and golden creeping Jenny (*Lysimachia nummularia* 'Aurea'). It also looks good with peppers and parsley or rosemary.

SWEET ALYSSUM

Sweet alyssum is one of the best edging plants. Its tiny blooms release a light but noticeable, fresh, honey-like fragrance that's especially delightful near porches, patios, and decks.

DESCRIPTION: Sweet alyssum produces branched or trailing plants that grow 4–6 inches (10–15 cm) tall and 9–15 inches (22.5–37.5 cm) wide. The slender stems carry 1-inch (2.5 cm) long, narrow leaves and clusters of tiny white, pink, or purple flowers. Sweet alyssum is an annual.

LIGHT NEEDS: Full sun is best, although plants can survive with a half-day of sun.

WATER NEEDS: Keep the soil evenly moist.

GROWING GUIDELINES: Grow sweet alyssum in well-drained, all-purpose container mix. Set plants 6 inches (15 cm) apart.

COMMON PROBLEMS: Plants tend to look ragged by midsummer. To encourage more flowering, shear plants back by half 4 weeks after the first bloom.

PROPAGATION: Sow seed indoors 6–8 weeks before the last frost date, or plant it directly into the container in mid- to late-spring.

COMMENTS: Sweet alyssum blooms in several colors, but the white flowers are by far the most fragrant.

COMPATIBLE COMPANIONS: Don't plant sweet alyssum by itself, since eventually it will need to be cut back. Good partners include petunias, bulbs, roses, ageratum, salvias (*Salvia* spp.), clematis, flowering tobacco (*Nicotiana* spp.), and eggplant.

CULTIVARS: 'Carpet of Snow' grows 4 inches (10 cm) tall and 8 inches (20 cm) wide and has white flowers.

| *Muscari armeniacum* | Liliaceae | *Myosotis sylvatica* | Boraginaceae |

GRAPE HYACINTH

FORGET-ME-NOT

Grape hyacinths bloom for only a short time, but their early spring color is definitely a welcome sight to winter-weary gardeners. They often self-sow and increase rapidly.

DESCRIPTION: Grape hyacinths grow from small, plump bulbs. The bulbs send up 4–8-inch (10–20 cm) tall, grassy leaves in fall or late winter, followed by hollow-tubed bloom spikes in early spring. The flower clusters look like bunches of tiny blue or white grapes. These bulbs are hardy in Zones 3–10.

LIGHT NEEDS: Full sun to light shade.

WATER NEEDS: Keep the soil evenly moist from fall through spring. Once the leaves die down, provide little or no summer water.

GROWING GUIDELINES: Plant bulbs in fall in well-drained, all-purpose container mix. Set the bulbs 2 inches (5 cm) deep and 3 inches (7.5 cm) apart. Allow the foliage to turn yellow before removing it.

COMMON PROBLEMS: Generally trouble-free. Bulbs can rot if overwatered in summer.

PROPAGATION: Divide the clumps when they get crowded.

COMPATIBLE COMPANIONS: Try grape hyacinths under shrubs or with other plants that don't need much summer water, such as nasturtium (*Tropaeolum majus*), rose moss (*Portulaca grandiflora*), lantana (*Lantana camara*), dwarf morning glory (*Convolvulus tricolor*), and creeping zinnia (*Sanvitalia procumbens*). For a special spring show, combine grape hyacinths with small tulips, daffodils, crocus, and pansies.

The dainty blue flowers of forget-me-not are traditional favorites for spring gardens. Add the bushy or sprawling plants to containers for a touch of early-season color.

DESCRIPTION: Forget-me-nots grow 6–12 inches (15–30 cm) tall and 6–9 inches (15–22.5 cm) wide, with narrow, hairy, green leaves. They usually grow as biennials, producing leaves the first year and flowering stems the second, but they can bloom the first year if started early indoors. The tiny blue or pink, white-centered flowers are borne in small clusters in May to June.

LIGHT NEEDS: Partial shade to a half-day of sun.

WATER NEEDS: Water often to keep evenly moist.

GROWING GUIDELINES: Plant forget-me-nots 6–9 inches (15–22.5 cm) apart in all-purpose container mix. To keep plants looking tidy, cut or snap off spent flower stems at the base.

COMMON PROBLEMS: If spider mites cause yellow stippling on leaves, spray the leaves with cold water or superior oil. Mildew can produce dusty-looking patches on the foliage; pinch off affected leaves and move the pot to an airier spot.

PROPAGATION: Sow outdoors in late summer to fall for bloom next spring or indoors in late winter for bloom the same year.

COMPATIBLE COMPANIONS: Forget-me-nots look great with many other early-blooming plants, including tulips, pansies, hostas, torenia (*Torenia fournieri*), nasturtium (*Tropaeolum majus*), periwinkles (*Vinca* spp.), rhododendrons (*Rhododendron* spp. and hybrids), and bergenia (*Bergenia cordifolia*).

Nicotiana spp.   Solanaceae

FLOWERING TOBACCO

One of the most fragrant garden plants, flowering tobacco forms a tall, stately accent for containers. The original species are mostly white, but the hybrids come in a range of sizes and colors.

DESCRIPTION: These shrubby, upright plants have large, soft, slightly sticky, green leaves and branched stems. The stems are topped with small, petunia-like, white, red, or pink flowers from summer until frost. Evening-blooming *N. alata* normally grows to 3 feet (90 cm) and has a good scent. In selecting for a more compact habit and daytime blooming, breeders have sometimes neglected fragrance. The 'Domino' series, for instance, grows only 10–12 inches (25–30 cm) tall, but it is not always fragrant. Night-flowering *N. sylvestris* is tall, with downward-facing, very fragrant, tubular blooms.

LIGHT NEEDS: Partial shade to full sun.

WATER NEEDS: Keep the soil evenly moist.

GROWING GUIDELINES: Grow flowering tobacco in all-purpose container mix. Space plants 10 inches (25 cm) apart. Pinch off faded flowers.

COMMON PROBLEMS: Mealybugs and aphids may feed on plants. Knock the pests off with a strong spray of water, or spray with insecticidal soap.

PROPAGATION: Sow seed indoors 4–6 weeks before the last frost date; leave it uncovered.

COMMENTS: Hybrids are often not fragrant at all. If fragrance is important to you, shop for plants that already have a few flowers, and sniff them to check the scent before you buy.

COMPATIBLE COMPANIONS: Try flowering tobacco with sweet alyssum, ferns, and petunias.

Pelargonium x *hortorum*   Geraniaceae

ZONAL GERANIUM

Justifiably known as the workhorse of the annual flowering garden, zonal geraniums are a mainstay for window boxes and other containers. They bloom cheerily from May until frost.

OTHER COMMON NAMES: Common geranium.

DESCRIPTION: Zonal geraniums are bushy plants that grow 15–36 inches (37.5–90 cm) tall and about 15–24 inches (37.5–60 cm) wide. They bear 3–5-inch (7.5–12.5 cm), velvety, scallop-edged leaves. The foliage is usually green, marked by various rings (zones) of green, brown, red, white, or gold. Clusters of pink, rose, red, salmon, or white blooms appear from spring through fall. Zonal geraniums are perennial in frost-free climates; elsewhere, grow as annuals or bring indoors for the winter.

LIGHT NEEDS: Full sun to light shade.

WATER NEEDS: Allow to dry out between waterings.

GROWING GUIDELINES: Geraniums thrive in a fast-draining, non-alkaline, peat moss-based mix. Space plants about 12 inches (30 cm) apart. Geraniums need little or no feeding.

COMMON PROBLEMS: Old plants tend to get woody; take cuttings from the stem tips and discard the base. Plants may stop blooming in hot weather but usually start again when cooler temperatures return.

PROPAGATION: Take cuttings of overwintered plants in spring. Sow seed indoors 10 weeks before the last frost date, after nicking the seed with a knife or nail file or soaking it in water for 24 hours.

COMPATIBLE COMPANIONS: Try them with petunias, dusty miller, dahlias, alyssum, edging lobelia (*Lobelia erinus*), or large periwinkle (*Vinca major*).

Pelargonium peltatum Geraniaceae	*Petunia* x *hybrida* Solanaceae

IVY GERANIUM

PETUNIA

Ivy geranium is an excellent choice for hanging baskets and window boxes. It offers bright green, ivy-like leaves, gracefully cascading stems, and delicately marked blooms.

Colorful and easy to grow, petunias are excellent for almost any container imaginable. Try them near a window or bench, where you can enjoy the light, sweet scent of the flowers.

DESCRIPTION: Ivy geraniums are shrubby plants with 2–4-foot (60–120 cm) long, trailing stems and five-lobed, ivy-shaped leaves. The glossy, green leaves grow 2–3 inches (5–7.5 cm) wide, sometimes with white or yellow veins. Clusters of single or double white, pink, red, or lavender flowers appear all summer. Ivy geraniums are winter-hardy in frost-free areas; elsewhere, grow them as annuals.

LIGHT NEEDS: Full sun to light shade.

WATER NEEDS: Allow the soil to dry somewhat between waterings.

GROWING GUIDELINES: Ivy geraniums grow best in a free-draining, peat moss-based mix. Space plants about 12 inches (30 cm) apart. Dead-head faded flowers. Pinch back growing tips several times in late spring and early summer to encourage branching. To keep plants from year to year in frost-prone areas, bring them indoors for the winter.

COMMON PROBLEMS: Lack of water can cause wilting and leaf drop; try to water more regularly.

PROPAGATION: Take cuttings from overwintered ivy geraniums in spring or from outdoor plants in late summer to early autumn. Start seed indoors 10 weeks before the last frost date.

COMPATIBLE COMPANIONS: Particularly good partners include zonal geraniums, petunias, dusty miller, clematis, and edging lobelia (*Lobelia erinus*).

DESCRIPTION: Petunias range from 6–18 inches (15–45 cm) tall, with a bushy or cascading habit. They have thick somewhat sticky leaves and single or double flowers that are shaped like Victrola speakers with ruffled edges. The 3-inch (7.5 cm) blooms may be red, salmon, pink, deep purple, lavender, blue, yellow, orange, cream, or white in solid colors or with contrasting edges, stripes, or veining.

LIGHT NEEDS: Full sun is best; tolerates half-day sun.

WATER NEEDS: Keep the soil evenly moist.

GROWING GUIDELINES: Grow petunias in well-drained, all-purpose container mix. Space plants 8 inches (20 cm) apart. Feed monthly. About 2 weeks after planting, pinch seedlings back by half to promote bushy growth. Remove faded blooms, along with the seedpod that develops at the base of each flower. Near the end of summer, cut plants back by half to encourage rebloom.

COMMON PROBLEMS: Botrytis blight—a fuzzy mold—is common on large-flowered (grandiflora) petunias. Pinch off affected parts.

PROPAGATION: Start seed indoors 6–8 weeks before the last frost date; leave it uncovered.

COMPATIBLE COMPANIONS: Petunias combine well with many plants, including dusty miller, geraniums, dahlias, parsley, ageratum, zinnias, periwinkle (*Vinca* spp.), edging lobelia (*Lobelia erinus*), and boxwood (*Buxus* spp.).

Portulaca grandiflora   Portulaceae

ROSE MOSS

Rose moss really shines in hot, dry spots, with small, rose-like flowers in neon colors over narrow, green leaves. If you tend to forget about watering and fertilizing, this is the plant for you!

OTHER COMMON NAMES: Portulaca.

DESCRIPTION: Rose moss is an annual that grows about 6 inches (15 cm) tall and 18 inches (45 cm) wide. Its trailing stems carry 1-inch (2.5 cm) long, succulent, needle-like leaves. The single or double, 2-inch (5 cm) wide flowers come in a range of colors, from vividly hot to soft pastels.

LIGHT NEEDS: Full sun.

WATER NEEDS: Allow the soil to dry between waterings.

GROWING GUIDELINES: Rose moss grows well in shallow containers of loose, free-draining, sand-based potting mix. Space plants 6 inches (15 cm) apart. Do not fertilize. Pinch off faded flowers.

COMMON PROBLEMS: Rose moss tends to rot if overwatered.

PROPAGATION: Sow seed indoors 6–8 weeks before the last frost date, or plant it directly into the container outdoors after the last frost. Either way, do not cover the seed; it needs light to sprout.

COMMENTS: Rose moss thrives in dry, hot conditions where nothing else grows. Its flowers are only open when the sun is out, closing in late afternoon and in cloudy weather.

COMPATIBLE COMPANIONS: Good container partners include yuccas (*Yucca* spp.), dusty miller, sage, thyme, and junipers.

CULTIVARS: 'Sundial' has double flowers that stay open most of the day.

Salvia splendens   Labiatae

SCARLET SAGE

Scarlet sage's fire engine red color adds an unmistakable accent to summer containers. It can easily eclipse more subdued companions. Tall types bloom longer than dwarf cultivars.

DESCRIPTION: These bushy annuals grow from 8–30 inches (20–75 cm) tall and have shiny, dark green leaves. The plants are topped with tall, long-lasting stems of tubular flowers from early summer until frost. Besides hot reds, they also come in pink, purple, salmon, and white.

LIGHT NEEDS: Full sun; tolerates partial shade.

WATER NEEDS: Keep the soil evenly moist.

GROWING GUIDELINES: Grow in all-purpose container mix, spacing plants 12 inches (30 cm) apart (slightly closer for dwarf types). Deadhead each flower stalk when it fades, reaching back into the plant so the cut end is hidden by the foliage.

COMMON PROBLEMS: Too much shade will lead to spindly growth and poor bloom; move the container to a sunnier spot.

PROPAGATION: Sow seed indoors 8 weeks before the last frost date; leave it uncovered.

COMPATIBLE COMPANIONS: Plant scarlet sage by itself, or combine it with gray foliage, such as dusty miller or lamb's-ears (*Stachys byzantina*). It also looks good with white flowers, such as 'Pretty in White' vinca (*Catharanthus roseus* 'Pretty in White').

RELATED PLANTS:
S. farinacea, blue salvia or mealycup sage, is another excellent container plant. It grows 18 inches (45 cm) tall, with tall, blue spires dusted with white powder. 'Victoria' is a commonly available cultivar.

Sanvitalia procumbens Compositae	*Senecio cineraria* Compositae

CREEPING ZINNIA

DUSTY MILLER

Creeping zinnia's trailing stems look wonderful cascading from hanging baskets and over container rims. This easy, drought-tolerant annual blooms from July until frost.

DESCRIPTION: Creeping zinnia grows only 4–6 inches (10–15 cm) tall, but it can spread to 2 feet (60 cm) or more. Its creeping stems carry small leaves and 1-inch (2.5 cm) wide, single- or double-flowered blooms in yellow or bright orange, with purple-brown centers.

LIGHT NEEDS: Full sun.

WATER NEEDS: Allow the soil to dry between waterings.

GROWING GUIDELINES: Grow creeping zinnia in light, fast-draining mix. Space plants 5–6 inches (12.5–15 cm) apart. Do not fertilize. Established plants need virtually no care.

COMMON PROBLEMS: Overhead watering can promote disease; try to avoid wetting the foliage when you water.

PROPAGATION: Creeping zinnia doesn't transplant well, so plant the seed directly in its container in late spring; leave the seed uncovered.

COMMENTS: Creeping zinnia is very resistant to both heat and drought.

COMPATIBLE COMPANIONS: Try creeping zinnia as an underplanting for Japanese maple (*Acer palmatum*), euonymus (*Euonymus* spp.), or yuccas (*Yucca* spp.). The yellow types look good with dwarf morning glory (*Convolvulus tricolor*).

CULTIVARS: 'Mandarin Orange' has orange flowers.

"Senex" is Latin for "old man," referring to the white whiskers that give this very useful foliage plant its woolly, silver-white appearance.

DESCRIPTION: Dusty miller forms clumps of finely cut, silvery white leaves. The clumps grow 8–24 inches (20–60 cm) tall and wide. Plants may survive winter outdoors and produce yellow flowers their second year, but they're really best as annuals.

LIGHT NEEDS: Full sun to a half-day of sun.

WATER NEEDS: Allow the soil to dry somewhat between waterings.

GROWING GUIDELINES: Dusty miller grows fine in well-drained, all-purpose container mix. Set plants 8–10 inches (20–25 cm) apart. Pinch off the shoot tips in early summer to encourage branching. If plants get leggy, shear them back by half to two-thirds to promote bushy new growth.

COMMON PROBLEMS: Second-year clumps tend to flop open if you let them flower; otherwise dusty miller is problem-free.

PROPAGATION: Sow seed indoors 8–10 weeks before the last frost; leave it uncovered

COMMENTS: The silvery foliage is especially effective in nighttime gardens.

COMPATIBLE COMPANIONS: Dusty miller makes a beautiful backdrop for bright flowers, such as red zonal geraniums and petunias. Other good companions include ivy geranium (*Pelargonium peltatum*), dwarf morning glory (*Convolvulus tricolor*), edging lobelia (*Lobelia erinus*), and rose moss (*Portulaca grandiflora*).

Tagetes spp.   Compositae

MARIGOLDS

These sturdy, dependable sun-lovers may be cliché to some, but they've earned a place in the "Annuals Hall of Fame." Pinching off spent flowers once a week can prolong the bloom season.

DESCRIPTION: Marigolds produce branching to semi-trailing plants with ferny, strongly scented foliage. The single or double blooms may be yellow, orange, gold, cream, brown, or maroon. For containers, look for compact species and cultivars. Signet marigold (*T. tenuifolia*) has small but profuse blooms on 8-inch (20 cm) plants. It has a trailing habit that is perfect for hanging baskets and window boxes. Other compact marigolds include the French types (*T. patula*), which grow 6–18 inches (15–45 cm) tall, and triploid hybrids, such as those in the 10- to 12-inch (25–30 cm) 'Nugget' series.

LIGHT NEEDS: Full sun to a half-day of sun.

WATER NEEDS: Keep the soil evenly moist.

GROWING GUIDELINES: Marigolds grow well in all-purpose container mix. Space dwarf types 6–9 inches (15–22.5 cm) apart; leave 12 inches (30 cm) between larger types.

COMMON PROBLEMS: Overhead watering may cause flowers to rot; pinch off affected blooms and water more carefully to avoid wetting the plants.

PROPAGATION: Sow seed indoors 4–6 weeks before the last frost date, or plant it directly into outdoor containers after the last frost date.

COMPATIBLE COMPANIONS: Marigolds look great with eggplants, peppers, parsley, basil, tomatoes, lettuce, cucumbers, mints, petunias, or blue salvia (*Salvia farinacea*).

Torenia fournieri   Scrophulariaceae

WISHBONE FLOWER

Look into the yellow throat of the little sky blue flowers, and you'll find the tiny, wishbone-shaped stamens. This rugged annual makes a fine container plant for partial shade.

OTHER COMMON NAMES: Bluewings.

DESCRIPTION: These bushy, compact, 8-inch (20 cm) tall plants have small, bronzy green leaves. Their fascinatingly marked flowers are light and deep blue, with yellow or white throats. They bloom from summer to fall.

LIGHT NEEDS: Partial shade.

WATER NEEDS: Water abundantly to keep the soil evenly moist.

GROWING GUIDELINES: Wishbone flower grows well in all-purpose container mix. Set plants 6–8 inches (15–20 cm) apart. In fall, you can bring the pots indoors and enjoy wishbone flower as a winter-blooming houseplant. Discard plants at the end of the winter.

COMMON PROBLEMS: Plants may sulk if the soil is cold.

PROPAGATION: Sow seed indoors 8–10 weeks before the last frost date, or plant it directly into the container outdoors after the last frost date.

COMMENTS: Wishbone flower is very resistant to heat and humidity.

COMPATIBLE COMPANIONS: Wishbone flower looks particularly good with hostas, sweet alyssum, edging lobelia (*Lobelia erinus*), golden creeping Jenny (*Lysimachia nummularia* 'Aurea'), forget-me-not (*Myosotis sylvatica*), and periwinkles (*Vinca* spp.).

CULTIVARS: Plants in the 'Clown' series have multi-colored flowers.

| *Tropaeolum majus* | Tropaeolaceae | *Vinca major* | Apocynaceae |

NASTURTIUM

Nasturtiums form lush clumps of bold, round, bright green leaves topped with neon-bright, spurred flowers. These colorful mounding or trailing annuals are easy to grow.

DESCRIPTION: Nasturtiums grow as bushy climbers to 6 feet (1.8 m) tall or compact clumps to 12 inches (30 cm) tall. Both types have wavy-edged, long-stalked leaves and fragrant red, orange, yellow, or red-brown, 2-inch (5 cm) flowers from spring to frost.

LIGHT NEEDS: Full sun is best; tolerates a half-day of sun.

WATER NEEDS: Allow the soil to dry between waterings.

GROWING GUIDELINES: Grow nasturtiums in light, well-drained mix with added sand. Space dwarf types 6 inches (15 cm) apart; plant other kinds 8–12 inches (20–30 cm) apart. Nasturtiums prefer poor soil, so do not fertilize. A common axiom for success is, "Be nasty to nasturtiums."

COMMON PROBLEMS: Aphids are a common pest, causing yellowed or distorted growth; spray plants with pyrethrin. Lush foliage but sparse blooms can indicate overwatering and/or overfertilizing. Plants may bloom poorly in hot weather.

PROPAGATION: Sow seed indoors 6–8 weeks before the last frost; use large containers to minimize root disturbance at transplanting time. Or just sow directly into outdoor pots in early spring.

COMPATIBLE COMPANIONS: Use nasturtiums to cover the fading foliage of spring bulbs. Nasturtiums also look good with forget-me-not (*Myosotis sylvatica*) and dwarf morning glory (*Convolvulus tricolor*).

LARGE PERIWINKLE

Large periwinkle's trailing habit makes it a must for hanging baskets and window boxes. It is beautiful, easy to grow, and resistant to heat and humidity.

DESCRIPTION: Large periwinkle spreads by trailing, rooting stems to form mounds 6–12 inches (15–30 cm) tall. The plants have 1–3-inch (2.5–7.5 cm) long, oval, glossy green leaves, accented by 1–2-inch (2.5–5 cm), lavender blooms in spring. There are white variegated forms, which need some shade. Large periwinkle is usually winter hardy only south of Zone 8, but it will sometimes overwinter outdoors in colder regions as well.

LIGHT NEEDS: Light shade is best; plants will tolerate full sun if well watered.

WATER NEEDS: Keep the soil evenly moist, especially if plants are in full sun.

GROWING GUIDELINES: Large periwinkle grows fine in all-purpose container mix, as long as it's not cold. If plants start to look stringy, shear them back to the ground to promote fresh new growth.

COMMON PROBLEMS: Generally trouble-free.

PROPAGATION: Take cuttings at any time.

COMMENTS: Large periwinkle is also commonly known as vinca. It is often confused with annual vinca (*Catharanthus roseus*), which has white or pink blooms.

COMPATIBLE COMPANIONS Try large periwinkle with petunias, impatiens, coleus, dahlias, dusty miller, geraniums, or browallia.

RELATED PLANTS:

V. minor, dwarf periwinkle, grows to 10 inches (25 cm) tall. It needs more shade and more water.

Viola x *wittrockiana*   Violaceae

PANSY

The fresh "faces" of pansies are a cheerful addition to spring containers. They are among the first of all bedding plants to flower, with a diversity of colors and markings on their velvety blooms.

DESCRIPTION: Pansies produce branching stems and oval leaves on plants to 8 inches (20 cm) tall. In most climates, they bloom in spring and again in fall; they may flower all summer in cooler areas. The 2–4-inch (5–10 cm) flowers come in white or shades of blue, red, pink, yellow, or purple; they may be solid, bicolored, striped, or blotched. Pansies are actually biennials, but they are usually grown as annuals.

LIGHT NEEDS: Part shade is usually best, although plants can take full sun if protected from midday heat.

WATER NEEDS: Keep the soil evenly moist.

GROWING GUIDELINES: Grow in well-drained container mix with added compost. Space plants 4–6 inches (10–15 cm) apart. Deadhead faded flowers often. Mulch to keep the roots cool.

COMMON PROBLEMS: Pansies tend to sulk in hot weather. If they start blooming, shear the plants back by half, or simply remove them and replace them with summer-blooming flowers.

PROPAGATION: Sow seed indoors 10–12 weeks before the last frost, or sow outdoors in mid-July to mid-August for next year's bloom.

COMPATIBLE COMPANIONS: Try them with dwarf snapdragons, grape hyacinths (*Muscari* spp.), and other spring bulbs, edging lobelia (*Lobelia erinus*), forget-me-not (*Myosotis sylvatica*), parsley, daylilies, or euonymus (*Euonymus* spp.).

Zinnia spp.   Compositae

ZINNIA

Zinnias are colorful annuals for sunny containers. To keep common zinnias looking their best, fertilize monthly and pinch off faded blooms.

DESCRIPTION: Zinnias come in two forms: common zinnia (*Z. elegans*) and narrow-leaved zinnia (*Z. angustifolia,* also listed as *Z. linearis*). Common zinnias grow 6–36 inches (15–90 cm) tall, with thick leaves and stems. Their single or double flowers appear all summer in a wide range of colors. Narrow-leaved zinnia forms 8-inch (20 cm) tall, trailing mounds of small, thin leaves topped with single, daisy-like flowers in shades of orange, yellow, and white from midsummer to frost.

LIGHT NEEDS: Full sun.

WATER NEEDS: Common zinnias prefer evenly moist soil. For narrow-leaved zinnia, let the soil dry out somewhat between waterings.

GROWING GUIDELINES: Narrow-leaved zinnia grows fine in all-purpose container mix; add compost to the mix for common zinnia. Space plants 6–12 inches (15–30 cm) apart, depending upon their height.

COMMON PROBLEMS: Common zinnia is prone to powdery mildew, a fungal disease that causes white patches on leaves. Try pinching off the affected leaves and moving the pot to an airier spot.

PROPAGATION: Sow seed indoors 6 weeks before the last frost date. You can also sow directly into outdoor containers in May to June.

COMPATIBLE COMPANIONS: Try zinnias with petunias, lettuce, tomatoes, flowering tobacco (*Nicotiana* spp.), or boxwoods (*Buxus* spp.).

Acer palmatum   Aceraceae

JAPANESE MAPLE

No other container tree can claim Japanese maple's exquisite combination of graceful form, delicate leaf texture, and blazing fall color. It can live in the same pot for years.

DESCRIPTION: This deciduous, many-stemmed tree can grow to 20 feet (6 m) tall in the garden, but it usually stays about 2–5 feet (60–150 cm) tall when grown in a container. Its green or red branches carry 2–4-inch (5–10 cm) long, deeply cut leaves that are reddish in spring, green in summer, and scarlet, orange, or gold in fall. Japanese maple is generally hardy in Zones 2–9.

LIGHT NEEDS: Filtered light to full sun.

WATER NEEDS: Provide plenty of water, but allow the soil to dry somewhat between waterings. Tap water may stress container plants; use rainwater instead.

GROWING GUIDELINES: Grow in a soil-based mix that contains sand for good drainage. Prune as needed in fall to midwinter to shape the plant.

COMMON PROBLEMS: Hot, dry wind can cause brown patches on leaves; move the plant to a more sheltered spot. Leaf edges may turn brown if salts build up in the soil; leach the container often with rainwater to prevent salt buildup.

PROPAGATION: Grow from seed, or take cuttings in late spring or winter.

COMMENTS: Thread-leaved and variegated types need more shade than others.

COMPATIBLE COMPANIONS: Underplant Japanese maple with grape hyacinths (*Muscari* spp.), rose moss (*Portulaca grandiflora*), creeping zinnia (*Sanvitalia procumbens*), or thymes.

| *Buxus sempervirens* | Buxaceae | *Camellia japonica* | Theaceae |

BOXWOOD

CAMELLIA

Boxwood is invaluable for adding year-round interest to container plantings. It grows slowly, and it's easy to clip into a variety of shapes, including geometric and animal forms.

OTHER COMMON NAMES: Box, English boxwood.

DESCRIPTION: Boxwood is a dense, branching, woody shrub with shiny, dark green, oval leaves to 1 inch (25 mm) long. Plants can reach 10–15 feet (3–4.5 m) tall and wide, but you can keep them at just about any size you want by trimming as needed. Tiny, pale green blooms appear in early spring. Boxwood is generally hardy in Zones 6–10.

LIGHT NEEDS: Full sun to part shade.

WATER NEEDS: Keep the soil evenly moist.

GROWING GUIDELINES: Grow boxwood in a deep container with well-drained, acid, peat-based mix. Set the plant in a spot that is sheltered from wind. Mulch to keep the roots cool. Prune in late spring to the desired height and shape, removing no more than a third of the stems at a time.

COMMON PROBLEMS: Mites may produce yellowish stippling on leaves; scales feeding on stems may cause leaves to turn yellow. Knock mites off with a strong spray of water; rub scales off with your fingernail or scrub them off with a brush and soapy water. If leafminers cause browned, blistered foliage, pinch off and destroy affected leaves. Alkaline soil can lead to poor growth or even death; check the soil pH every year or two.

PROPAGATION: Take cuttings in summer.

COMPATIBLE COMPANIONS: Combine boxwood with bedding dahlias, zinnias, petunias, or roses.

In cold climates, you'll need to bring potted camellias indoors for the winter. You'll enjoy their large flowers from November to April and their polished, dark green leaves year-round.

DESCRIPTION: Camellias are woody shrubs that can grow to 20 feet (6 m) tall. They produce leathery, oval, 4-inch (10 cm) long leaves, accented in winter by single, semidouble, or fully double, white, pink, or red blooms to 5 inches (12.5 cm) across. Most camellias are hardy in Zones 8–10.

LIGHT NEEDS: Partial shade.

WATER NEEDS: Allow the soil to dry slightly between waterings.

GROWING GUIDELINES: Plant in wooden tubs or half-barrels filled with lime-free, well-drained mix that contains at least 50 percent organic material. Mulch with a 2-inch (5 cm) layer of wood chips. Repot, prune out any dead wood, and thin stems as needed after bloom.

COMMON PROBLEMS: Yellowed leaves with green veins indicate that the plant needs iron. Over-fertilizing may cause leaf edges to turn brown or whole leaves to drop; leach the soil with rainwater to remove any salt buildup. Brown or dropping flowers are a sign of petal blight; destroy all fading blooms and remove and replace the mulch. Flower buds may drop if the soil is too dry.

PROPAGATION: Take cuttings of the current season's growth in late summer, or air layer a stem.

COMPATIBLE COMPANIONS: Underplant camellias with English ivy, pansies, or lettuce.

| *Chamaecyparis* spp. | Cupressaceae | *Clematis* x *jackmanii* | Ranunculaceae |

FALSE CYPRESS

JACKMAN CLEMATIS

Compact forms of false cypress come in a variety of growth habits and colors. Their evergreen foliage provides interest all year long. Prune plants as needed in spring.

These slender, perennial vines have large, starry, rich purple blooms. They flower mainly in June and July but may repeat in fall. Add a trellis to their pot so they can climb.

DESCRIPTION: These evergreens are available in a wide range of shapes and sizes. Hinoki false cypress (*C. obtusa*) is best for containers, with horizontal deep green branches. 'Nana' grows slowly to 8 inches (20 cm) tall and wide, with an irregular, globular shape. Sawara cypress (*C. pisifera*) tends to have a more open habit. 'Compacta Variegata' grows to 20 inches (50 cm) tall and 30 inches (75 cm) wide, with green foliage that's marked in cream-yellow. Plants are hardy in Zones 5–8.

LIGHT NEEDS: Full sun to partial shade.

WATER NEEDS: Allow to dry slightly between waterings.

GROWING GUIDELINES: Plant in well-drained, light, soil-based mix. Place the container in a protected spot for winter. If shoot tips turn brown in winter, wrap the plant in burlap during cold weather.

COMMON PROBLEMS: Spider mites produce yellowish stippling on leaves; knock the pests off the plant with a strong spray of water. Soft, cone-like cocoons are a sign of bagworms; remove and destroy the cocoons. Overwatering may lead to root rot. Dead foliage in the center of the plant indicates too much shade.

PROPAGATION: Take cuttings in fall.

COMPATIBLE COMPANIONS: Underplant with grape hyacinths (*Muscari* spp.) for spring interest; add dwarf morning glory (*Convolvulus tricolor*) or creeping zinnia (*Sanvitalia procumbens*) for summer color.

DESCRIPTION: Jackman clematis is a deciduous vine with dark green leaves and twisting, curling leaf stalks. The vine can climb to 10 feet (3 m) in a season and has deep violet-purple flowers that are 4–5 inches (10–12.5 cm) wide. Jackman clematis is generally hardy in Zones 5–9.

LIGHT NEEDS: Partial to full sun. The general rule for success is to plant clematis with its "head in the sun and feet in the shade."

WATER NEEDS: Keep the soil evenly moist.

GROWING GUIDELINES: Grow in a 3–5-gallon (13.5–22.5 l) tub of loose, quick-draining, peat-based mix that contains added compost and lime. Mulch the soil or set lower-growing plants around the base to keep the roots cool and shaded. Fertilize monthly from spring to late summer. Prune the vines down to just above the lowest pair of strong buds in late winter or early spring.

COMMON PROBLEMS: Clematis borers tunnel into vines, causing wilting or broken stems; prune out damaged parts and seal the cuts with paraffin. Even unaffected vines can be brittle, so tie them to the trellis if necessary to prevent damage.

PROPAGATION: Take cuttings in spring or early summer. Layer the stems to the ground in spring.

COMPATIBLE COMPANIONS: Jackman clematis looks marvelous with roses, impatiens, wax begonias, petunias, or edging lobelia (*Lobelia erinus*).

Euonymus fortunei   Celastraceae   *Hedera helix*   Araliaceae

WINTERCREEPER

ENGLISH IVY

This tough, tolerant evergreen can climb or cascade. It makes an excellent accent shrub, with rich green foliage that may be marked with gold or white.

This hardy garden classic comes in many colors and sizes. Let it trail to soften the edge of a pot, or train it to grow upward on a trellis or wire topiary form.

DESCRIPTION: Wintercreeper grows as an evergreen vine or shrub with broad, scallop-edged, elliptical leaves to 2 inches (5 cm) long. Its upright growth is usually around 2–3 feet (60–90 cm); as a vine, it can climb or spread to 20 feet (6 m) by clinging stems. Plants are generally hardy in Zones 5–9.

LIGHT NEEDS: Full sun to full shade.

WATER NEEDS: Allow the soil to dry between waterings.

GROWING GUIDELINES: Wintercreeper prefers a mix that's on the sandy side, but it can adapt to all-purpose container mix as long as it has good drainage. Prune as needed in late spring.

COMMON PROBLEMS: Wintercreeper is particularly prone to scale; if you notice small bumps on the leaves or stems, spray plants with superior oil. Anthracnose can cause blackened leaves and shoots or brown spots on leaves; prune off and destroy affected parts. Leaves turn yellow and brown if exposed to harsh cold; move the container to a sheltered spot for the winter.

PROPAGATION: Take cuttings in late summer from mature wood. Sow seed outdoors in fall. Air layer stems, or transplant rooted stem sections.

COMPATIBLE COMPANIONS: Variegated, trailing types are effective surrounding upright forms of false cypress (*Chamaecyparis* spp.). Other possible partners include grape hyacinths (*Muscari* spp.), lantana (*Lantana* spp.), and junipers (*Juniperus* spp.).

DESCRIPTION: This evergreen, woody vine produces clinging stems that can travel as much as 30 feet (9 m). The thick green leaves have lobed, ruffled, or curled edges and may be marked with yellow, gray, or white. English ivy is generally hardy in Zones 5–10, although fancy-leaved types may not be as cold-tolerant as plain-leaved kinds.

LIGHT NEEDS: Full sun to full shade.

WATER NEEDS: Allow the soil to dry out a bit between waterings. Established plants are drought-tolerant.

GROWING GUIDELINES: Grow ivy in well-drained, peat-based container mix, and water well at planting time. Once established, ivy grows easily with little fuss. Fertilize with fish emulsion in early spring and again in August. Trim stems as needed to control the plant's size and shape.

COMMON PROBLEMS: Slugs and snails may chew holes in leaves. Pick pests off plants at night, or place the pot on a table or pedestal to get the plants off the ground. Water sitting on leaves can promote dark patches caused by bacterial leaf spot; remove and destroy infected leaves, and water early in the day so leaves dry quickly. Leaves may turn brown where plants are exposed to harsh winter weather.

PROPAGATION: Take cuttings at any time.

COMPATIBLE COMPANIONS: English ivy looks great with petunias, geraniums, and many other container plants.

JUNIPERS

Junipers are tough and drought-tolerant, placing them among the best evergreens for container planting. There are many dwarf, trailing, or horizontally branched types.

DESCRIPTION: While some species of junipers can grow into tall trees, the dwarf types are the best choice for container gardens. 'Compressa' common juniper (*J. communis* 'Compressa') grows 2 inches (5 cm) per year in a perfect, tight, upright column to 15 inches (37.5 cm) wide and 4 feet (1.2 m) tall. 'Emerald Sea' shore juniper (*J. conferta* 'Emerald Sea') grows to about 1 foot (30 cm) tall, with blue-green foliage and a trailing habit. Creeping juniper (*J. horizontalis*) has many low-growing cultivars, including 6-inch (15 cm) tall 'Blue Mat'. Most junipers are hardy in Zones 2–9, although the hardiness can vary by cultivar.

LIGHT NEEDS: Full sun is best; tolerates light shade.

WATER NEEDS: Allow the soil to dry between waterings.

GROWING GUIDELINES: Set plants 3–4 feet (90–120 cm) apart in well-drained, all-purpose container mix. Cover soil with mulch. Do not prune.

COMMON PROBLEMS: Spider mites can cause yellow stippling on leaves; control them with superior oil. Browned branch tips may be due to fungal blight or twig borers; prune off damaged tips.

PROPAGATION: Take cuttings in late summer; layer low growers in summer; sow seed in fall.

COMPATIBLE COMPANIONS: Good juniper partners include tulips, dwarf morning glory (*Convolvulus tricolor*), rose moss (*Portulaca grandiflora*), and wintercreeper (*Euonymus fortunei*).

BAY

This handsome, glossy, evergreen shrub does double duty by letting you enjoy the beauty of the plant all year and use the leaves to flavor your dinner.

OTHER COMMON NAMES: Grecian laurel, sweet bay.

DESCRIPTION: Bay is a multistemmed, upright, woody shrub that can grow to 7 feet (2.1 m) tall in pots. The dark green, 2–4-inch (5–10 cm) leaves are leathery and aromatic. The inconspicuous flowers are followed by 1/2-inch (12 mm), black berries. Bay is hardy in Zones 8–10.

LIGHT NEEDS: Filtered shade.

WATER NEEDS: Allow the soil to dry between waterings.

GROWING GUIDELINES: Plant in well-drained container mix that contains added compost. Bay responds well to pruning, so you can trim it as needed into formal or informal shapes. You can even train it to grow on a single stem with a rounded, tree-like top. North of Zone 8, bring the container indoors for the winter.

COMMON PROBLEMS: Scale insects may attack, causing yellowed leaves; look for black bumps on leaves and stems. Rub the pests off with your fingernail or a brush, wipe them off with a cotton swab soaked in isopropyl alcohol, or spray with superior oil.

PROPAGATION: Bay can be difficult to propagate. Cuttings can take 6 months to root; seed must stay at 75°F (24°C) for a month to sprout.

COMPATIBLE COMPANIONS: Set off bay's dark green leaves against silver-foliaged plants, such as dusty miller. Or, for a more colorful container, underplant bay with creeping zinnia (*Sanvitalia procumbens*).

| *Passiflora caerulea* | Passifloraceae | *Rhododendron* spp. | Ericaceae |

PASSIONFLOWER

Passionflowers add an exotic touch to any container planting, and they are productive, as well. Their spectacular flowers are sometimes followed by small, orange or yellow fruits.

OTHER COMMON NAMES: Blue passionflower, passion vine.

DESCRIPTION: Passionflower produces lobed leaves on vigorous, heavy vines that climb to 12 feet (3.6 m) by means of tendrils. They bear fragrant, 5-inch (12.5 cm) wide flowers that are a combination of blue, purple, and white. The flowers may produce small fruits, which are edible but not particularly flavorful. These vines are usually hardy in Zones 7–10.

LIGHT NEEDS: Full sun to light shade.

WATER NEEDS: Keep the soil evenly moist.

GROWING GUIDELINES: Grow passionflowers in 10–15-gallon (45–67.5 l), wooden planters with well-drained, all-purpose container mix. Site the container in a warm spot, and provide a strong support, such as a trellis, for the vine to climb. Mulch the soil to keep it moist. Prune the stems to just above the ground each year to promote vigorous new flowering stems. Trim in fall if you're bringing the plants indoors for the winter (north of Zone 7), or prune in late winter if you leave your plants outdoors.

COMMON PROBLEMS: Buds may drop if the plant isn't getting enough light; move it to a brighter spot.

PROPAGATION: Take stem cuttings in spring or fall; sow seed in spring.

COMPATIBLE COMPANIONS: Passionflower grows best when planted in its own pot.

RHODODENDRONS AND AZALEAS

Low-growing rhododendrons and azaleas can make excellent container plants for shady decks and patios. Make sure you choose a container that has plenty of drainage holes.

DESCRIPTION: Rhododendrons and azaleas are closely related and share the same growth needs. These spring-blooming shrubs are generally hardy in Zones 4–9. Particularly good container rhododendrons include 'Ginny Gee', a 2-foot (60 cm) mat former with pink flowers; 'Carmen', a 12-inch (30 cm) tall, red-flowered cultivar; and *R. impeditum,* with silver gray foliage and blue-purple blooms. If you're looking for a container azalea, consider 'White Nymph', a low grower with heavy, midseason bloom. Purple 'Violetta' and orange 'William Van Orange' have a cascading habit that's perfect for hanging baskets.

LIGHT NEEDS: Filtered shade.

WATER NEEDS: Keep the soil evenly moist. Rainwater is beneficial.

GROWING GUIDELINES: Plant in fast-draining, acid mix with added perlite and compost. Mulch with wood chips. Use acid fertilizer in spring before and after flowering. Prune shoot tips as needed after bloom.

COMMON PROBLEMS: Yellow leaves with green veins indicate chlorosis; give the plant iron.

PROPAGATION: Take cuttings in midsummer. Layer in summer. Sow seed indoors in winter.

COMPATIBLE COMPANIONS: Both rhododendrons and azaleas are shallow-rooted, so it's best not to disturb the roots by planting annual companions.

MINIATURE ROSES

YUCCA

With perfectly scaled leaves and flowers, the everblooming miniature roses have taken the container gardening world by storm. More than 200 types are now available.

DESCRIPTION: These diminutive, shallow-rooted bushes grow 4–18 inches (10–45 cm) tall, with 1/2–2-inch (12–50 mm) blooms in nearly every color but true blue. Also available are patio tree roses grafted on 24-inch (60 cm) trunks, and mini tree roses, on 18-inch (45 cm) trunks. Most container roses are hardy in Zones 4–9.

LIGHT NEEDS: Plants need at least 6 hours of full sun.

WATER NEEDS: Keep the soil evenly moist.

GROWING GUIDELINES: Grow mini roses in a 6-inch (15 cm) or larger container, with a blend of 2 parts well-drained, all-purpose mix to 1 part compost. Fertilize monthly. Prune in early spring. In cold-winter regions, sink the pot into the ground for the winter.

COMMON PROBLEMS: Knock aphids off leaves, buds, and stems with a strong spray of water, or apply insecticidal soap or neem. Superior oil works against both aphids and spider mites, but avoid getting it on the flowers. Knock off Japanese beetles into a jar of soapy water. If you notice spots on the leaves, pick off the affected parts, move the pot to an airier spot, and avoid wetting the foliage.

PROPAGATION: Take cuttings in summer. Layer in spring or fall. Sow seed in spring or fall.

COMPATIBLE COMPANIONS: Try them with alyssum, clematis, or boxwood (*Buxus sempervirens*).

Few plants make as dramatic an architectural statement as yuccas. The spiky clumps are crowned by spectacular flower spikes in early summer.

OTHER COMMON NAMES: Adam's needle.

DESCRIPTION: Yucca produces bold rosettes of evergreen, sword-shaped, light green leaves with sharp points. The clumps may be to 3 feet (90 cm) tall and 5 feet (1.5 m) wide. Tall spires of 2–3-inch (50–75 mm) white flowers bloom above the rosettes in June. Yucca is hardy in Zones 5–9.

LIGHT NEEDS: Full sun.

WATER NEEDS: Allow the soil to dry between waterings.

GROWING GUIDELINES: Plant yucca in a large container of well-drained, all-purpose mix; added sand is a plus. Cut down faded flower stems in fall.

COMMON PROBLEMS: Overwatering can lead to wilting and root rot. Other than that, yuccas are usually problem-free.

PROPAGATION: Sow seed outdoors in fall, or remove rooted offsets from the base of the parent plant.

COMMENTS: Since the leaves have dagger-like points, make sure the container is not near walkways or children's areas. Yucca is easy to grow and drought-tolerant.

COMPATIBLE COMPANIONS: Plant yucca by itself, or give it an edging of creeping zinnia (*Sanvitalia procumbens*) or rose moss (*Portulaca grandiflora*).

CULTIVARS: 'Golden Sword' has yellow-striped leaves.

Ocimum basilicum   Labiatae

BASIL

Green or purple, smooth or ruffled, basil looks as beautiful in containers as it is tasty in salads and sauces. Pinch off flower stems as they appear to encourage leafy growth.

OTHER COMMON NAMES: Sweet basil.

DESCRIPTION: This annual herb grows to 18 inches (45 cm) tall, with branching stems. The aromatic foliage is usually bright green, but purple-leaved types are also available. Spikes of small, white flowers rise above the leaves in summer.

LIGHT NEEDS: Full sun.

WATER NEEDS: Water regularly, allowing the soil to dry somewhat between waterings.

GROWING GUIDELINES: Grow basil in warm, light, sandy, well-drained mix. Space plants 10 inches (25 cm) apart. Fertilize once during the summer.

COMMON PROBLEMS: If you set basil plants out too early, their growth may be stunted, or they may die. Wait until after the last frost date, when the weather is settled and the container soil is warm. Lack of water causes wilting; try to keep the soil evenly moist.

PROPAGATION: Sow seed indoors in early spring. To have a continuous supply, sow again every 2 weeks until early summer.

COMPATIBLE COMPANIONS: Green basil looks great with marigolds and sage. The purple-leaved types are effective with silver or white leaves or flowers; try dusty miller, sweet alyssum, or licorice plant (*Helichrysum petiolatum*).

| *Phaseolus* spp. | Leguminosae | *Vaccinium* spp. | Ericaceae |

BEANS

BLUEBERRIES

Container gardens can support many kinds of beans, from the dwarf types of edible bush beans to the beautiful climbing vines of scarlet runner beans.

Blueberry bushes bear luscious sweet berries, and the plants are attractive, too. Hardy dwarf types are excellent for containers, with three-season interest.

DESCRIPTION: Bean plants may be bushy or vining, with heart-shaped, green leaves and 1-inch (2.5 cm), red or white summer flowers. The flowers are followed by edible green, yellow, or purple pods about 60 days after sowing. Bush string beans grow 12–20 inches (30–50 cm) tall; ornamental vine can climb to 8 feet (2.4 m).

LIGHT NEEDS: Full sun.

WATER NEEDS: Keep the soil evenly moist.

GROWING GUIDELINES: Fill a 10–20-gallon (45–90 l) container with well-drained, all-purpose mix that contains added compost. The mix should have a nearly neutral pH. Set up stakes or a bamboo teepee for climbing types before planting, or place the container against a wall with a trellis. Fertilize once after growth starts, then again when pods are forming. Harvest beans weekly to keep the plants productive.

COMMON PROBLEMS: Whiteflies and aphids may cause yellowed leaves and/or distorted growth. Knock the pests off with a strong spray of water, or spray with insecticidal soap. If powdery mildew produces gray patches on leaves, pinch off affected parts and move the container to an airier spot.

PROPAGATION: Sow seed directly into the container a week after the last frost date.

COMPATIBLE COMPANIONS: Beans grow well with many other sun-loving flowers and herbs.

DESCRIPTION: These shrubby plants produce small leaves that are bronze in spring, green in summer, and scarlet or gold in fall. Clusters of tiny, white-pink, bell-shaped blooms appear in spring, followed by the attractive and edible fruits. Blueberries are normally hardy in Zones 3–9, although the range can vary depending on the species.

LIGHT NEEDS: Full sun is best. Plants tolerate some shade but tend to be leggier.

WATER NEEDS: Keep the soil evenly moist.

GROWING GUIDELINES: Set one plant in a large tub of well-drained, acid mix that's been amended with plenty of compost, peat moss, ground bark chips, and sand. Mulch the soil to keep the shallow roots cool and moist.

COMMON PROBLEMS: Blueberries are generally trouble-free.

PROPAGATION: Blueberries are difficult to propagate, so it's usually easiest to buy new plants.

COMMENTS: Most blueberries produce better crops if cross-pollinated. Grow at least two different cultivars, or choose a cultivar that is self-pollinating.

COMPATIBLE COMPANIONS: Since blueberries have shallow roots, it's best to plant them in their own container, without any companions.

CULTIVARS: 'Elliott' grows to 12–18 inches (30–45 cm) tall and is self-pollinated, so you only need one plant.

| *Daucus carota* var. *sativus* | Umbelliferae | *Allium schoenoprasum* | Liliaceae |

CARROT

CHIVES

If you water containers regularly to keep the soil moist, they can provide perfect growing conditions for these tasty root crops. Try the short-rooted kinds in standard-sized pots.

DESCRIPTION: Aboveground, carrots produce fern-like, green foliage to about 9 inches (22.5 cm) tall. The foliage grows from a thick, juicy, orange taproot.

LIGHT NEEDS: Full sun.

WATER NEEDS: Keep the soil evenly moist.

GROWING GUIDELINES: Grow in fairly large containers—a 7-gallon (31.5 l) planter works well for most kinds—in loose, sandy mix. When the seedlings are 2 inches (5 cm) tall, thin them to 1 inch (2.5 cm) apart. Avoid high nitrogen fertilizers. Harvest at 45–70 days, when the roots are large enough to use.

COMMON PROBLEMS: If you let the soil get too dry and then too wet, the roots may split; try to keep the soil evenly moist.

PROPAGATION: Sow seed directly into the container outdoors in early spring. If you want a steady supply of carrots through the season, sow additional pots every 2 weeks until mid-July.

COMMENTS: Carrot seed may take 3 weeks to germinate.

COMPATIBLE COMPANIONS: Try carrots with tomatoes, chives, or lettuce and other greens.

CULTIVARS: 'Minicor' grows to 4 inches (10 cm) tall and has slender, finger-like roots. 'Thumbelina' and 'Planet' have small, rounded roots; they can even grow in window boxes. Other short-rooted types include 'Nantes', 'Chantenay', and 'Lady Finger'.

Chives grow in grass-like tufts of slender leaves and stems adorned by lavender-pink, pompon flowers in spring. Both the leaves and the flowers have a mild onion flavor.

DESCRIPTION: Small, underground rhizomes with bulb clusters produce 8–12-inch (20–30 cm) tall clumps of hollow, grassy leaves. Separate stems hold the clover-like blooms over the foliage in spring. Chives are hardy in Zones 3–10.

LIGHT NEEDS: Full sun to light shade.

WATER NEEDS: Keep the soil evenly moist.

GROWING GUIDELINES: Chives thrive in well-drained mix that contains added compost, but they can grow in regular all-purpose mix. Add a mulch of compost to the soil surface each spring. Snip leaves as needed. Divide the clumps every 3–4 years if they get crowded.

COMMON PROBLEMS: Chives are generally trouble-free. If the clumps look ragged, cut them to 2 inches (5 cm) tall in midsummer to promote a flush of new growth.

PROPAGATION: Divide clumps after bloom. Sow seed indoors in late winter; it germinates slowly.

COMMENTS: The flowers add a colorful touch to salads.

COMPATIBLE COMPANIONS: Good partners include carrots, tomatoes, and marigolds. Chives reportedly help repel aphids from companions.

RELATED PLANTS:
A. tuberosum, garlic chives, is an outstanding ornamental, with flat leaves, mild garlic flavor, and beautiful, edible, white flowers.

| *Cucumis sativus* | Cucurbitaceae | *Solanum melongena* | Solanaceae |

CUCUMBER

You don't need a big garden to grow a season-long supply of cucumbers; try the compact bush types in containers! Even though the plants are smaller, they still produce full-sized fruits.

DESCRIPTION: Bush-type cucumbers produce 1–3-foot (30–90 cm) tall mounds of heart-shaped, lobed leaves. Their small, funnel-shaped, yellow flowers are followed by slender, green fruits all summer.

LIGHT NEEDS: Full sun.

WATER NEEDS: Keep the soil evenly moist.

GROWING GUIDELINES: Grow bush cucumbers in a large planter filled with well-drained mix that's been enriched with compost. If the mix is on the acidic side, add lime. Mulch seedlings with compost when they are 6 inches (15 cm) tall. Provide a dose of low-nitrogen fertilizer when the first flowers set fruit, and continue to fertilize every 2 weeks while the plants are actively growing.

COMMON PROBLEMS: Overwatering may encourage seedling diseases, preventing germination or killing young seedlings. Covering the container with a floating row cover can prevent cucumber beetles from feeding on young plants. (Remove the cover once plants start to flower, since they need pollination to set fruit.)

PROPAGATION: Sow seed 1/2 inch (12 mm) deep directly into the container. Wait until the last frost date or a week or two after, when the soil is warm.

COMPATIBLE COMPANIONS: Bush cucumbers tend to fill their container, but you could tuck in a few marigolds or lettuce plants.

EGGPLANT

Eggplant is easy to overlook in the garden, but it makes a handsome addition to a container planting. Enjoy its bushy habit, pretty lavender flowers, and glossy fruits.

DESCRIPTION: Eggplants produce handsome 2–3-foot (60–90 cm) tall bushes with large, lobed, felt-like green leaves that often have a purple tinge. The starry purple flowers are followed by oval or cylindrical fruits, which range in color from white to light lavender to deep purple-black.

LIGHT NEEDS: Full sun.

WATER NEEDS: Allow to dry slightly between waterings.

GROWING GUIDELINES: Eggplant prefers well-drained, all-purpose container mix that contains extra compost. Grow 1 plant in each 16-inch (40 cm) container. Fertilize when the first flowers appear, then twice a month afterward until the weather turns cold. Pinch off some of the flowers to prevent overbearing. Harvest fruits when large enough to use; they're most tender when small.

COMMON PROBLEMS: Knock aphids and whiteflies off the plant with a strong spray of water, or spray with insecticidal soap. If whiteflies tend to be a problem each year, place a floating row cover over the transplants and leave it on until early summer. Plants chilled early in the season don't recover well; wait until very warm weather to set out your plants.

PROPAGATION: Sow seed indoors 10–12 weeks before the last frost date. Set transplants out a week or two after the last frost date, when the soil is warm.

COMPATIBLE COMPANIONS: Pair eggplant with lettuce, sweet alyssum, ageratum, or marigolds.

GREENS

Mesclun mixes, lettuce, chard, and spinach add diverse leaf colors and textures to container gardens. Snip the leaves as needed for salads or garnishes.

Lettuce is easy to grow in containers as long as you keep the soil evenly moist. When the leaves start to taste bitter, pull the plants out and sow a new crop.

DESCRIPTION: Many kinds of edible leaf crops—commonly grouped together as greens—are perfectly suited to growing in container gardens.

Lettuces come in either heading or loose-leaf types. Heading lettuces produce firm clumps of tightly packed foliage; leaf lettuces have loose foliage that's picked as needed. Among the prettiest of loose-leaved lettuces are 'Reine de Glaces', with deeply notched, frosty green leaves; 'Red Oak Leaf', with lobed, reddish green leaves; and 'Lollo Rosso', with green-margined, rose-pink leaves. 'Buttercrunch' is a tender, small heading type.

Mesclun mixes are various combinations of lettuce with other low-growing salad crops.

Spinach and chard also make easy and productive container plants. Spinach's dark green, oval leaves may be smooth or savoyed (crinkled); try semi-savoy 'Indian Summer' or 'Melody'. Chard is taller, growing to 18 inches (45 cm), with ruffled leaves and broad stalks. 'Fordhook' chard is dark green with white stems; 'Rhubarb' chard has red stems and reddish green leaves.

LIGHT NEEDS: Full sun is best for most greens, but they do appreciate a bit of shade during midday heat.

WATER NEEDS: Water regularly to keep the soil evenly moist.

GROWING GUIDELINES: Grow greens in loose, well-drained, all-purpose container mix. Thin to 4 inches (10 cm) apart. Fertilize with fish emulsion once or twice a month. Shade plants in hot weather. Harvest the leaves as needed before the plants bolt (flower and set seed).

COMMON PROBLEMS: Mulch can provide a good hiding place for leaf-eating slugs and snails, so don't use it. Leafminers can produce winding tunnels in chard and spinach leaves; pick off affected foliage and cover the remaining plants with a floating row cover until hot weather arrives. (Prevent damage next year by covering seedlings earlier.) Hot weather encourages plants to bolt.

PROPAGATION: Sow seed directly in the outdoor container; leave the seed uncovered. Make the first sowing in early spring. If you want a steady supply of greens, sow additional pots every 2 weeks until early summer; then start sowing again in late summer.

COMMENTS: Once greens send up a flower stalk, their leaves get bitter; pull out the plants and replace them with something else or sow more seed.

COMPATIBLE COMPANIONS: Create a beautiful and productive salad garden by planting several types of greens together in one large container. Greens combine well with just about any flower or vegetable that also enjoys moist soil. Taller companions are helpful, since they can provide some shade for the greens.

| *Mentha* spp. | Labiatae | *Origanum heracleoticum* | Labiatae |

MINTS

OREGANO, GREEK

The fresh scent of mint adds an extra-special touch to a container garden. Make sure you place the plants where you can easily pick the leaves or brush by them to release the fragrance.

DESCRIPTION: Mints are prized for their small, scented leaves, which grow on creeping or upright stems. There are a number of species and cultivars, most of which adapt well to life in containers. Among them is golden ginger mint (*M.* x *gentilis*), which grows to 2 feet (60 cm) tall, with rounded, yellow-marked, green leaves. Peppermint (*M. piperita*) also grows to 2 feet (60 cm), with pungent, pointed, green leaves. Corsican mint (*M. requienii*) is a rapid-growing, ¹/₂-inch (12 mm) tall, mossy creeper that needs extra moisture. Mints are generally hardy in Zones 3–9, although the preferred conditions vary among the species.

LIGHT NEEDS: Partial shade.

WATER NEEDS: Keep the soil evenly moist.

GROWING GUIDELINES: Mints will grow well in all-purpose container mix, although they do appreciate some added compost. Add bonemeal in spring. Harvest the leaves and stems as needed. Pinch off flowers as they appear. After 3 years, plants may be worn out and need replacing.

COMMON PROBLEMS: Mints are generally trouble-free, except that they can become invasive.

PROPAGATION: Divide clumps in spring or fall. Take cuttings during the growing season.

COMPATIBLE COMPANIONS: Low-growing mints can be used in just about any container to fill space. Try taller mints with tomatoes or marigolds.

This low-growing mint relative makes a handsome dark green "groundcover" for container plantings, and its pungent leaves are a flavorful addition to tomato sauces.

DESCRIPTION: Greek oregano has a semishrubby habit, with thin stems and small, oval, dark green, aromatic foliage. Clusters of small, pink or white flowers appear from August to September. Greek oregano is generally hardy in Zones 5–10.

LIGHT NEEDS: Full sun.

WATER NEEDS: Allow the soil to dry out between waterings

GROWING GUIDELINES: Grow Greek oregano in well-drained, all-purpose container mix. Pinch off flowers to promote leaf production. Plants tend to get woody with age; replant every 3 years.

COMMON PROBLEMS: Generally trouble-free.

PROPAGATION: Take cuttings in fall. Divide clumps in spring.

COMMENTS: Compared to common oregano, Greek oregano is lower growing and less invasive, and it has more flavor.

COMPATIBLE COMPANIONS: Pair Greek oregano with other herbs, such as sage, rosemary, and thyme, or use it as a green backdrop for colorful flowers, including marigolds, creeping zinnia (*Sanvitalia procumbens*), and dwarf morning glory (*Convolvulus tricolor*).

| *Petroselinum crispum* | Umbelliferae | *Capsicum annuum* var. *annuum* | Solanaceae |

PARSLEY

PEPPER

Parsley has such an attractive form that you may forget it's also useful as a flavoring. Curly-leaved types are especially ornamental. Parsley is high in iron and vitamins A and C.

DESCRIPTION: Parsley produces compact, 6–12-inch (15–30 cm) clumps of bright green, frilly foliage. This popular herb is a biennial, which means it produces its flavorful leaves the first year and then flowers and sets seed the second year. If plants have good drainage, they can overwinter in Zones 3–10, but since you really want the leaves and not the flowers, it makes sense to set out new plants each spring.

LIGHT NEEDS: Partial shade to full sun.

WATER NEEDS: Keep the soil moist, but don't let it get waterlogged.

GROWING GUIDELINES: Set plants 1 foot (30 cm) apart in all-purpose container mix that contains extra compost. Harvest outer leaves first, as needed.

COMMON PROBLEMS: Leaves get tough the second spring, which is normal; replace plants each year for a steady supply of tender foliage. Parsley may grow poorly in hot weather.

PROPAGATION: Soak the seed 24 hours before sowing directly into outdoor containers in early spring. The seed may take 6 weeks to germinate.

COMPATIBLE COMPANIONS: Parsley's tidy green clumps look great combined with pansies, lettuce, marigolds, edging lobelia (*Lobelia erinus*), impatiens, petunias, and tomatoes.

RELATED PLANTS:

P. crispum var. *neapolitanum,* flat-leaved or Italian parsley, is much larger, to about 2 feet (60 cm) tall.

Peppers make excellent container plants, especially when covered with their colorful fruits. Fertilize once or twice a month, especially just before and during fruit set.

DESCRIPTION: These many-stemmed, bushy plants grow about 2 feet (60 cm) tall, with oval, green leaves and small, white flowers. The flowers are followed by edible green, yellow, red, purple, or even chocolate-colored fruits from summer until frost.

LIGHT NEEDS: Full sun is generally best, although plants appreciate shade from midday sun.

WATER NEEDS: Allow the soil to dry slightly between waterings, but water often, especially in hot weather.

GROWING GUIDELINES: Peppers grow well in warm, well-drained mix with added compost and some dolomitic limestone (for magnesium). Give each plant its own 5-gallon (22.5 l) container, or set plants 18 inches (45 cm) apart in larger planters. In mid- to late-June, cover the soil with a dark-colored mulch.

COMMON PROBLEMS: Knock aphids and whiteflies off plants with a strong spray of water, or spray with insecticidal soap. If plants are too hot (over 80°F [26°C]) or too cold (cooler than 60°F [15°C]), they may stop growing and be vulnerable to disease and insects. Blossom end rot results from uneven watering or a nutrient imbalance.

PROPAGATION: Sow seed indoors 8–10 weeks before the last frost date. Set plants out a week or two after the last frost date, when the soil is warm.

COMPATIBLE COMPANIONS: Good pepper partners include lettuce, sage, marigolds, and zinnias.

Rosmarinus officinalis   Labiatae

ROSEMARY

This beautiful Mediterranean shrub thrives in hot sun and dry spots, with delicate, little leaves on graceful stems. Trailing types are excellent for softening the edge of containers.

DESCRIPTION: Rosemary is a shrubby herb that grows 2–6 feet (30–180 cm) tall, with narrow, thick, glossy green leaves that are grayish underneath. Clusters of small, lavender flowers appear in spring and sometimes in fall; plants also bloom in winter when grown indoors or in warm areas. This herb may survive the winter outdoors in Zones 7–10; in Zones 7 and north, bring the pot inside in the fall.

LIGHT NEEDS: Full sun.

WATER NEEDS: Allow the soil to dry between waterings; water only in drought.

GROWING GUIDELINES: Plant in well-drained, soil-based mix with a neutral to slightly alkaline pH; add lime if needed to raise the pH. A nutrient-poor, dry mix is better than a moist, rich one. Don't fertilize. Pinch shoot tips back several times a season to control the plant's size or shape, and occasionally thin out crowded stems.

COMMON PROBLEMS: Lanky growth indicates either overfertilizing or overwatering.

PROPAGATION: Take cuttings at any time. Layer the stems to the ground. Rosemary will grow from seed, but it is slow to germinate and grow.

COMPATIBLE COMPANIONS: Grow rosemary with other herbs, including sage, thyme, and oregano, or with colorful, drought-tolerant flowers, such as creeping zinnia (*Sanvitalia procumbens*).

Salvia officinalis   Labiatae

SAGE

Sage's shrubby habit and aromatic leaves are a lovely complement to other herbs and colorful flowers. Try it in a pot near a bench or path, where you can easily brush the leaves.

OTHER COMMON NAMES: Garden sage, culinary sage.

DESCRIPTION: Sage is a shrubby herb that develops a woody base over time. It forms upright or sprawling clumps, growing 1–2 feet (30–60 cm) tall. Elliptical, gray-green, aromatic leaves are 1½ inches (3.7 cm) long. Spikes of purple-lavender flowers appear in early summer. Sage is normally hardy in Zones 4–8, although this may vary some by cultivar.

LIGHT NEEDS: Full sun.

WATER NEEDS: Allow the soil to dry between waterings; sage tolerates drought.

GROWING GUIDELINES: Plant in well-drained, nutrient-poor mix. Add lime. Do not fertilize. Shear off the flower stems after bloom. Pick leaves as needed. In early spring, prune away dead wood. Divide plants every 3–4 years.

COMMON PROBLEMS: Sage is generally trouble-free.

PROPAGATION: Take cuttings in early summer. Layer the stems to the ground in spring. You can grow sage from seed, but it is very slow to mature.

COMMENTS: The youngest, unflowered topgrowth has the highest-quality leaves.

COMPATIBLE COMPANIONS: Combine sage with rosemary, basil, thyme, oregano, lettuce, or rose moss (*Portulaca grandiflora*). Tricolor types are very pretty with silver foliage plants such as dusty miller. Avoid planting with cucumber, which it inhibits.

Fragaria spp.   Rosaceae   *Thymus vulgaris*   Labiatae

STRAWBERRIES

THYME

With their sprawling habit, pretty foliage, and prolific, sweet, red berries, strawberries are beautiful and rewarding container plants for small gardens.

Thyme is great for carpeting the soil in containers. Its spreading stems and silvery or gray-green leaves complement taller, more colorful plants. Pinch the growing tips to keep plants bushy.

DESCRIPTION: Strawberries produce long runners and three-lobed leaves on spreading plants that are 6–8 inches (15–20 cm) tall and up to 1 foot (30 cm) wide. White flowers are followed by the juicy, red berries. Some strawberries (called June-bearers) produce one large crop in early summer. Everbearing types yield a moderate main crop in June and a scattering of berries through the rest of the season. 'Brighton' garden strawberry is an everbearing type with showy blooms and mild-tasting berries; it is excellent for hanging baskets. Strawberries are usually hardy in Zones 3–9.

LIGHT NEEDS: Full sun to partial shade.

WATER NEEDS: Water frequently and deeply.

GROWING GUIDELINES: Grow strawberries in well-drained mix with added compost. Space plants 14–18 inches (35–45 cm) apart in 3-gallon (13.5 l) or larger containers. Make sure the crown (the point where the leaves meet the roots) is at or just above the soil surface. Mulch the soil. Fertilize with high-phosphorus fertilizer twice yearly—when growth starts and then after the first crop.

COMMON PROBLEMS: Snails and slugs may feed on leaves and fruit; prevent damage by setting the pots up on a table or a pedestal.

PROPAGATION: Detach and plant offsets from runners.

COMPATIBLE COMPANIONS: Strawberries grow best when planted alone.

DESCRIPTION: Thyme is a small, shrubby herb that grows to 12 inches (30 cm) tall, with $^1/_4$-inch (6 mm), oval, gray-green leaves. Tiny, lavender blooms appear from May to October. Thyme is hardy in Zones 5–9.

LIGHT NEEDS: Full sun to light shade.

WATER NEEDS: Allow the soil to dry between waterings.

GROWING GUIDELINES: Thyme prefers warm, well-drained, average to nutrient-poor mix. Set plants 6–12 inches (15–30 cm) apart. Fertilize with fish emulsion in early summer. Harvest shoots as needed; pick before bloom for the most intense flavor.

COMMON PROBLEMS: Thyme rots if kept too wet; avoid overwatering.

PROPAGATION: Take stem cuttings at any time. Divide clumps in spring. Thyme grows slowly from seed; sow indoors in late winter.

COMMENTS: Common thyme is the most flavorful, with the most fragrant flowers as well.

COMPATIBLE COMPANIONS: Grow thyme as a groundcover under potted Japanese maples (*Acer palmatum*). It looks good with other herbs, as well as with marigolds, dusty miller, and grape hyacinths (*Muscari* spp.).

RELATED PLANTS:

T. citriodorus, lemon thyme, is a 4–12-inch (10–30 cm) tall spreader that's great in pots and hanging baskets.

Lycopersicon esculentum Solanaceae	*Cucurbita pepo* var. *melopepo* Cucurbitaceae

TOMATO

ZUCCHINI

You don't need a big garden to grow this popular vegetable. Tomatoes now come in dwarf types that can produce tasty fruit even in small containers.

DESCRIPTION: Tomatoes are bushy or vining plants with a main thick trunk and many branches. Indeterminate types climb to 6 feet (1.8 m) or more and produce fruit over a long season. Determinate tomatoes grow to a certain height, then flower and set fruit; dwarf types may be as small as 6 inches (15 cm) tall. Small, yellow blossoms develop into red, gold, or pink fruits.

LIGHT NEEDS: Full sun.

WATER NEEDS: Water deeply and generously, especially before fruits begin to ripen.

GROWING GUIDELINES: Plant tomatoes in well-drained container mix with added compost. Smallest types can fit in a 1-gallon (4.5 l) container. Give dwarfs a 3–5-gallon (13.5–22.5 l) container and standards a 30-gallon (135 l) planter or half-barrel. Mulch after the soil is warm. Fertilize twice monthly after blossoms appear.

COMMON PROBLEMS: Uneven watering and nutrient imbalances can produce blossom end rot (dark patches on the base of the fruit); try to keep the soil evenly moist and add dolomitic limestone. Fruit may not set if temperatures are over 90°F (32°C).

PROPAGATION: Sow seed indoors 8 weeks before the last frost. Set out transplants after the last frost date.

COMPATIBLE COMPANIONS: Try tomatoes with mint, parsley, basil, marigolds, or lettuce.

Avoid the "zucchini, zucchini, and more zucchini" syndrome by planting a bush type in a container. You'll still get a good harvest, but you probably won't be overwhelmed by excess fruit.

DESCRIPTION: Zucchini grows on bushy or vining plants with thick stems and broad, green leaves. The large, funnel-shaped, yellow flowers quickly develop into elongated, green fruits.

LIGHT NEEDS: Full sun.

WATER NEEDS: Water often, especially after fruit set.

GROWING GUIDELINES: Grow zucchini in well-drained mix that's been enriched with compost and/or aged manure. Add dolomitic lime, too. Set one plant in each 3-foot (90 cm) wide container. When the soil is warm, cover it with a dark mulch. Provide a dose of low-nitrogen fertilizer when the flowers form, then twice a month afterwards. Harvest the fruit often, while it is still fairly small.

COMMON PROBLEMS: Squash-vine borers burrow into stems, leaving sawdust on the ground and causing sudden wilt; inject BT (*Bacillus thuringiensis*) into the affected stem. Gray mold and powdery mildew are common at the end of the season. To prevent these problems as long as possible, place the pot in an airy spot and avoid wetting the foliage or watering plants at night.

PROPAGATION: Sow seed indoors in April, or plant directly into outdoor containers in mid-May.

COMPATIBLE COMPANIONS: Zucchini plants usually fill their container, but you may try tucking in a few marigolds for extra color.

USDA PLANT
HARDINESS ZONE MAP

The map that follows shows the United States and Canada divided into 10 zones. Each zone is based on a 10°F (5.6°C) difference in average annual minimum temperature. Some areas are considered too high in elevation for plant cultivation and so are not assigned to any zone. There are also island zones that are warmer or cooler than surrounding areas because of differences in elevation; they have been given a zone different from the surrounding areas. Many large urban areas are in a warmer zone than the surrounding land.

Plants grow best within an optimum range of temperatures. The range may be wide for some species and narrow for others. Plants also differ in their ability to survive frost and in their sun or shade requirements.

The zone ratings indicate conditions where designated plants will grow well and not merely survive. Refer to the map to find out which zone you are in. In the plant-by-plant guides, you'll find recommendations for the plants that grow best in your zone.

Many plants may survive in zones warmer or colder than their recommended zone range. Remember that other factors, including wind, soil type, soil moisture and drainage capability, humidity, snow, and winter sunshine, may have a great effect on growth.

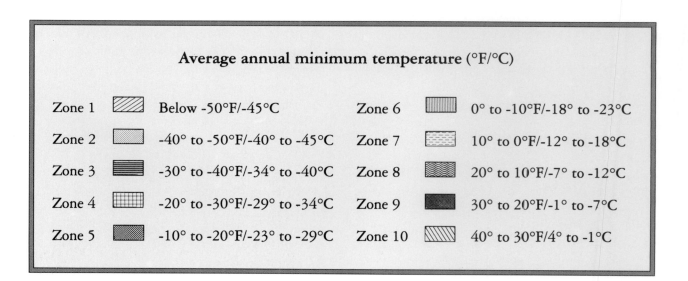

Average annual minimum temperature (°F/°C)

Zone 1		Below -50°F/-45°C	Zone 6		0° to -10°F/-18° to -23°C
Zone 2		-40° to -50°F/-40° to -45°C	Zone 7		10° to 0°F/-12° to -18°C
Zone 3		-30° to -40°F/-34° to -40°C	Zone 8		20° to 10°F/-7° to -12°C
Zone 4		-20° to -30°F/-29° to -34°C	Zone 9		30° to 20°F/-1° to -7°C
Zone 5		-10° to -20°F/-23° to -29°C	Zone 10		40° to 30°F/4° to -1°C

INDEX

The numbers in bold indicate main entries, and the numbers in italic indicate illustrations.

ACKNOWLEDGMENTS

Photo Credits

A–Z Botanical Collection: photographer Anthony Cooper: page 55 (right); photographer P. Etchells: page 22 (top right); photographer K. Jayaram: endpapers; The Picture Store: back cover (bottom) and page 57 (right); photographer Andy Williams: page 15 (bottom right).

Gillian Beckett: pages 11 (right), 57 (left), 59 (left), 60 (left), 66 (left), 67 (right), 68, 70 (left), 71 (left), 72 (right), 74 (left), 76 (left), 78 (left), 83 (left), 85 (right), 86 (left), 88 (right), 89 (left), 90 (left and right), 120 (left), 126 (right), 132 (left), 136 (left), 146 (right), and 150 (right).

Bruce Coleman Limited: photographer Hans Reinhard: pages 22 (bottom right) and 151 (left).

Thomas Eltzroth: pages 16, 24 (left), 32 (right), 43 (bottom right), 52, 53 (right), 54 (left), 56 (left), 59 (right), 64 (right), 67 (left), 69 (left and right), 74 (right), 76 (right), 77 (right), 82 (right), 87 (left), 89 (right), 103 (top right), 118, 119 (left), 124 (left), 125 (right), 127 (left and right), 133 (left), 134 (right), 135 (right), 141 (right), and 146 (left).

Derek Fell: pages 18 and 46 (right).

The Garden Picture Library: photographer Lynne Brotchie: back cover (top) and pages 12, 33 (left), and 43 (top right); photographer Linda Burgess: page 17 (top right); photographer Brian Carter: page 60 (right); photographer John Glover: opposite contents page and pages 17 (top left and bottom right) and 26 (left); photographer Michael Howes: pages 19 (bottom left) and 28 (left); photographer Lamontagne: pages 42 (top), 94 (right), and 140 (right); photographer Jane Legate: page 112; photographer Zara McCalmont: page 34; photographers Mayer/Le Scanff: pages 20, 27 (top), and 42 (bottom); photographer Sidney Moulds: title page; photographer J. S. Sira: pages 31 and 40 (right); photographer Brigitte Thomas: front cover; photographer Steven Wooster: pages 47, 48 (top right), 95 (top right), and 106 (right).

Holt Studios International: photographer John Adams: page 27 (bottom); photographer Nigel Cattlin: pages 23 (bottom right), 25, 30 (left, center, and right), 33 (top right), 58 (right), 61 (right), 62 (right), 65 (right), 66 (right), 73 (left), 79 (left), 80 (left), 120 (right), 128 (right), 135 (left), 147 (left and right), 148 (left and right), 149 (right), and 153 (left); photographer Bob Gibbons: pages 85 (left) and 130 (right); photographer Primrose Peacock: page 131 (right); photographer Inga Spence: page 56 (right).

Andrew Lawson: pages 7 (top left), 15 (left), 41 (bottom left), 43 (left), 48 (left), 50, and 95 (top left).

Stirling Macoboy: pages 62 (left), 63 (right), 130 (left), and 136 (right).

S & O Mathews: pages 14, 41 (top left), and 49 (right).

Clive Nichols: half title page, opposite title page (designer Anthony Noel), copyright page, pages 22 (bottom left), 49 (left), 63 (left), 65 (left), 92, 95 (bottom right), 96 (left), 97 (left and right), 98 (left), 99, 100 (bottom, designer Anthony Noel), 101, 102 (designer Julie Toll), 103 (left, designer Sue Berger), 104, 107 (bottom left, designer Anthony Noel, right), 108 (left and right), 109 (left), 110, 111 (top right, designer Jill Billington, left, and bottom right), 113 (top and bottom), 114 (top, designer Jill Billington, bottom), 115, and 142 (right).

Jerry Pavia: pages 11 (left), 26 (right), 28 (right), 48 (bottom right), 73 (right), 84 (left), 98 (right), 103 (bottom right), 122 (left), 124 (right), 126 (left), 128 (left), and 140 (left).

Photos Horticultural: back cover (center) and pages 7 (right), 17 (bottom left), 19 (top and bottom right), 21, 23 (left and top right), 24 (right), 29 (left and right), 32 (left), 33 (bottom right), 40 (left), 41 (right), 44, 45 (top and bottom), 46 (left), 53 (left), 70 (right), 87 (right), 91 (right), 95 (bottom left), 100 (top), 122 (right), 133 (right), 138 (left), 144, 145 (left), and 152 (right).

Harry Smith Collection: pages 15 (top right), 42 (center), 54 (right), 55 (left), 58 (left), 61 (left), 64 (left), 71 (right), 72 (left), 75 (left and right), 77 (left), 78 (right), 79 (right), 80 (right), 81 (left and right), 82 (left), 83 (right), 84 (right), 86 (right), 88 (left), 91 (left), 119 (right), 121 (left and right), 123 (left and right), 125 (left), 129 (left and right), 131 (left), 132 (right), 134 (left), 137, 138 (right), 139 (left and right), 141 (left), 142 (left), 143 (left and right), 145 (right), 149 (left), 150 (left), 151 (right), 152 (left), and 153 (right).

Graham Strong: pages 8, 94 (left), 96 (right), 106 (left), 107 (top left), and 116.

Weldon Russell: pages 7 (bottom left) and 109 (right).